Luca Fer

CW00766123

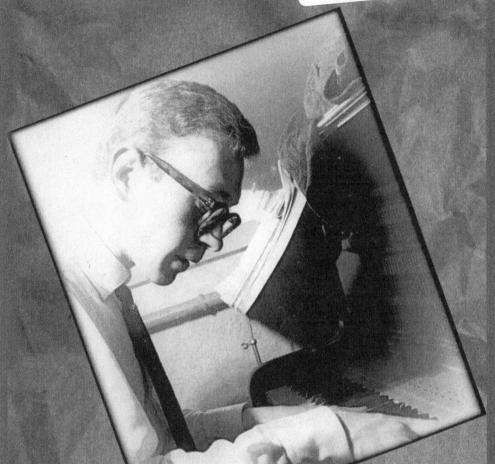

OUT OF NOWHERE
the uniquely elusive jazz of
MIKE TAYLOR

Typeset by Jonathan Downes,
Cover and Layout by SPiderKaT for CFZ Communications
Using Microsoft Word 2000, Microsoft Publisher 2000, Adobe Photoshop CS.

First published in Great Britain by Gonzo Multimedia

c/o Brooks City,
6th Floor New Baltic House
65 Fenchurch Street,
London EC3M 4BE
Fax: +44 (0)191 5121104
Tel: +44 (0) 191 5849144
International Numbers:
Germany: Freephone 08000 825 699
USA: Freephone 18666 747 289

© Luca Ferrari MMXV

All rights reserved. Without limiting the rights under copyright reserved above, no part of this
publication may be reproduced, stored in or introduced into a retrieval system, or transmitted,
in any form of by any means (electronic, mechanical, photocopying, recording or otherwise),
without the prior written permission of both the copyright owners and the publishers of this
book.

ISBN: 978-1-908728-48-7

O n a visit to London a few years ago I met up with Dave Tomlin. During our subsequent conversation he urged me to listen to the music of Mike Taylor, and when I heard his *Trio* album for the first time I couldn't believe my ears.

It was "All the things you are" and it really impressed me. Of course I had been listening to other versions before, in particular the versions played by Bill Evans and Lennie Tristano, but Taylor's arrangement, from the very first seconds left me literally beyond words. Where had this innovator come from? Those first hesitant notes, never heard before? That gifted balance between empty and full; the breaks, the unpredictable silences among his careful tones?

I discovered subsequently, reading the very few articles in print about him, his fleeting life, with its tragic and unexpected epilogue, but what little testimony survives is surely enough to give him the status of a real 20th Century jazz meteor.

This unpredictable star that so briefly touched our planet disappeared, taking with him a musical cornucopia of fruitful promise that he had discovered, achievements and possibilities so near.

This is his story.

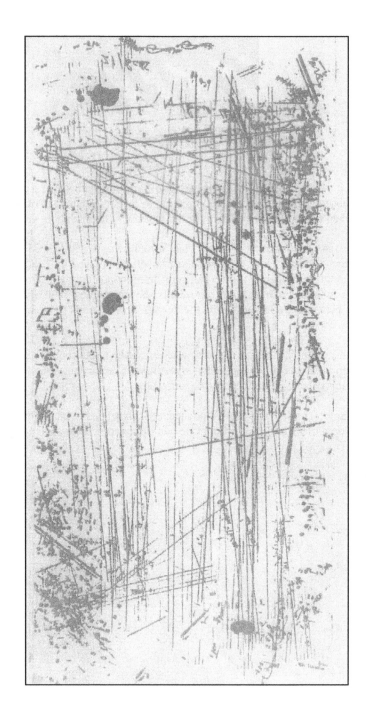

**Mike Taylor's' blotter drawn for the concert programme at London I.C.A. Gallery
(December 1st 1965)**

Contents

Foreword

"We need to be able to hear in the depths of any music,
the theme without notes that is created for us,
the theme of Death."

(Louis-Ferdinand Céline)

Beginning of January 1969.

Fully dressed he slowly walked into the sea. Someone noticing this called the police who arrived and dragged him to the shore, his clothes soaking wet. He was taken to the local police station where he was dried out and given a cup of tea. Having then been given a stern lecture, he was told to keep out of the water and sent on his way. He walked a mile or so along the coast, then - this time unseen - went back into the water...

Mystery Of Body In Creek

"Police are still trying to identify a man whose body was washed up at Leigh Creek on Sunday. Investigations ruled out thoughts that he was one of three wildfowlers lost off Foulness a fortnight ago, and a possible link with a cabin cruiser found wrecked on Shoebury Beach has also been discounted. He is aged between 25 and 30, 5ft. 8in. tall, of medium build, with shoulder-length dark brown hair, auburn moustache, a long and straggled beard, straight nose, blue eyes and large ears with small lobes. He was wearing a cream striped shirt, two white vests, two pairs of trousers and brown shoes. The body had been in the water for about six or seven hours - perhaps less....".

A short piece in a local newspaper, the *Southend Standard*, reported that on January 20th a body had been found, but nothing more. The autopsy on the body revealed no violence or any other cause of death and a couple of weeks later detectives established through medical records the identity of a body recovered between Leigh-on-Sea and Southend-on-Sea directly opposite the boat, *Lady Saville*, at that time moored nearby and used as a clubhouse for the Essex Yacht Club.

Then, on February 6th, Guy Y. Jerman, H. M. Coroner for the county Borough of Southend-on-Sea, archived the file, reporting simply: "Drowning in the sea". An open verdict, which was written on the death certificate. Accident or suicide? Either was possible.[1]

For some time, Taylor had been going around that area, unknown to the local residents of the village, which is nowadays a small town of twenty thousand inhabitants. There, the Thames flows into the sea and ducks float dreamily on its surface. No-one there would have known Mike Taylor, by now a composer and jazz pianist of some repute, although he had, towards the end of his short career, played there in the local jazz clubs several times.

Cesare Pavese, an Italian writer who killed himself in August 1950, wrote: "You astonish the others who move near to you and they don't know, when you are close to many people in whom you are not interested and don't know well, to them it is a secret pain?". [2]

What was Mike Taylor's secret pain?

Mike's friends in London were much upset when news of his death reached them. Ron Rubin, double-bass player who from 1961 had played on some of the rare recordings which have survived, and a few of the live gigs, wrote in his journal: "I had some very bad news a few weeks ago. Mike Taylor was washed up on the beach at Leigh-on-Sea. He'd been in the sea a matter of weeks, and nobody knew what he was doing round those parts".

Tony Reeves, who had played bass with the *Mike Taylor Quartet* in 1965: "I was quite sad. Although I had not played with him for several years, and in the meantime he had become rather strange, he was a very original musician, and I would like to have spoken to him and played with him one more time".

Southend-on-Sea, Sutton Road Cemetery, February 7th, 1969

> "Here lies one whose name was writ in water".
> (John Keats, epitaph for himself)

The funeral at the Southend-on-Sea cemetery, as reported in his diary by Rubin, who just the night before had played a gig in the town was, he says, a real disaster. "Mike's funeral today at Leigh-on-Sea. Nobody seems to know what he was doing there. His grandparents lived in Herne Bay and maybe his body was washed across the estuary by tides? The funeral, like much of Mike's life was a bit of a fiasco – apparently most of the mourners went to the wrong cemetery. Interesting chat there with Charles Fox who had favourably reviewed our LP "Trio". Mike Taylor RIP ".

And again: "As I was working near Leigh-on-Sea with Humph the night before, I stayed the night at Leigh to go to the funeral which was a very sad little affair. It was so depressing and rather a shambles. The atmosphere was not enhanced by a windy out of season little seaside town...". [3]

The gravestone number 23588, a stark rough slab of dark marble, with the name Michael R. Taylor, followed by "composer – musician", also the date of birth and just a presumed date of death: January 19th 1969. [4] An inscrutable inscription seemingly taken from something he had once written:

"I dive from a springboard
Into cool clear water
And yet I furnish my springboard
With my experience
So that my life
Is more than my action."

Ron Rubin in a letter to the author (January 2014): "I can't trace the provenance of the inscription, but I'd guess it's something rather lovely from his own mind".

Who could say they really knew Mike Taylor?

Sunday Times, February 9th 1969

"Mike Taylor would have been 31 this year", the *Sunday Times* reported that day. "In another year or two, he might have been recognised as the startlingly original pianist and composer that many British jazz musicians already knew him to be".

Speaking of the death, the newspaper defined his life as "elusive", admitting that "he changed in the last six years or so from a conventional young man into an unpredictable eccentric".

Even though his friends admitted he was a difficult man to know, "they all agree on one thing – from the start he had a completely individual talent".

Southend Standard, February 13th 1969

The local newspaper again asked for reasons for the pianist's death. Under the headline "Jazz man's mystery death" it dares to attempt an explication about the end of the musician. Just a few words alluding to the coroner's medical report: "The Southend Coroner said death could have been accidental or deliberate, and added: "The evidence does not disclose the means by which death arose"".

Then, quite surprisingly, a word came from Taylor's sister Muriel Hogbin who reveals that her brother: "tried to gas himself two and-half years ago, due to his inability to be recognised as a musician".

A statement which was immediately retracted in evidence to the Coroner she had reported: "I saw him at the beginning of January and he was much better because he was now recognised".

Her only explanation for his presence in the area was that, although having no money and unemployed, he had come to attend to a concert and therefore had no reasons to kill himself...

1
Looking like a tramp.

"You can escape but you cannot hide away"
(Sheldon Kopp)

Two fleeting images to define a life slipping away; elusive, swallowed up in a senseless end when Mike Taylor was still convinced that he could resist the dark forces which were taking over inside him. Forces which wanted to make him feel shut off from life, without hope, past redemption.

Fairfield Hall, Croydon (London), August 29th, 1965

Just a few years before the sea swallowed him up at Leigh-on-Sea, a day came when an unexpected kind of consecration came upon him. He, a jazz pianist and composer leading a new group of musicians, was just beginning to make a name for himself. By day he earned a living helping his grandfather to sell paint and wallpapers all around London.

To Croydon's Fairfield Hall comes the American free-jazz legend Ornette Coleman, a musician everyone is watching as a revolutionary of the so-called *new thing*. Fans and jazz critics had been astonished by a sequence of powerful albums such as *The shape of jazz to come* (1959), *Tomorrow is the question!* (1959), *Change of the Century* (Atlantic 1959), *Ornette on tenor* (1962) and, most of all, *Free Jazz* (1960), the New World Jazz manifesto.

That evening the *Mike Taylor Quartet* (Mike at piano, Tony Reeves on bass, Dave Tomlin on soprano sax and Jon Hiseman on drums) had been selected to open the concert.

"Ornette Coleman arrived in London in August 1965 as a tourist, for he was far too dubious a commercial proposition for any British promoter to risk engaging his trio", Alan Bates, one of the promoters, wrote. "However Coleman did want to appear in public, so he simply became his own promoter; he persuaded me to organize a concert for him and financed the whole operation himself. Within three weeks of his arrival, his European premiere had given him his first taste of unqualified acclaim from listeners and reviewers; the impact was so profound that Coleman was elected "Musician of the Year" in the 1965 *Melody Maker* Critics' Poll (their first-ever Poll victory) (…) on the strength of just the one solitary performance, and later the

Melody Maker remarked that "the concert has already assumed almost legendary status"". [5]

Prestigious BBC Jazz Awards winner in 2008, Alan Bates is a legendary jazz character, and promoter of concerts from the Fifties onwards. He had been the founder of jazz labels such as Black Lion and Candid Records that have produced and published albums played by artists such as Thelonious Monk, Charles Mingus, Sun Ra, Cecil Taylor, Steve Lacy and more. It was he that Coleman asked to manage the concert, as he writes on the album notes of the record that documents the evening: "The aura of expectancy surrounding the concert certainly helped. Apart from the fact that music of the Coleman school had never performed here, several other considerations heightened the suspense: Coleman had made no records for four years; he had only recently emerged from retirement; neither his composing for chamber ensembles nor his playing of violin and trumpet had yet been recorded at all; he had never been outside the U.S.A. before, and his arrival in London was a complete surprise". [6]

But in spite of the tension the musician's charisma had generated, at least initially things took a turn for the worst.

"The announcement that a Coleman concert would take place in two weeks' time seemed almost incredible in a country where, unless the visiting musician is classified as a "concert artist" (one who plays European-style compositions or Asian-style improvisations) by the Ministry of Labour, he is not allowed to perform without a reciprocal exchange of British musicians having been expensively and laboriously arranged beforehand. Coleman was classified as a "concert artist", the first time a black American playing his own music had been granted this status, but the British Musician's Union then made certain arbitrary and unjust demands to Coleman and myself which would have had the effect of cancelling the concert. Two penalties were imposed for our refusal. Firstly, the Union prohibited its members from accepting engagements from or either New Departures review (which present experimental works in all the arts in both print and performance, and had helped with organisation) or myself; in fact the Union has not even allowed us to plead our case. Secondly, the *New Departures Quintet*, which was to have played the first part of the concert with the poets Mike Horowitz and Pete Brown, was prohibited from appearing; the musicians who eventually appeared with Horowitz and Brown were guitarist John Renbourn and the Mike Taylor Quartet". [7]

An occurrence confirmed by Victor Schonfield, the other promoter of the event: "Although I organised the August 1965 Ornette Coleman concert", he says, "I was never involved with Mike Taylor. His appearance at the concert was a last-minute arrangement, when the Musicians' Union here instructed their members not to take part (because of complicated industrial politics). It was the poet (and many other things) Pete Brown who arranged for the Taylor group to substitute for the *New Departures Quintet*".

Some days after the event jazz critic Ronald Atkins wrote a well-structured review about the evening on the austere *Tribune*: "BRITAIN usually lags behind in its awareness and appreciation of the newer trends in jazz. Quite apart from our national conservatism, the regulations under which American musicians are allowed to perform here preclude the casual,

"I'm in town and I want to play" attitude whereby a relatively uncommercial jazzman can work for months at a time in a continental club.

On August 29, however, Ornette Coleman made his European debut, not at the Olympia in Paris nor the Cafe Montmartre, Copenhagen, but in Croydon's Fairfield Hall.

Coleman, a 35-year-old alto-saxophonist from Fort Worth, Texas, was practically unknown before his quartet was booked into New York's Five Spot Café in November 1959.

Within a few months he had changed the course of jazz. Before him, the jazz solo had evolved in a rigid framework of chorus lengths, pre-stated chords and a regular rhythmic pulse. A gifted musician was able to move easily enough within this structure, and there have been many recent attempts to lessen the dependence on chord changes, or to use different time signatures and many shifts of tempo.

Coleman just stepped into the midst of these trappings and blew them away. His solos follow a logic that is quite free from chord restrictions and his bassist and drummer provide a supple, often contrasting rhythm in which a fixed tempo is never stated. For ears not attuned to his music all this seemed perverse and wilfully incoherent; now, as is the case with innovators, one cannot imagine how or why the validity of his music was ever questioned.

Having undergone in two years the basic processes which jazz reserves for its few geniuses — being discovered, condemned, praised and exploited - Coleman left the rabble to fight over the pieces while he practised and studied. He now plays the trumpet and violin as well as the saxophone, and has composed a string quartet and a film score.

Coleman was self-taught, defiantly so, and obsessed with music as being something natural, personal and unforced. His blues background gives strength and passion to his music as it has done to the greatest soloists but, whether blues or avant-garde European, he has absorbed and assimilated rather than learnt. Already acknowledged as an outstanding thematic composer, his newer works, showcasing musical pointilliste and episodic silences, show him capable of expanding his talent without sacrificing the indigenous unity of his music.

As a soloist, the range of this most empirical of improvisers encompasses microtones and distortions of pitch but, unlike some of his disciples, Coleman is essentially a melodist.

With no harmonic chains to fetter him, he can transfix the audience with a few seconds of astounding melodic inventiveness which we know is created then and there. His concert solo on 'The clergyman's Dream' was replete with moments where the rules of thematic development were swept asunder by these continual spontaneous eruptions.

Coleman's tone is warm and incessantly varied, with the most opulent low-register sound ever heard on an alto-saxophone (he insists on using a plastic rather than a metal instrument). The languid and poignant sheen of his playing on slow ballads — on Sunday, a stunningly beautiful version of sadness — has an austere sensuousness that sets it apart from the familiar saxophone romanticism.

A programmatic composition of a different kind, the headlong 'Falling Stars', featured Coleman on trumpet and violin. Astringent and totally rhythmic, his conception of the latter instrument is truly expressive of another side of his musical ego.

David Izenzon, double-bass, and his drummer Charles Moffett supported Coleman with unflagging concentration and technical brilliance. Izenzon must be the leading exponent of bowed bass in jazz and his blending with the saxophone, both in unison passages and in moments of calculated dissonance, was a high point of the concert.

Before the trio appeared, the *Virtuoso Ensemble* gave the first performance of Coleman's wind quintet, 'Forms and Sounds'. For a man of his background to write so fluently in the post-Schoenberg tradition is remarkable in itself. While the piece does not make the revolutionary impact in its own field of Coleman's work in jazz, it stands as another landmark in the development of one of the most gifted and uninhibited minds in Western music". [8]

The specialist *Jazz Monthly*, reporting the event, emphasized the presence of Ornette Coleman in England for the first time, and talked about a "miracle". Journalist Jack Cooke wrote: "Miracles sometimes do happen, and though after Ornette Coleman's return to active participation in jazz there always existed the possibility that some day we might see and hear him and his group in this country that possibility was always remote enough to have been classed as a miracle. Well, now it's happened, and though I suppose what took place at the Fairfield Hall on August 29th won't have much, if any, effect on the English jazz scene as a whole there was inescapable proof, for anyone who cared to go along, that Ornette's work is still the most vital and essential single force in contemporary jazz. There was never a moment's doubt that we were in the presence of a great jazz musician". [9]

This writer minimized the role of the "support" band with a severe opinion on Taylor's quartet, also misnaming it as the "Mike West Quartet".

"The substitute group was the *Mike West Quartet*, who accompanied Brown but not Horowitz, and who also filled out the first set with a tiring and heavy-handed imitation of some of the most obvious characteristics of the *John Coltrane Quartet*". [10]

Jazz Journal did a little better with a pair of pages signed by Barry McRae who just at the end of his piece wrote: "In addition there were several numbers by the *Mike Taylor Quartet* – a group of young British musicians working in the Coltrane manner. Although a good musician, soprano saxophonist Dave Tomlin was rather too formal in his approach to this style of jazz and there were times when the leader's piano was a little static. On the whole, however, they played in an imaginative way and showed the kind of potential that bodes well for the future of British jazz. It is doubtful whether the well known musicians originally booked would have made a greater impression in the face of Ornette Coleman's inspired playing". [11]

As you can see, just a few lines on Taylor's quartet, but without any comment on their music, the group, no doubt somewhat overshadowed by Coleman's shock performance, being defined in the jazz magazine *Change* as "semi-professional".

Yet, in those days, everything seemed to be handy. The dream of a music passion that coincides with the life and becomes a job, a way of self-subsistence, public recognition, money. Life.

Dave Gelly: "Obviously, Ornette Coleman was the big attraction. Mike's quartet opened the concert – in effect, the 'support act'. There was also the problem that Ornette was appearing without a work permit, and the British Musicians' Union had banned any of its members from taking part".

According to Pete Brown, "Mike's direction was so different from Coleman's (which the critics were only just getting used to) that they didn't understand it. I seem to recall that even then there was animosity towards Coleman. Brit critics are very puritanical. And then of course later, people have their turn if they are rediscovered. Everyone now loves Joe Harriott, but there were times he couldn't get a gig and none wrote about him, even though he was a tremendous innovator and player. And he died without a bean. I guess that's jazz!"

Unfortunately, today the main characters attending that evening remember little of it. Jak Kilby, a photographer who was soon by chance to meet Taylor, admits the event "was one of the bigger festivals at the time".

"I was not allowed to take photographs. I got into the backstage of the theatre with Johnny Dyani and Mongezi Feza of the *Blue Notes*. We were in the backstage dressing room just before the concert and went down with the band as they went on stage, but hid in the wings. But the security came and pulled us out, well, Mongezi and myself - they put us back in the dressing room where we could see and hear nothing. Johnny managed to stay at the side of the stage as they did not see him. We crept back and were seen and thrown out of the theatre".

Asking Tony Reeves what was the mood of that evening, he says: "As far as I can remember, the mood was OK. When you are supporting anyone, by definition the audience is not there to see you, of course, but I think we went down quite well. Coleman was more brash, connected quickly with the audience, in a funny way he was 'more commercial', but I still feel the *Mike Taylor Quartet* was an appropriate choice of opening act. We played first, as far as I remember. I'm sure someone in the audience would have covertly recorded the gig, but I've no idea if it still exists".

Jon Hiseman, commenting on the impact Coleman's music made on him that evening, says that he had a real revelation about the value of Taylor's project: "I was surprised for the simple reason it never occurred to me that anybody was doing anything like we were doing anywhere else in the world at the time. There weren't any musicians coming into London playing that sort of music and 'living in suburbia'. I didn't have access to any esoteric recording that might be in some famous jazz record shop in the centre of London. I had no idea that there was this movement in New York playing free music". [12]

The drummer, while denouncing the short–sighted reading of Coleman's music by the British critics, is sure that the *Mike Taylor Quartet* was playing avant-garde music, a very original sound never heard before. "In fact, people around me, including musicians who were my contemporaries, would come and listen to this strange Mike Taylor thing and didn't get it all. So, the Ornette Coleman concert was a bit of a surprise from me from that perspective". [13]

However in spite of Hiseman's certainty, some months pass and nothing seems to happen. Basically the Quartet doesn't play much anymore, "in some little London clubs", as Reeves remembers, and the next thing is the group splits up and Mike is alone again.

Ronnie Scott's Old Place. 39, Gerrard Street, London W1, Friday the 27th October, 1967

It's another brief picture of a life running into thin air: Mike Taylor at the piano, round-shoulders, a long beard, entranced and absorbed, as if in symbiosis with his instrument.

Jak Kilby portrayed him in this way, two years after the Croydon concert. He got only seven shots, all black & white and more or less variants, "taken in extremely bad lighting conditions - pushing the limits of what was possible with film at the time" - he points out.

Kilby was a freelance photographer, winding up by chance to take pictures of musicians around the London clubs, after an attempted career in a photography studio, but left because the job was underpaid.

He says: "In 1967 I had been working in a photography studio for four years, straight from school as a trainee then eventually as a junior photographer. This was the old way - college was almost non-existent then and what there was, was not well regarded. We worked long hours for very low money. In 1967 I left the company hoping to find a better job but was immediately asked to do freelance work. So I became freelance and that was the case for the rest of my life. At the same time I was a music fan. We had a lot of blues musicians in London in the 1960's and I heard a lot of that. When I worked for the company several of us of the same age used to go to a local record shop at lunchtime - you could listen to the records free of charge in booths so we went through every blues record we found and when we used them up started on the Jazz section. I really liked that music! We also used to read *Melody Maker* which featured news and stories about many types of music at that time, not just the output of the commercial record companies but Jazz, Blues and Folk music."

"I was doing many kinds of work as a freelance photographer but early on met drummer John Stevens and saxophonist Evan Parker walking down a street. I recognized them from *Melody Maker*. So I talked to them and was then invited to their gigs. This started me photographing their music events, particularly at the Little Theatre Club which John ran. The Theatre Club would run 'casting' theatre productions, with new plays every two weeks so I also got the job of photographing their theatre productions. I was helping in the Jazz side of the club, taking money on the door, taking photographs of the musicians and driving them to gigs outside London, which got me to other locations for Jazz. Ronnie Scott's Old Place was something of a rival club. So, I did not just photograph Jazz. But it was something I did speculatively, that is, usually unpaid, but hoping to get something from any photographs published later. I also did some work with a few rock musicians but that was usually only if I was hired."

So that afternoon Kilby ended up almost by chance at Ronnie Scott's: "The location is not the place known as Ronnie Scott's Club today, it was the older premises in Gerrard Street in London, Chinatown - at the time, lots of Chinese but not as much as now. When Ronnie Scott moved to his new better and bigger space the old club was at first closed and then re-opened to present British Jazz, but only for a short time as (I was told this by drummer John Stevens who was offered to run the Old Place but turned it down) they were planning to open a gambling club for Chinese but needed time to get the license, and to show something else happening meanwhile.

"When I went to the club that time, it was because I'd been told the *Archie Shepp Quintet* (Shepp, Roswell Rudd, Grachen Moncur III, Jimmy Garrison and Beaver Harris) would be rehearsing that afternoon. They were and I took photographs of them. But when they finished Mike Taylor arrived to rehearse. They only played a short time. His trio was with Ron Rubin (double bass) and Laurie Allan on drums. When they finished the *Chris McGregor Group* (*Blue Notes*) arrived to rehearse, so it was quite a day!"

Ron Rubin wrote in his journal that day: "Good to see Mike wearing shoes and playing piano again. His demeanour much improved. Fingers crossed. Jimmy Garrison and Archie Shepp rehearsing when we arrived. Interesting chat with them - more Black Flower than Black Power...".

As to Kilby, even if today his memory is sketchy and he struggles to focus on a clear picture, he remembers that day and Taylor's music as something "different and quite unlike anything he'd been hearing on record, not straight bebop, or any of the British or American free/avant-garde new music. It was quite original and in that respect it had what people like myself wanted - the sound of surprise. Yes, Taylor was the focus of the group I heard. But that is not unusual with a piano trio".

On another occasion, describing the image of Taylor: "I didn't know who he was. He looked like a tramp, hunched over the keyboard. But he had the longest fingers I had ever seen and I was mesmerized by them as they worked. I had never heard nor seen anyone play like that. I realized that I was witnessing something special". [14]

"Looked like a tramp" is the picture of Mike Taylor Kilby has fixed on his memory, and on the few photographs which survive. A 'tramp', a 'hobo', a 'homeless'... man with no roots, a drop-out, adrift...

How could this have happened?

2
The artist as a clandestine.

"The artist is a clandestine"
(Marcel Duchamp)

Looking at the first twenty years of Mike Taylor's life we grope in the dark; fragments, scraps of news, some data repeated by jazz magazines and the few fans of his music that remember him and search for his very rare records.

With such lack of direct evidence, it's always the legends and myths that come alive. They spread like wildfire, becoming certainty even if they have only the frail consistency of suggestion.

And it's an old paradox, when you think about it, because Mike Taylor was born and lived in the twentieth century. So, as with the most extraordinary stories of artists dealt with by unpredictable fate, apparently no videos of him exist, just a handful of black and white photos (some made by his brother Terry, who also disappeared into thin air...) a few recordings of his music, even if he stated that he composed more than 200 pieces. No interviews. No writings or diaries. Nothing in the public domain. As with Robert Johnson, no one knows the full story...

So few of us left to give back the dignity of a musician of dazzling intuitions and obscure, disorienting fragility, just personal data to fix the facts of his life - birth, marriage, and death. Among these, his existence becomes elusive, evasive, and even clandestine.

The birth certificate reveals that Ronald Michael Taylor was born at St. Faith's Nursing Home, 24 Mount Park Road in Ealing, West London, on June 1st, 1938. His parents, Ronald Harry Frank and Joan Mary (nee Kift) lived at 5 Park Hill Court, in the same area, in a respectable apartment block.

When Mike was born, Ronald Harry Frank is 26 and according to the civil registry is "a Company Secretary", more specifically "an accountant" in the family's company, specialized in selling wallpapers and paints. The company holder is the paternal grandfather Philip Harry, who some years before started the business at 70, Swyncombe Avenue where he lived with his wife Violet Irene. [15]

Mike's Father and Mother married just few months before in 1935. That year Muriel Mary was born, and after Ronald Michael, in 1941 followed Terence Frank (Terry). In 1941, when by now England is at war, Ronald Harry Frank entered West Middlesex County Hospital in Isleworth (Middlesex), where he died on October 20th, a victim of Aplastic Anaemia, an acute blood disease. [16]

Three years later, half-way through 1944, when Mike is 6, the exhausted family was struck by the unexpected death of Joan Mary, the mother. [17] Social services then gave the custody of the children to the paternal grandparents, who after some years living at Swyncombe Avenue, in 1952 moved to 19 The Common, Ealing (London W5), in a big Victorian house just in front of Ealing Common.

Ealing, now as then, has all the main traits of a rural village in London, with typical red brick Victorian houses. Favoured during the Industrial Revolution for its calmness and the clean air, this area embodied the ideal residential area for the middle-classes.

This is where Michael, his brother and his sister lived during their childhood and teens; a quiet location, which we could suppose helped to overcome the serious shock of the loss of both parents in the twentieth century's darkest period, when England was being lacerated by the tragedy of the Second World War.

After a golden isolation during the 1930's, with relative stability and economic development, from the Summer of 1939 onwards England had to confront the severe international scenario. After taking over the government of Germany, Hitler occupied the Sudetenland and the Rhineland, before moving to occupy Poland; Mussolini moved to invade Abyssinia; 38 million gas masks were distributed to the British population; food, petrol and clothing were rationed. Hundreds of thousands of children were transferred from the main towns to the countryside.

After a first phase of Luftwaffe air attacks on ports and airports and some main towns, an attempted invasion by the Germans was made in August '41 which was repulsed. In the Summer-Autumn of 1944, after the so-called *German Blitz* and later with a shower of V1 and V2 bombs, England had to count many thousands of victims among its population.

As in many other London areas, Ealing didn't avoid the bombings. It was in ruins and everyday life was influenced by fear and anxiety.

It's not that when the war ended that things were better. Not for nothing an old English adage says: "Enjoy the war, because the peace will be terrible".

England, trying to pick itself up after the world conflict had to deal with a heavy post-war debt, that in 1949 entailed currency devaluation, lack of raw materials and food, and an acute energy crisis. The country had to endure severe winters without adequate supplies of fuel. In London public transport was affected, in schools lessons take place in chilly classrooms. Food was still rationed (and will be until 1954!) the area where Mike was living had become crumbling and exhausted. [18]

When destroyed or damaged, property needed renovation. Building materials were scarce, and bureaucracy slow in issuing building permits.

In this evident crisis, the Taylor family's commercial company was one of the few which were busy in the Ealing area, and there was no lack of work, even if Philip Harry was now without the help of his prematurely deceased son and the grandchildren were still too young to replace him.

Unfortunately no memories or documents seem left about Mike's teenage years. The thing we know [19] is that after some hesitant lessons on the piano which he had as a child, Mike started to play clarinet. During the two years of compulsory military service in the RAF, from 1956 to '58, where he became an officer, Mike came back to the piano, with a passion for jazz that would blossom very soon.

The only relevant anecdote about the experience that reveals Mike's reluctance to adapt himself to the RAF, comes from a memory of Jon Hiseman, one of the musicians who were to spend much time with him: "I think he told me he had been in the RAF at a time when all men aged 18 had to go for national service. I had no idea that Mike was an officer in the RAF and when I tried to talk to him about it he simply said that it wasn't an interesting experience. He hated it and had learnt to play piano there".

Dave Tomlin, with a past in small jazz groups playing traditional and be-bop with a passion for Johnny Griffin and Charlie Rouse's sax, knew nothing of Mike's having been an officer in the RAF, comments: "This goes some way to explain his formal manner". And in fact, in some rare photos surviving from just a few years later this can be confirmed by the well-trimmed hair, glasses and usual clothing-style of a middle class European of the '60s, "He looked like a bank clerk and acted like a mystic". [20]

Dave Tomlin says that the reason there was so little information about Taylor's life is that jazz musicians rarely spoke of their personal lives, as amongst them this was considered "not done". He says: "I'm not going to be much help here. I didn't know he had other brothers apart from Terry, and certainly I had never heard of a sister. We never ever spoke of such things being so fanatically into music".

"Fanatically into music" tells us more than any detailed descriptions about the passion of Mike's for music, suggesting that his personal universe at the time was almost totally absorbed by musical interests.

One old friend, Mike Burke says: "Mike was a close friend of mine from 1960 to 1964 when he had his quartet. My wife, Dianne, and I, and Mike and his wife Ann became very close friends and we would see each other just about every weekend. Mike and his wife were living in Richmond, Surrey at the time, and my wife and I lived in West Hampstead. Dave Tomlin also became a close friend, and one weekend he said he was going to score some weed, and we should all come to his flat in Tufnell Park Road in Holloway. It was the very first time I got stoned, and it opened up some very wide doors for me, which reverberated for the rest of my life, especially for listening to, and understanding, jazz and classical music. From then on we'd meet every weekend, sometimes more, to smoke grass and listen to music - *Jazz Messengers*, Miles, Coltrane, Monk - we'd absolutely consume it!".

I asked Burke, now a pensioner after a long career as Art Director and Graphic Designer, to be more precise. Does he remember which Mike's favourite albums were? He says: "I don't remember that Mike had any records, I'm sure he must have had a few. The only record I can remember Mike owning was *Explorations* by the Bill Evans Trio. I do recall being at a record store with him when he couldn't decide whether to buy *Explorations* by Bill Evans Trio or a Horace Silver album. I think he bought the Bill Evans... The albums we listened to a lot were *The Big Beat, Mosaic, Meet You at the Jazz Corner of the World* by *Art Blakey and the Jazz Messengers*; *My Favourite Things, Olé* by John Coltrane, *Monk at Town Hall, An Electrifying Evening with Dizzy Gillespie, Afro-American Sketches* by Oliver Nelson. There were many others, I had a fairly large collection, which is now enormous!!!"

When Michael Burke started to hang out with him, Mike was freshly married to Ann Summersby [21], a receptionist in wholesale textiles, and they lived in a terraced house at 20, St. Stephen's Gardens in Twickenham, a suburb on the west side of London.

"I believe it was a 1-bedroom flat, about 1/2 mile walk from Richmond train station", he remembers. "We only visited them there a couple of times. Mike usually drove over to our place in West Hampstead or we'd meet at Dave Tomlin's flat. Mike had a car, which at the time was unusual for most young people in England and drove us around frequently to visit various friends".

Mike drove a grey Austin A35 (the model manufactured in 1956) because, after he had taken a degree, he earned a living as a salesman for his grandfather's company. Trombonist John Mumford, describes it as "a very small car, on the back seat of which could be seen samples of wall-paper, as he was at that time, I think, working as a travelling-salesman". Dave Tomlin is still amazed about how instruments and persons could fit into so small a space: "How we all got into Mike's tiny car plus drums I don't know but it was really a great squeeze; probably we were all too stoned to notice". It was uncommon in those days that a 'wannabe' jazz musician had a car, but the car belonged to his businessman grandfather, a man about whom, as for most of Mike's life, we have just a few memories.

"I recall being introduced to his grandfather once, but just to say hello", Burke remembers. "Mike looked very much like him. He was a smart, almost military looking man, with a moustache, and I recall thinking how much he was like Mike, even though the meeting had been very brief."

"I also met his brother Terry a few times. In fact I was upset with Terry, because I loaned him a very wonderful book of jazz photographs, but he never returned it and I never saw him again after that. I never met Mike's grandmother."

"He never spoke about them to us, in fact we got the feeling that we shouldn't ask him about them, it was a subject he'd prefer to avoid", Burke confirms. "Since we know today his parents both died when Mike was very young, it explains a great deal about his personality. He was so introverted, and in many ways cold about that kind of personal and intimate communication. We knew he was brought up by his grandparents, but never found out about the details."

A man of few words and although focused entirely on music, he had one other interest: art movies, mostly all European: "I agree that Mike was totally and almost exclusively into music – listening, composing, playing...", Burke confirms. "The only other thing I thought he was somewhat interested in was he liked movies, especially "art movies": foreign or literary. The kind that show at more specialized cinemas. Definitely not action or comedy or "blockbuster" sort of films."

From these few clues we can think, maybe too superficially, that Mike had an approach to life more cerebral than physical. Anyway, he was reflective, though often subverted by a marked sense of irony.

Another memory of Burke seems to reveal this other really unexpected aspect of Mike's personality: "We did sit around listening to a particular record by Lenny Bruce over and over, every time he came to our flat, it had us all in hysterics – Dr. Sholem Stein and Shorty Petterstein - a comedy 45 that I had. But otherwise it was always music. Mostly modern Jazz, sometimes progressive classical, too. As I said, I had a large collection of records even back then".

Published in England by Vogue in 1960, the quoted single had been originally realised in the USA five years before under the title *Two Interviews Of Our Times* (Fantasy Records EP-4051). It contains two fake interviews created and performed by the famous multi-media artist Henry Jacobs (assisted by Woody Leafer), one for each side, with Doctor Sholem Stein and a jazz hipster musician called Shorty Petterstein. On his radio programme, Henry Jacobs used to interview some expert ethnic-musicologists about the origins of certain ethnic music and it could have happened that he invented an episode with a fake expert and very bizarre theories. In the case of Doctor Sholem Stein, overtly Jewish, during the eight minutes of recordings he pushed himself to state that the origin of calypso were contained in Talmudic writings. He stated this through paradoxical and philological references.

Surely more funny, even if of a sardonic and slang humour, was the Jacobs' interview with Shorty Petterstein, an introverted jazz musician (a French hornet player) reluctant even to get close to the microphone. In the beginning, to the pedantic questions of the interviewer ("How do you like Dixieland?", "What about Tchaikovsky?"...) Petterstein replies clumsily, in monosyllables, repeating as in a trance some words and overlying the interviewer's voice: "So they like your music?", Jacobs asks: "They come man, they come man, they come, they come, they come...".

"Where you will play in the future?" "Well... like... Man I am here I mean... I mellow swinging groups... I like... I like Frisco the most, man, because I mean the town... I like the seems man... I mean it's like that, you know...". To the following question, "would you suggest to the young artists to have an academic education or to play haphazard, freely?" Petterstein replies: "Man I mean... I'm a musician... To me, the most important thing is... like I should blow, I mean... like academic Julliard, man... and it's a real bad scene, you know man... bad scene..."

"Bad scene?"

"Yeah man, well I mean it's not, you know... like nothing happened..."

However towards the end, to a new question, Petterstein comes on very angry and becomes irascible and aggressive to the point where the interviewer is forced to advise him to "take it easy" and sit down and listen to the music...

Burke says: "I think you have to understand the way a hip jazz man thinks to get the humour. And of course there's a language as well as a cultural barrier here. Shorty Petterstein talks with a certain kind of jargon, and way of thinking that the interviewer has difficulty understanding, and I can't really explain it adequately to you... For instance, when Shorty says that "nothing happened" at Julliard Music Academy, he means he can't relate to the emphasis on advanced modern music teaching by composers like Bartok or Shostakovich, or 'some bit' (music of that kind) like that".

And again: "The interviewer has no idea of what Shorty is talking about and keeps asking him these annoying questions while Shorty really only wants to listen to the music. When Shorty says "A blow is like an instrument" he means that whatever the jazz musician plays - sax, trumpet, piano, bass, drums – it's all "blowing." The interviewer can't understand that and Shorty loses his temper, says he didn't want to keep answering this square's stupid questions, and the interview comes to an end".

About Mike's sense of irony: "Mike did have a great sense of humour and laughed at jokes and funny situations along with us. He was just a regular guy, but was serious about his and other people's music. He did take music seriously, though, but was always open to a good laugh".

By now London is enthusiastically discovering American Blues, while John Lennon derides the jazz enclave with a typical wry sneer (he'll say scornfully in '65: "Jazz is just a lot of old blokes drinking beer at the bar, smoking pipes and not listening to the music"). Maybe there was a kind of satisfaction among the jazz players in those years, to be citizens of a world apart [22]. Mike laughs at it, sure, but his laugh has more the flavour of self-irony.

Taylor appeared on the London jazz scene in '60 - '61, where, differing from the expected course of such a very individual artist, it seems that he found a useful, low-profile role by taking part in jam sessions. Nothing epic or extraordinary, in other words. Making no decisions as yet to form his own band, he went to places where playing jazz informally was the only aim. This was what many jazz musicians did in London, including trombonist John Mumford, who says: "I remember Mike from many occasions when he came to late-night sessions in the basement of the Nucleus Coffee Bar. My impressions of him at that time were, I think, very much as others have described him: tidy, very conventional in his clothing, appearance and manner... quietly spoken, polite".

The Nucleus Coffee Bar, located in Monmouth Street, in London's Covent Garden, was the right place for the comings and goings of jazz musicians interested in developing their abilities in the skills of improvisation. "Keeping the *chops* in good shape by having several hours experience of performance-situations a couple of times a week... People unpredictably coming and going so frequently during the Friday and Saturday all-night sessions, each weekend over perhaps a two or three year period...", Mumford explains. "All the 'Usual Faces' might look in, musicians who appreciated a chance to tackle improvisation and group harmony, using Classic Song Structure as a medium, in a different environment to that of their regular commitments. There were some other places where, varying with the music-preferences of the owner, late-night playing of one kind or another was possible, but the Nucleus was my favourite because (as we were not being paid) we were given a good spaghetti Bolognese when we stopped at around 5.30 in the morning".[23]

It was at the Nucleus, above all, that Mike could play with different musicians, getting used to the different styles and learning new harmonic dimensions while hazarding different approaches to well-known American standards.

"Piano players would come, have half an hour or so at the keyboard, (it wasn't a very good piano) and then give place to another", Mumford says. "From this aspect Mike was, grouped amongst others, a useful player".

Although the sessions usually took "standards," as the basis for improvising, some elements of Taylor's piano style (a style that will make him unique) were already there.

"In the context of a jam-session repertoire", he affirms, "mostly using tunes best described as 'American Songbook', his playing style, although clearly reflecting his awareness of the realistic need to make accompaniment that participating players will find useful, was very rarely 'ten-finger chords'. The most similar sound which I had heard at that time (and perhaps even now, too) that seemed to relate to his minimalist approach was that of Erik Satie".

An individual approach, it seems, that didn't impress double-bass player Goudie Charles who in that period (it's the beginning of 1960) was selecting a piano player for his quintet: "I auditioned twelve pianists for my group, we rated them all and he was third on our list, so he didn't get the gig. He used to turn up to the odd gig by my quintet, and we would invite him to sit in for a number or two, as you do".

In those months, before the wedding with Ann and the new house in Twickenham, Taylor was still living with his grandparents in Ealing. Even Charles, meeting him, recognised Taylor as a discreet person, "pretty introverted and intense". And as everyone admits "He was a man of few words... Mike never spoke to me about his personal life".

So his lips were sealed on that subject and there were no clues as to his previous story.

Why, for example, he decided to call himself simply "Mike", since his first name is "Ronald", as was that of his father...?

Tomlin: "Anyone named Ronald would change it as fast as possible as it would be too embarrassing to admit to. Shortening it to 'Ron' would be even worse as it would be too common - working class and very naff. So any English person would know immediately why he changed it..."

So Taylor didn't pass the examination made by Charles to become a pianist for his quintet, and continued to hang out at jazz clubs, attending with his friends the gigs available in London. And anyway, he was perhaps beginning to feel the first stirrings of ambition and the idea that he had something exclusive and unique to offer. Or maybe, as Tomlin's detailed testimony that follows regarding an evening at the Nucleus, Mike simply wanted to play after witnessing an abruptly finished performance.

"I first clapped eyes on Mike Taylor in about 1961 or thereabouts. I was playing tenor sax there with pianist Mike Butcher and trumpet player Chris Bateson one evening when Mike Butcher had one of his attacks of madness, standing up and shouting obscenities at the wall behind the piano and then stalking of into the night still muttering to himself. At this point a very straight and conservatively dressed man came over and asked if he could play with us. He then sat down at the piano and began playing a blues somewhat in the style of Bill Evans, which pleased Chris and I as this was the kind of music we admired most of all. At the end of the piece the pianist, who introduced himself as Mike Taylor, said that he was forming a group and asked if we were interested in joining him, however, he insisted that he only wanted musicians who could read music. This Chris was unable to do but I could just about get by and said that I was interested".

There are a some details in Tomlin's memory that shed light on Taylor's embryonic artistic ideas and the desire to form a band with musicians able to read from a score. These are the basis of a precise musical poetic, already an artistic, manifesto.

Jazz can be thought of as music of the spirit; free, with few structures. In those years, America had been central to ideas of a new musical territory, questioning outdated rules. *Free-jazz* carried the vehemence of a force of nature, Europe was still struggling with modern jazz forms - be-bop and hard-bop, and strangely, London was experiencing a recovery of tradition: skiffle, folk, and popular songs.

In England jazz music had been personified by American legendary figures, resulting in a "new tradition " of musicians playing hard bop as an established style. In the London of 1957 one of the most famous groups was Ronnie Scott and Tubby Hayes' quintet called Jazz Couriers – double-bass, drums, piano and two sax tenors – a simplification, sure, compared with the harmonic somersaults of bebop, but a new way to rethink the rhythm and find connections with blues and gospel. It was not by chance that Ronnie Scott (with his friend

Pete King) in '59 had the idea to open a club in Gerrard Street, Soho, where American jazz stars could play: the original project included plans to support local young bands but for some reason this didn't work. [24]

As we have seen, Bill Evans was one of the first pianists to be heard by Mike Taylor, *Explorations* (published that year, in 1961) being one of the records he owned. Enrico Pieranunzi, one of the best Italian jazz pianists, is not wrong in a biographic essay written some years ago on Evans, when he observes *Explorations*, in which Evans' revolution went through a new interpretation of the ballad.

He writes: "The 'romantic' aspect of jazz (a term that the pianist wasn't crazy about, at least in its superficial and obvious sense) had been, before Evans, the almost exclusive domain of singers and horn players (Coleman Hawkins, Ben Webster, Davis himself, Chet Baker, Helen Merrill). Never, in the history of jazz, had the piano been used as a vehicle to 'sing' stories from the heart – or their sad endings either – like a trumpet, sax or human voice had been. Evans was a revolutionary in this. He changed a solidly established tradition, expanding it to include the piano which, before them, had been thought of either as a percussion instrument or as an 'imitator' of the trumpet or sax, the most visible jazz instruments". [25]

While the aesthetics of the time was radically changing into unstructured, timbre and harmonic aggressions; digressing into atonal free forms, Evans chooses the 'low-profile' of the internal dialogue with the trio, reducing instruments and musicians while the opposite widespread tendency is to play with ensemble. A choice that seems to have seduced Mike in the same way.

So it's easy today to imagine Taylor reading intently the record cover notes written by producer Orrin Keepnews who tells of the rise of this young pianist elected for two years (1958 & 1959) by the critics of the prestigious *Downbeat* "New Star Pianist", third in the rank of the best pianist in 1960. Look at the stark picture on the cover, with that close-up of Evans in a white shirt and glasses, according to the fashion of the time, and the modest expression of one who, reluctant to exhibit himself, wants to 'communicate' with his music alone.

How to explain Taylor's need to count on musicians able to read written music conceived in detailed form as if it were a classical composition?

Tomlin is self-evident in his flat explication of it and maybe, conscious or not, this was the most plausible of Taylor's demands: "The reason was that he was writing music on paper, so to learn the pieces you had to be able to read".

After the meeting with Tomlin and Bateson at the Nucleus, Taylor's first step was to form a quintet and rehearse at his grandparents' house in Ealing. Goudie Charles, who some months before rejected him for his band, became the bass player of Taylor's quintet. The circumstances of their meeting, as often happens, was a matter of chance: "I joined Mike's quintet about a year after he auditioned for my group", Goudie Charles remembers. "Dave Tomlin asked me to join, not Mike. Dave lived near me and heard me practising and knocked on the door - I didn't know him before that. Bass players were in short supply in London then, so casual hirings like this happened a lot".

The first drummer of the band was Peter (Ginger) Baker, soon to be a star with *Cream* and one of the most famous rock drummers ever, but so overwhelmingly loud that coexistence with the double-bass soon became impossible. The next drummer to join was a young 17 year old named Randy Jones, later to emigrate to the USA and become the regular drummer for more than twenty years with Dave Brubeck' s band.

Goudie Charles again: "Baker was incredibly good but phenomenally loud. There was no amplification then. We were all acoustic and he just overwhelmed us. (…) My fingers used to be bloodied because ridiculously you just pull so much harder with a loud drummer. It's a waste of time but everybody does it. I said, 'Who's replacing him?' He said, 'Oh this great 17 year old drummer from Slough called Randy Jones.' If I'm going to be brutally honest, personally, I preferred playing with Randy. I'm not putting Pete down because he was a great drummer, and if we had all been amplified it would have been okay, but Randy was so much better for me personally to play with because he was very quiet and a wonderful player even at the age of 17". [26]

Taylor now started to compose some new tracks, also influenced by hard bop giants such as the *Horace Silver Quintet* and *Art Blakey's Jazz Messengers*. One of them miraculously emerged in 2012 from a live recording taken at Modern Jazz Workshop in Herne Bay (near Whitstable, Kent) on May 1961, a place where the band begun to play often in those days and quite sinisterly near to the place where years later Taylor would meet his tragic end.

Titled "Phrygie", it's documented on a compilation of rarities published in 2012. [27] Even if Dave Tomlin admits now that, "There's nothing I can say about the track. I've no idea where or when it was recorded. So of course I have no memories of it", he explains that "the name "Phrygie" comes from the Phrygian Scale upon which the tune was based".

"I do remember it was a piece we played often around the clubs and was a composition by Mike Taylor".

The quintet - Mike Taylor on piano, Dave Tomlin on sax, Randy Jones on drums, Frank Powell on trumpet and Charles Goudie on double-bass - plays the tune with a be-bop attack, showing the acquisition of modal structures alternate to the more traditional chord changes used at the time. Apart for Randy Jones' quite grave rhythm, that marks the tune more with the drum bass than the other instruments, notable are the solos of Tomlin, who plays the theme and the following reprise, and Taylor's long piano solo before the last reprise, where the reference to Horace Silver's blues structure and discreet skill on the keyboards is quite evident.

Even if the recording is quite modest, it attests to Taylor's poetic approach, while still well rooted in the tradition of contemporary British jazz.

Charles is to the point when he affirms: "Mike was just one of dozens of young musicians trying to play the music, and although I know this whole mini-industry has grown up around his legend, at the time I played with him, he wasn't regarded as anything special; at that time his writing was more interesting than his playing. In my opinion, easily the best young piano player around at that time was a guy called Richard Rushton, who eventually emigrated to the USA - I don't know what became of him".

In fact, in those days the London jazz references were basically two, and Taylor didn't escape the environmental conditioning: "There were two main USA groups influencing the young UK musicians at that time", Charles recalls, "one was *Art Blakey's Jazz Messengers* and the other was Horace Silver's quintet. Mike didn't particularly play like Horace Silver (who does?), but his writing was influenced by him..."

Silver passed away in June 2014 from natural causes at 85, having made his debut in 1950 playing with Stan Getz on tour, before going to New York, and two years later joining the Art Blakey's band. From '56 he formed his quintet going from standards to his own compositions and obtaining a progressive success in Europe, above all in France, thanks to his brilliant and syncopated style that combined hard-bop elements with references to be-bop, gospel and blues: "A crisp, chipper but slightly wayward style, idiosyncratic enough to take him out of the increasingly stratified realms of bebop piano", as Richard Cook and Brian Morton write in the influential *The Penguin Guide to Jazz on CD*. "Blues and gospel-tinged devices and percussive attacks give his methods a more colourful style, and a generous good humour gives all his records an upbeat feel". [28]

A kind of jazz that embodied the idea of mainstream music; easy to listen to, shiny and immediate, able to alternate ballads with a strong pianistic impact (as the wonderful "Sweet Stuff" from *Finger Poppin'* published in 1959 or "Sister Sadie", from *Blowin' the Blues Away*, published the same year) with a mid and up tempo hard-bopping compositions as the eponymous "Finger Poppin'" or "The Preacher", his first recording success.

When Silver's records started coming to England, the impact of his music was so strong as to surprise and influence more or less all the London jazz scene. Ian Carr will come to include him as one of his most important influences, with other clear references found in such bands as *Chris McGregor's Blue Notes*. [29]

Above all, critics give to Silver the credit for having refined the conception of the jazz quintet with tenor trumpet at centre stage while several groups of the period were moulded on his recordings.

In the Nucleus at that time some other main references would have been John Lewis & Milt Jackson's *Modern Jazz Quartet*, Ahmad Jamal, Westcoast pianist Carl Perkins, Harold Land (an influential pre-Coltrane sax player) and Moondog. Burke recalls that on some occasions Mike had expressed negative opinions about the Red Garland's piano style, by now a legend of John Coltrane's quintet, coming to realise that "he hated the way he played piano". The memory, even if suggestive, doesn't reveal anything about the process of selection by which Taylor chose his original models.

Another possible interpretation is that the supposed 'hatred' for Garland's piano technique reveals that Taylor was sure he would never play the instrument in that way, that delicate and slim blues style derived from the declared love for Art Tatum, Nat Cole, Bud Powell and the shining style of Erroll Garner. A common thread of pianistic aesthetic that, though deeply rooted in the blues, maybe Taylor felt to be quite irrelevant, attracted as he was by European classical forms (for example, Satie, Debussy, and Ravel...), he probably heard these as a teenager, or by other styles he heard on the air (Evans, Monk, Nelson...). For now anyway, his approach to the keyboards was still so conventional that he didn't create any particular impressions around. Clear evidence of this is another live piece, miraculously recorded during an evening at Herne Bay by Charles. It's a 9:53 rendition of the Thelonious Monk classic "Straight, No Chaser", a benchmark in the American pianist repertoire composed in 1951: a great solo by Tomlin, the real centrepiece of the band, Jones' drums precise even if elementary, scarcely creative as usual, an essential piano that duets with sax until 5.34, when it plays a solo supported only by drums. A solo characterized by a blues mould, clearly rooted in tradition, with a bopping style, an enthralling groove, even if not too original.

Goudie Charles is right when he says: "As you will note from "Straight, No Chaser", there was nothing particularly remarkable or legendary about the Mike Taylor group in which I played. In my opinion, Dave Tomlin's tenor sax and Randy Jones's drums were the best things about that group."

Tomlin introduces some very interesting observations about the role of certain music critics anxiously looking for style-comparisons in order to label the music: "Well, Horace Silver was one of our favourites. Although Hank Mobley was one of my favourite tenor players (amongst others) the *Mike Taylor Quartet* tried not to sound like anyone else - very difficult as so many players had already broken most of the new ground so to find spaces in between them was hard, but we did try. Many other players at the time modelled themselves on the 'greats', for instance had you heard Trevor Watts playing alto-sax you would have thought it was Bird himself he was so good at it..."

And again: "Writers about jazz always try to find these sort of connections so that they can say who the different musicians modelled themselves on. Whenever I've been interviewed the interviewers have suggested all kinds of people, for instance - Dave Brubeck/Paul Desmond, which is ridiculous, so I have to say again that although the *Mike Taylor Quartet* appreciated people like Horace Silver, Bill Evans etc., Mike's compositions where not consciously based on any of them".

Pete Brown, who had known Taylor through Burke, remembers he listened to him for the first time at The Troubadour (Coffee House) in Brompton Road, London Earl's Court, another important club at that time, from 1963 characterized by a scheduling of gigs, mostly folk. Brown thinks Taylor's way of playing initially was a mix of Silver and Monk: "We were all big jazz fans. I think I first saw him play at the Troubadour with a line-up that included my friend John Mumford on trombone and Randy Jones on drums. I knew that Mike was very serious about his music - his early bands played a lot of Horace Silver, Monk and Blakey tunes. His very adept piano playing was firstly a mix of Monk and Silver influences, until it evolved into his own style. I don't know anything about his early days, when I met him he was a commercial artist, still not a professional musician. Very well-dressed, and either married or about to be married to a very attractive girl. I think I went to their place once, I recall it as being very smart".

Despite the work of brother Terry, then road manager and photographer of the *Graham Bond Organization* [30], who in his free time helped Mike, the quintet got few gigs with Jones preferring to play full time with his own group which was proving to be of more interest to promoters: "*The Mike Taylor quintet* didn't do that many gigs, and I was fitting these in with my own quintet's gigs, which were more plentiful. I left Mike's quintet amicably when I came under the spell of Coltrane and was lucky enough to have in my group a West Indian tenor saxophonist called Milton James, who was just about the first guy in London doing the Coltrane thing (we later became the Milton James Quartet, I was still on bass.)".

Concerts aside, it's another precious memory of Burke that recalls the climax of excited apprenticeship in these first months of activity: "I didn't actually attend any concerts by Mike and his bands. It was far less formal than that. Mostly suburban pubs with dance facilities, and most of the other people there were either with the band, (us, friends, musicians, wives, girlfriends) or other than that they were young people who were more interested in dancing than listening to the actual music. A lively crowd, but not really that interested in the music, more about dancing, meeting each other, stuff like that. As I said, a young crowd, mostly teenagers..."

So just a few people, mostly friends. "The only people who were interested in the music were us. It was never a formal concert situation with rows of seats".

Money... forget it.

According to Burke, "Anyway Mike didn't seem too worried by reactions of the audience, just focused on his music: I also think, that these dates were 'just another gig' to Mike, when I was there, and he was really more interested in the music than in the audience reaction. Anyway, he never had a huge outgoing ego about himself as long as I knew him..."

Also a memory by double-bassist Ronald *Ron* Rubin, who had met Taylor at "a very atmospheric coffee house in Soho called *Sam Widge's*, where the likes of John Mumford, Chris Bateson and Dick Heckstall-Smith liked to jam into the early hours", confirms the prevalent condition of informality of that period: "We used to go down there in '61 and '62 and play at the Modern Jazz Workshop. In the afternoon, we'd smoke ganja and eat ice cream on the pier, then we'd go to Mike's grandparents' house for tea and scones. Later at the gig we'd play our way-out stuff to a small audience of enthusiasts".

Just a few black and white pictures taken by brother Terry remain to testify to it now.

It's the first of July 1962, and by now Rubin has joined the quintet after having come up to London from his native Liverpool, where he had received his first experiences with some jazz local bands. In London he had already played with the *Glyn Morgan Band, Dick Williams Band* and Brian Leake.

These are among the few photographs circulated through the years that document one of the many sessions at the Jazz Workshop in Herne Bay; Mike on piano, Rubin on double-bass, Tomlin tenor sax, Chris Bateson trumpet and Jones on drums.

On a couple of these Taylor, wearing striped suit and heavy black-rimmed glasses, with a short haircut as worn at that time, is intently following the score on the keyboard; on another, taken during a break, Taylor and Rubin are bent over a score. Mike has his hand placed on his mouth, it's evident he's looking for a development of the tune he's rehearsing.

These pictures emanate seriousness and evidence of a passion that by now attempts to acquire the characteristics of a profession.

Although the finding of these photographs attests to the existence of some well-defined line-ups, in these first months of activity it is difficult to retrace accurately what was happening. The London scene, now so vibrant with emerging talent, seemed to be founded on a collusion of musicians and bands inside a closed but highly dynamic microcosm.

Tomlin: "Jazz musicians in those days nearly all knew each other because temporary groups formed all the time to do gigs. For instance I knew John Mumford because we played in a group which went on tour to Denmark with Sister Rosetta Tharpe, Mumford (trombone), Ginger Baker (drums), Diz Dizley (guitar), Bob Wallace (trumpet), myself clarinet etc. (this was long before meeting Mike.) Those kind of groups were forming all the time and then dissolving when the job was done".

John Mumford remembers he played with Taylor in some small bands where it was not certain that the pianist was the leader: "I do remember playing in a small band-formation with Mike, but at that time (probably before his first recordings) he had not yet developed his personal compositions/materials. I'm not even sure if it was *his* gig, so we would have been using "standard" jazz tunes".

Mumford is persuaded that Taylor, bearing in mind his financial independence, "Would be quite selective about where and in what company he would feel comfortable playing" and that "a year before his first album was recorded, he would be have been mostly "sitting in" with bands in a low-profile way".

This was an attitude that could have misled some biographers, causing them to imagine stable line-ups following a rigid chronological order, when they were simple jam sessions, random encounters, or quick collaborations.

As in the case of that unusual line-up with Chris Bateson and Frank Powell on trumpets, John Mumford on trombone [31], who comments: "Don't recall that event, very unusual to feature two trumpets and trombone, I'd think there must have been at least one reed player as well. Leads me to think that it would have been mostly jazz standards being played, as in Mike's carefully constructed compositions, where multiple front line instruments are used, written parts and rehearsals would be necessary, but I do not remember them happening..."

Surely more suggestive is the hypothesis, circulating through those years, of a trio with Ginger Baker on drums and Jack Bruce on bass (future rock legends with *Cream*) between 1962 and 1963. Tomlin considers this circumstance rather absurd: "I've never heard of a trio with that line up. Jack Bruce did do some rehearsals with the quartet but Ginger Baker? No...."

Mumford: "I don't recall this trio formation. Did you learn about this from someone? At that time, Jack I think would have been moving between Cyril Davies, Alexis Korner, *Johnny Burch Octet*, and early *Graham Bond Organisation*. Ginger Baker was probably not yet involved with Jack on any full-time group commitments. A couple of names who had begun to take a managerial & agency interest could be: Robert Stigwood and Giorgio Gomelsky, both of whom appear to have possibly had contractual dealings at around that time. It would be a typical 'Management Move' to suggest the 'Taylor/Bruce/Baker' line-up, maybe even going as far as organising a recording experiment... I am a bit surprised by the thought of Jack Bruce and Ginger Baker working together with Mike in a trio, as whenever I heard the two of them (Jack and Ginger) there was always a very pronounced 'Powerhouse' kind of approach. Mike's compositions were not along those lines. Although I haven't got as much information as you have, I always think of the John Hiseman/Tony Reeves version of the trio as being the definitive sound".

As both Dave Tomlin and John Mumford agree; "There was a lot of interaction between all the names mentioned above, all focused in London, everyone hearing everyone else. I do not remember doing any "introducing", as it really would not have been necessary".

If it is sure, as I've documented, that Baker would have played with Taylor in one of the first line-ups with Goudie Jones on bass, it also allows that Jack Bruce had by then met Taylor. Anyway, in February '63 the two future stars would join the *Graham Bond Trio* (later the *Graham Bond Organization*), according Pete Brown "One of the three or four greatest British bands ever" [32], and just years later they would have collaborated with Taylor in 1967.

In any case, a fact is cleverly highlighted by Duncan Heining in his biography about Taylor, that "For a relative unknown Taylor certainly seemed able to pull some highly talented musicians into his orbit" [33]. An orbit where, in different times, it will merge also drummers Jon Hiseman and Laurie Allan, saxophone player Trevor Watts and trumpeters Henry Lowther, bassists Martin Gail and Ron Rubin, who will become his friend until the end of his life.

At this point we have only Ron Rubin's journal to help us.

After the days with Goudie Charles' quintet, on June 26th, 1962 Taylor was on stage at Piedmont Restaurant, in Frith Street, Soho. With him, also Rubin on double-bass, Tomlin on tenor, Bateson on trumpet and Randy Jones on drums. A line-up that will last for some months, playing most of all at the Modern Jazz Workshop in Herne Bay - "really a kind of upmarket shack", in Ron Rubin's words.

"This was to be a regular fortnightly gig until I joined Sandy Brown and Al Fairweather. Highest gig money was two quid apiece, lowest five bob, but we had a ball!" the double-bassist noted after the evening of 1st July.

After a rehearsal on 5th at Piedmont Restaurant, in fact, from July to October the quintet played gigs at the Modern Jazz Workshop, with some occasional appearances at Bernie's Club in Acton, at Club Octave in Southall and at Richmond Community Centre.

The line-up with Martin Gail on double-bass instead of Rubin, who meanwhile joined Sandy Brown's band, survives thanks to a sequence of black and white shots taken by Burke at the Richmond's Jazz Cellar in November 1962. He says: "These were not taken at a concert... it was a jazz club that met on Friday evenings at a pub in a London suburb. I took my camera but didn't have any special lights and I never use flash because I think it flattens the image too much and gives it an unrealistic appearance. That explains why the photos tend to be very dark and patchy, but I think that makes the photos more like the atmosphere and ambience of the smoky jazz basement environment".

Actually the photographs show us the mood of a typical jazz club in London at the beginning of the Sixties; narrow and smoky, chaotic and packed with writhing bodies. A sense of climax wonderfully described by Julio Cortazar in *The Pursuer*, a novel published in 1959 placed in Paris in the Fifties, where it shows the psychophysical decline of Johnny Carter, a character inspired by the legend of Charlie Parker.

And it's not difficult to imagine the intense interest experienced, regardless of any lack of commercial status, at that time. Dave Gelly, musician and jazz journalist who met Taylor some years later, in a 2007 reminiscence tells that, "There was quite a lot of jazz about in London and the south-east at the time, although it was mostly shoestring stuff, played in the back rooms of pubs, with musicians collecting a share of the door money. Nobody made a living from it. Nevertheless, the *Melody Maker*, *Jazz News* and other papers did at least attempt to cover this activity by publishing brief live reviews and profiles. There was also a certain amount of live jazz on the BBC Light Programme and Third Programme, which, unlike today's celebrity-obsessed media, were mildly receptive to new and untried talents." [34]

In another picture taken at that club, there are Gail, Powell and Tomlin. A relevant detail is the music stand in front of Powell that confirms Taylor's use of 'the dots'.

A music stand with scores lies next to the piano and Mike is playing, his eyes focused on the keyboard. On this shot, again he wears a white shirt and tie, the same heavy-rimmed glasses, his hair now longer. He is looking relaxed, and his posture tensed as if ready to catch the sounds almost with surprise. His jacket is balled up on top of the piano, with the hem hanging down to the keyboard, this says it all about the informality of that evening and about Taylor's indifference to his image.

There's much of the early years of Taylor on this photograph. Quiet, and absorbed in the music, a poised young musician, striving to express himself through the jazz. *"Self-contained, reticent, remote* would be words descriptive of my impression of his persona", Mumford says.

Another picture in the same photographic session portrays Mike again at the piano, this time his attention is directed towards Burke's camera. At his back Powell has his head bent down and Gail is intent on the double-bass. Now, while smoking a small cigar, Mike's look is of a dreamy pensiveness, as if his mind were absorbed in other kinds of thought.

Michael Burke remembers in that same period "Mike wrote the music for a short movie I wrote and was directed by my friend Ron Ostwald (who later changed his name to Mark Petersen). He wrote and played a wonderful hard-bop score, and the rehearsals took place in the bedroom of my parents' house in Belsize Park, London".

"Ron Ostwald, and I", he follows, "were particularly interested in movies and movie-making, especially the new kinds of film that were coming out of New York, (John Cassavates), the French New Wave, Truffaut, Chabrol, and Italian movies by Fellini and Antonioni. We both thought we could try to make a short movie ourselves, and I showed Ron a story I'd written some months previously, and he was enthusiastic enough to decide to film it".

The short film (just 16 minutes long) is still available at the British Film Institute of London that financed a part of the work. Titled *The Party,* the movie starring actors Martin Asbury, Pat O' Rourke and Peter Brown, later famous poet, musician and lyricist for the Cream, and it tells the story of "a young man at a party which symbolises his whole attitude to life, with both disappointments and new beginnings". [35]

Mark Petersen, now living in London Highgate, recreates the event: "I first met Mike through Mike Burke in 1960. Mike Burke and I were hoping to make a film together based on a short story of his. We had shot and edited a 16mm test sequence in order to submit it to the British Film Institute for funding. Mike Taylor was recruited to supply the score for this sequence. I got on very well with him and I admired his music and thought it ideal for the sequence. The film was financed partly by the BFI and partly from my grant as an art student at St Martins School of Art. When the whole film was eventually finished, Mike created the music which ran throughout the film (about 10 themes). I'm not sure what titles Mike chose for these themes, but I do remember that one was called "Anacleto's Theme". The theme had a vaguely Mexican feel to it (Anacleto was a Mexican bandit played by Dirk Bogarde in a movie called *The Singer not the Song*). The recording was a primitive affair - we recorded it on Mike Burke's domestic tape recorder through a single microphone - not ideal".

The movie recordings took several weeks. "Ron took over the direction, with some assistance from me", Burke says. "The film was shot on 16mm, in black and white with sound. We decided we wanted original background music, particularly hard-bop jazz which I loved. I played Ron a track from Mingus *Ah-Um,* namely "Goodbye Pork Pie Hat" which we thought set the mood for the movie. I thought Mike Taylor might be the perfect musician and could possibly be interested in writing some tunes and playing them, with his quintet. So I invited them over to my parents flat, where I was still living, and played them the Mingus track, said that was the kind of thing we'd like. Mike sat down at the piano I had in my bedroom and within 10 minutes came up with a song that fit the bill perfectly! His tenor sax player hadn't arrived yet, so I played the melody on flute, by ear, not very well, I admit!"

"When Dave arrived, Mike had already made a musical notation and Dave played it with so much style that we were all knocked out! They, the quintet, that is, Frank Powell on trumpet, Dave, tenor, Mike on piano, Martin Gail on bass and Randy Jones, drums, recorded 6 or 7 wonderful original numbers, all composed by Mike Taylor, a complete background soundtrack for the movie. Ron succeeded in getting a grant to finish making it from the British Film Institute, and it was later shown at the National Film Theatre in London. Unfortunately, by that time Ron Ostwald and I had had a falling out and I never got to see the film until many years later on a home projector. Glad to say we soon settled our differences and have now been friends for many, many years!"

I asked Burke to be clearer about those tunes: "I have already answered, with the way he sat down at the piano in my room and formulated the first song. The others were more or less typical hard bop kind of tunes like the ones we were listening to by the Jazz Messengers, or Horace Silver. I wasn't present when he wrote them, but heard them performed by the quintet". A memory confirmed by Pete Brown: "I just watched some of *The Party*... Music sounds great, typical hard bop, before the real Mike Taylor emerged".

Petersen realised the tracks were the basis of *Pendulum*, the first album Mike Taylor would record later, when he accidentally heard of the tragic end of the pianist. He says that "in 1969 I was driving home with the radio on and the compère said that the next number was in tribute to the late Mike Taylor - I thought it must be another Mike Taylor, but then the number they played was one of the main themes from *The Party* I had to pull over - it really hit me hard".

The valid partnership should have accomplished another project around the end of that year, but unfortunately everyone seems to have lost the tracks: "Later in 1962 Mike Taylor and I worked together on another film sequence which I directed. This was a 35mm 'teaser' for a proposed feature film called *Conflict*. The music was exciting and very cinematic (Mike was by now getting a real feel for film scores). Again it was recorded on a domestic tape recorder through a single mike. Spurred on by this experience I built a primitive sound mixer for Mike - a little black box which could accommodate three microphones each with its own volume control. I'm not sure whether he ever used it, since shortly after I gave it to him we began losing touch".

As we can see, this artistic cooperation was practised within the small circle of friends. And if it seems true that brother Terry was the first manager of Taylor's band, and as the author of the few photos of Mike which have survived, Michael Burke, for instance, surprisingly was the main designer of the first concert posters of the quintet. He remembers: "I designed and printed some silk-screen posters for the band. I believe his grandfather owned a paint factory in West London and that's where I printed the posters... We, that is Mike and I, went to the factory on Sundays when nobody else was there and made use of the facilities. I have absolutely no idea where the paint factory was, maybe somewhere in Ealing, but I'm not sure. Mike drove us there, but it was a part of London that I was completely unfamiliar with..."

At the beginning of 1963 a crucial defection from the quintet was when Frank Powell, "much more interested [in moving] into a Tad Dameron style jazz" (Tomlin's elucidation), left the band for good. The fact had a decisive consequence because at that point Mike decided to do away with trumpet altogether and just run a quartet.

Tomlin: "Frank didn't last long since he was really into Tad Dameron and kept trying to introduce some of his pieces. Mike wasn't interested and was only into playing his own compositions which I too began to recognise as something rather special. So Frank left and Henry Lowther (trumpet) joined us for a while, but he was much in demand and soon took a different path. It was at this point that Mike decided to reduce the group to a quartet, something I was a little nervous about since I didn't think I was really up to being the solo front-man. However Mike thought I was capable so I took the plunge..."

So, the first quartet line-up consisted of Mike Taylor on piano, Dave Tomlin on tenor, Ron Rubin on bass, and at first Randy Jones on drums.

First official gig at *Bernie's Club* (Acton) on Sunday 21st April ("Take-home pay: ten bob", Rubin writes); then, on Sunday 12th May at the prestigious *Marquee Club* in London's Oxford Street.

"I remember Mike's quartet had a gig at the *Marquee Club*, on Oxford Street in the West End of London", Burke says. "They were playing the upstairs lounge, while *The Jazz Couriers* (Ronnie Scott, Tubby Hayes) were playing the main room downstairs. Before the gig started we went outside and attempted to smoke a joint in the doorway of a next-door shoe store, but Ronnie and Tubby had beaten us to it and were already there puffing away! We had to find somewhere else to get high!" [36]

Tomlin: "Occasionally other bass players would take Ron's place, Jack Bruce for example and eventually Jon Hiseman took over on drums and Tony Reeves became the regular bassist and we began playing at small out-of–town jazz clubs around the London suburbs".

Reeves states that he doesn't remember anything about that period (apart from the fact that, he says, "I think Jon Hiseman may have brought us together"), but he can offer us a clear picture of Mike the first time he met him: "A gentle, quietly spoken, rather introverted man, but with a strong 'inner flame'".

More or less the same first impressions got by Ron Rubin who described him in his diary as "a gaunt mélange of inspiration and inadequacy, hipness and naiveté". [37] And years later to Richard Morton Jack: "You could hardly have found a more immaculate and polite chap than Mike. He was almost in the Ivy League mould: highly intelligent, well-read and thoughtful, as well a being totally uncompromising musician". [38]

Henry Lowther, who years after met Taylor again, described his first meeting with him and gives an interesting psychological interpretation that reveals the pianist's determination to preserve his integrity of image. He says: "I do remember Mike being very smartly dressed, obsessionally so, in traditional English clothes; blazer with brass buttons, striped shirt and tie, smartly creased grey flannel trousers and polished black shoes".

Here the focus is clearly on that "obsessionally so", and on "traditional English clothes", since in those years English jazz musicians exhibited a more bohemian look; Taylor was anything but classic.

The same impression free sax player Evan Parker received when he met Taylor for the first time: "He and Dave Tomlin came to the house of a friend in Staines, a town to the west of London. The house was large enough so that we could play without disturbing anyone. They were much better players than me and my friends and were very "hip" - Ivy League clothes, *de rigueur* in Modern Jazz at that time, and a lot of justified attitude.

"I think they came there to be introduced and to jam. They were pretty disappointed at the low level we were playing at. They were for want of a better word "cool" or "hip". The modern jazz scene was very much about who you had played with as much as what you knew - of course these two things are connected!"

"I added the detail of clothes because I know the expression *bella figura* and in each culture and sub-culture at any given time in history what constitutes *bella figura* is at least in part determined by the choice of clothes. In case you think I was being superior I should make it clear that I also went through a similar change of look. You only need to see the photographs of Miles Davis, Bill Evans, Charles Lloyd and others across the dates 1964 - 1970 to observe the same transition. The *zeitgeist* as the Germans say".

So a smart look that seemed to coincide with a precise gesture control, to a refined style.

This is confirmed by Burke, who reveals: "I do know that Mike never would drink wine; he never got up and danced when the rest of us did, especially when we smoked and listened to records. Mike would sit and watch us, usually with an amused look on his face, but we didn't really know what he was thinking".

This is also more or less memory of Dave Tomlin: "Mike at that time was only smoking dope and we all used to get stoned together after gigs back at my flat we also used to dance there with his wife and various girl friends the Twist to Chubby Checker records which were very popular at that time, and we used to line up, one in front of the other and twist. Mike never danced, he used to stand in front watching us through a faceted prism from a chandelier which he carried in his pocket - he was too straight to let himself go and dance. In another room was a bowl filled with grass which we would help ourselves to, which puzzled any girlfriends we brought back who often wondered how we could enjoy ourselves falling about laughing without any drink in evidence".

Focused on his music,, careful of appearance, in a way quite abstinent, "too straight to let himself go and dance". His only concession, the cannabis. An attitude moreover very widely held by young people, since using a joke told by actor Nigel Havers, London "was a fragrant haze of Brut aftershave and cannabis". [39]

With an amusing anecdote Tomlin tells how easy it was to get it: "There was this guy called Jimmi Fox, a trumpet player, we mostly used to get it from. No one ever heard him actually play the trumpet. He had a false bottom in his case, so people would think he was a musician, but when he took his trumpet out he had all these deals in there. It was a good cover". [40]

With Taylor it seems the consumption of grass may have been simply a reaction to his middle-class origins, or was it a way of adopting the bohemian life style connected with the jazz music scene?

Dave Gelly remembers the first meeting between Jon Hiseman and Mike, dating it towards the end of 1963, he seems to prefer the second option: "Jon told me that he had met this remarkable pianist-composer, unlike any he had heard before, and had started rehearsing with him in Ilford. Jon was aged 19 or 20 at the time, living with his parents in Eltham, south-east London. To get to Ilford meant a complicated drive to the other side of the river Thames, through the Blackwall Tunnel. I don't remember what Jon said about Mike, except that he was very dedicated and different from anyone else on the London scene. At the time, Mike was working in his grandfather's business, delivering paint, wallpaper etc. in a van..."

This memory later amended by Hiseman: "Dave is confused, that was Peter Lemer, another pianist. No, I drove to an empty shop in Ilford where the quartet rehearsed. I sensed this was important for me. I felt conscious of being original when I played with Mike - he forced it upon me by playing the way he did".

Philip John Albert Hiseman, to everyone simply *Jon,* after his name was published in the *Melody Maker* by error, and who was still earning a living at the Television Audience Measurement (TAM) - a market research company - had met Taylor through Jack Bruce; and even if he believed in the existence of a Taylor-Baker-Bruce trio, says: "Mike telephoned me when Ginger and Jack left his trio to join Graham Bond. Jack had recommended me. When we finally got to meet he seemed very quiet and unassuming but very sure of himself. He appeared to have a wisdom that came from clarity of purpose. He did not seem to make choices as there were no choices for him. He did what he did and was not interested in the consequences. He was always smoking a lot of dope - he never played unless he had smoked a lot before. He was composing and playing whenever he could".

In the beginning of 1964, Ron Rubin went to Palma de Mallorca (Spain) where from April to October he played bass at the Indigo Jazz Club (between sharing the bill with Rendell, Scott and a young, still unknown Robert Wyatt). Mike's band was now made up of Taylor, Tomlin (tenor saxophone), Hiseman (drums) and Jack Bruce (bass). Again a few concerts in small clubs, playing for peanuts, but with a very peculiar form.

As Hiseman says, it was "small gigs with very small audiences most of the time. Very few people understood what he was doing. The melodies were usually obscure if he had adapted a standard tune, although his own melodies in his own compositions were actually very tuneful. I suppose you could tap your feet to the music that you wouldn't necessarily know where the beat actually was".

A recollection of Digby Fairweather, jazz cornettist, author and broadcaster gravitating on the scene, confirms it: "I remember very well the first - and only! - time I heard Mike. It was at the *Studio Jazz Club* in Westcliff-on-Sea, one Friday night in (I think) 1964, and the last time I spoke to Jon Hiseman he remembered the night too, if I remember rightly. Resident at Studio Jazz on Friday nights was the *Southend Modern Jazz Quintet* (SMJQ) led by tenorist Kenny Baxter. Quite later on in the evening my recollection is of a quite sudden and probably unscheduled 'invasion' by the Mike Taylor Quartet: Dave Tomlin, Jack Bruce, Jon Hiseman and the leader. They took the stage to play what - to us - sounded to be some very contemporary Coltrane style jazz, and as we were more used to Parker, Rollins and Adderley their arrival created quite a stir and some lively controversy too! Whether the group had been 'booked' I'm not sure but my impression is that they just came in for the heck of it - and blew the club apart in the process".

An anecdote that we find on the retrospective written by Bolton for *Jazz Journal* in 1974: "Mike's group did play gigs at a Westcliff-on-Sea club where audience could get close up to the stage, and this helped in getting across the new dimension in music which the pianist was striving for. But elsewhere the 'new school' had to fight established ideas of what kind of jazz should be presented". [41]

A concept sustained in some way by Hiseman when he says "Mike recognised clearly that a lot of his contemporaries were simply mimicking the greats, especially the Americans. He knew he was different. I never heard him play a conventional piece of music on the piano, and don't even know if he knew how to. Instead, he'd reduced standards to a few notes, then improvise around them. He was interested in extending chords as far as he possible could, not playing tunes at parties. He had no interest in those forms". [42]

And again: "Playing clever things over a chord sequence wasn't enough. There had to be more to it – more depth, more emotional communication. When we were working on a piece in rehearsal he would sometimes sit absolutely still and silent at the piano until he came to a considered view on exactly what he wanted. And that would be it". [43]

"He wouldn't play other's people rubbish to get a gig", Pete Brown says. "Mike was an accomplished pianist, but certainly after a certain time he didn't want to play standards in bars just to earn a living. He only wanted to play his own music. Before that, his bands played Monk tunes and stuff that Blakey's various composers had written - Horace Silver and Benny Golson were examples. He learned from those and then did his own thing. But he was very uncompromising".

The uniqueness of Taylor's music is attested also by the words of Dave Tomlin: "He'd got his finger on something that was utterly unique and different. His compositions were just unlike anything else. It was so utterly beautiful but it was still jazz. It was an honour to play his music because nothing else was like it". [44]

Around the second half of 1963, there's a story that doesn't reveal anything about Taylor's personality but could be significant in the perception that the pianist was starting to have about himself. At a party organised at Ron Ostwald's home, Mike refused to play.

Ostwald: "My parents moved out of their flat leaving it empty. I decided to take advantage and to throw a party. Mike said he would bring his musicians and supply the music for the party if I could supply the piano. I hired a piano for him at some expense and then on the night Mike refused to play for some reason. Stupidly, I had no back-up in the form of a record player so there was a party without music. Strange behaviour from Mike, perhaps a foretaste of what was to come".

This is Burke's memory: "At one party, at Ron Ostwald's parents flat (they were away on vacation), Mike and his band was supposed to play, but when it was time, he refused, and just sat in a corner, while his drummer, a guy named Sammy Stone, stood and played very loudly on one snare drum for what seemed like hours, and made everyone at the party, especially Ron Ostwald, pretty angry. In fact, my wife Dianne, Ann Taylor and I left, and went for a long drive and got totally stoned in Ann and Mike's car...!"

I askeed Burke whether he thought this was strange behaviour. "Why Mike refused to play at that party that night? I have no idea why. I guess he just didn't feel like playing. Sometimes we just don't feel like we want to do what people expect us to do..."

A reply that reaffirms the image of a quiet man, with no manifest idiosyncrasies. So, no clues that prefigure the radical changes in his personality that would happen years later. Maybe the mood of the party wasn't so ideal, maybe Taylor felt he didn't want to 'waste' his music. Maybe...

Another memory by Burke offers us a clue or example of Mike's psychology, as on some occasions he surprised his friends with behaviour in some ways 'bizarre': "One small, possibly insignificant incident I recall was at our flat in West Hampstead one night. Mike, Ann, and Dave Tomlin were over, it was our usual Saturday night - listening to jazz, and smoking pot. My wife Dianne made us all tea, and served it in our usual mugs. Mike rejected his and said he couldn't face such a huge quantity of liquid, too much... almost intimidating... Could he have his tea in a small teacup? We found that a little strange, but Dianne gave him a smaller cup of tea and he was satisfied!"

With the band stabilized as a quartet, Mike Taylor's music began to change drastically into something really new, a never-before heard form of modern jazz came about at rehearsals where musicians could experiment freely. The Horace Silver hard bop soon became a very distant memory.

Tomlin: "After a while I began experimenting with the soprano sax and Mike decided I should give up the tenor on all of our gigs and this is when the group began to build an original repertoire based on a reworking of familiar standards and original compositions by Mike. These compositions interested me greatly since they seemed to have an almost classical quality, reminiscent perhaps of Chopin's *Nocturnes* or Eric Satie's *Gymnopedies* and *Gnossiens*".

And again: "The workouts were broken at his grandparents' house by genteel tea breaks. It is difficult to say how the music really came out, mostly the melodies would start with just one phrase, then every possible direction would be explored until the right one became obvious. There was absolute freedom as regards conception and rules, I believe it is no exaggeration to say that Mike's stature was as great as Chopin's but there was scant romance about the dreary suburban pubs which were his main outlet. But the music had us fast in its grip and we only occasionally caught glimpses of the grey world outside".

The musical ideas of Mike were in limbo until the early Sixties. By 1964 he developed his project basing it on a different use of the piano pedals - "repetitive harmonic patterns underneath the score", as Robert Bolton wrote.

"His own writing and arranging began to impress others", he follows, "chiefly at this stage in finely re-shaped interpretations of "Greensleeves" and the re-working of tunes like "Night in Tunisia" and "But not for me", both of which appeared on the first of two albums he made...".
[45]

Jon Hiseman was forced into a personal revolution about the way to play his drums: "The nature of much of his improvisation was not chord sequences but modal shifts. That meant piano and bass could be very free and I instinctively responded to this by developing the idea of playing pulse without bar lines and then without regard for the on and off beat. I wasn't sure what I was doing at first, but it was what the music seemed to demand and again, it was seen as innovative. Since much of the music had more to do with intertwined textures than solos, I needed a way to play a continuous tone with my feet, while my hands were free to improvise. So, about this time, I upgraded my drums to a Ludwig Silver Sparkle kit, with two bass drums." [46]

Pete Brown, as well as Burke, recognised the uniqueness of the quartet's music, considering that it was so innovative that it was ostracised by parts of the London jazz establishment, promoters and operators: "Because I was always going to jazz clubs, I then became aware of the classic quartet, with Tomlin, Reeves and Hiseman. This was a very original and forward-looking band. Mike was, as I understood it, a little bit of an outsider on the modern jazz scene, but then most people were except for a small establishment based around Ronnie Scott and Tubby Hayes, who seemed to regard Jack, Ginger, Graham and Dick and perhaps Mike and his team as the enemy because they were going much further than bebop and hard bop (although their roots were in this music)".

We cannot say if Brown is right or wrong about this, but it's a fact testified by some available sources that the Mike Taylor's quartet never played at the original *Ronnie Scott's Club* nor at the Richmond National Jazz & Blues Festival, which was the main festivals promoted in those years, where from 1961 to 1964 the most important English jazz bands (Chris Barber, *Ken Coyler's Jazzmen, Don Rendell Quintet, Tubby Hayes Quintet, Joe Harriott Quintet*, Mose Allison, and the *Ronnie Scott Quartet,* for example) played on stage.

During this period, as Tony Reeves clarifies, just after joining the band on bass instead of Gail, the repertoire of Mike Taylor "was always a mixture of standards and originals, perhaps 60% originals, 40% standards". And what about his *modus operandi*?

"Most of the work was done by Mike (and Dave Tomlin) beforehand, they would arrive with a sketch of how the piece would start, and sometimes its ending, and we would play it through together, finding our own parts. On a tune like "Pendulum" itself, Mike asked me specifically to play the left-hand piano part in unison with him. Much of it was improvised, and so became very much the product of the four people who were playing it".

Sharing the same flat for some months, Tomlin confirms their method when he says that Taylor "would just play an idea on the piano first and then write it down. I didn't watch him do this as there wasn't much to watch, anyway he worked in his own room and I in mine".

Hiseman, however, remembers the relaxed way Taylor used to communicate his musical ideas to the other fellows of the band: "Mike had a very quiet, sure way of expressing his opinions. He never raised his voice, never told you what to do, but trusted you to feel your way. He taped everything, and when we listened back, I'd know if he'd liked something I'd played because he'd grin." [47]

Reeves: "Playing with Mike was a double-edged sword. The music was highly original, but could be very difficult. He was an introverted man, not a tutor, but absolutely able to communicate what he wanted in a rational, musical way". [48]

Another proof about the uniqueness of Taylor's music was testified by journalist Robert Bolton who, writing the first proper retrospective on the pianist published in two parts in December 1974 and in January 1975, could listen to some recordings of the period ("Folk Song n. 1" and "Half Blue", recorded between the end of 1963 and the beginning of '64), which, unfortunately, now are lost: "I am more than ever convinced that the pianist was well ahead of his time", he wrote, "in the creative aspect of his music. He was developing a group sound that had fresh textures, out of time signatures and freedom for soloists". [49]

In those days of enthusiastic research, Mike also painted and drew his gig posters, as documented by one of the few photos of him survived taken by his brother Terry and published for the first time just on *Jazz Journal* magazine in the retrospective edited by Bolton.

In one of these, on his knees, Mike is painting a little rectangular square with white rounds and curved lines as in a Paul Klee artwork.

On the carpet, in addition to dishes of colours, a pack of cigarettes, a screwdriver and a wooden or cardboard flier fixed on two wooden beams can be seen. On the poster we can see the writing in red lettering "Mike Taylor quartet" and a glued paper strip with "TONIGHT". [50]

In white shirt and trousers, he fully expresses all the passionate naivety, the attention to detail in which he tries to become professional.

The care with which Mike drew the staves for his scores has become proverbial. Sometimes this inclination has been explained as a clue to his madness. Dave Tomlin does not agree with this interpretation: "I read somewhere someone had said that Mike's way of writing music down was the result of his madness. This is not true. Instead of using normal printed staves he drew them himself and the length of his staves were drawn with a five pointed manuscript pen to accommodate the length of the musical phrasing... I know this since I was living with him at the time and I also used this method myself for some my tunes... I'm pretty sure people who say that did not know Mike very well..."

For Gelly, this was a possible expression of his tendency towards perfectionism: "The music had to look a certain way to satisfy him. His scores and the individual instrumental parts were carefully bound in spring-back folders."[51]

Thanks to Trevor Watts, the English jazz free-improvising alto and soprano saxophonist who later would play a few times with Taylor, we have now a complete collection of four of Taylor's scores composed around the end of 1964. He says: "I have one of his original scores that he used to write all out himself, everything by hand and very neat on tissue paper. Wrote his own staves and everything". Asked originally to describe it he responded: "Haven't seen it since the '60's and as you can guess my music room is full of my own scores and music and tapes and instruments etc., etc. In actual fact this score I have are the arrangements for four tunes Mike did, all in the one book. The tunes being three of his and an arrangement of the Vernon Duke tune "Taking a chance on Love". His tunes in this book of scores are "Brown Thursday", "Triangle Waltz" and "Rama". The arrangements are for soprano sax, trumpet, alto sax, trombone, bass, piano & drums throughout. He hand drew the staves and everything on it in neat pen & ink on a thickish tissue type of paper. The book is also self made with a stiff orange cover and clips to keep it all together".

These compositions, copied by Mike on 25th September 1964, are contained in a handmade binder with a cardboard cover and barrettes to hold together the papers. One is impressed by the tidiness, the order of the pages, the precision of the work, a carefulness that reveals a deep love for the music, but also the need to have a strong control over his work, as if he were afraid of being overwhelmed by the force of the musical ideas moving inside him.

Tomlin has a further explanation that would conjugate aesthetics and functionality: "Mike drew his own staff lines with a five pointed pen for aesthetic reasons. I did the same, if you look at 'Lark Rise' you will see this. This way the staff lines ended when the music ended wherever that was on the paper. Using shop bought manuscripts was expensive and didn't look so good when finished..."

Was this a common usage among English jazz musicians, I ask Tomlin? "No, it is not common practice. I suppose I was influenced by Mike in that. It didn't really have anything to do with expense, it's more like not wanting to eat processed food - staying outside the control of 'industry' - conforming to common standards. But most of all it was very satisfying to draw the staves to fit the music and not having lines of empty staves with nothing on - it looks aesthetically pleasing".

Except that artists who used the score as a sort of 'pretext' for making a visual project (for example, *Erratum Musical* penned by Marcel Duchamp in 1913, or to *Avoir l'apprenti dans le soleil* of 1914, a cyclist drowned with black ink and pen on a score...) or those musician-painters who painted scores on their artworks (as composer Arnold Schonberg with *Green Self-portrait*, an oil painting from 1910), there are very few composers who have drawn their own scores rather than using music paper.

Apart from some isolated cases from the beginning of 1900 (as German Max Reger with *Quartet for violin, viola, cello and piano* op. 133 composed in 1914), usually they are experimental classical music composers, working from the second half of the last century as the polyhedric Sylvano Bussotti – Italian composer, painter, poet, writer, theatre director – who from 1965 elaborated a graphic system of musical notation with a strong visual impact; or musicians as Brown (*December* 1952 or *Four Systems* 1961), Moran (*For Visions Nos 2 and 2* 1964), Ligeti (*Volumina* 1967), Crumb (*Spiral Galaxy (Aquarius)* 1972), Donatoni and Stockhausen who in 1971 composed *Mantra* setting up on a score designed with coloured pencils and integrated to the music as a part of the work itself. These composers are more or less directly borrowers with John Cage who from the Fifties revolutionised the conception of music composition imagining it as a dimension of the artwork itself. So the score was not only a mere technical illustration of the music, but a 'multidisciplinary object' with unlimited possibilities.

Taylor, anyway, designed his compositions with a traditional approach, but he did it by hand, although he used a music paper bought in a shop, enjoying making his music as an artisan. And it was as if his music composition, by its nature a work of pure abstraction, would acquire a material identity, personal and unique, that one-off, 'aura' quoted by Walter Benjamin on a famous essay. [52]

About these compositions, as Watts remembers, "I rehearsed Mike's tunes and maybe did one gig, but cannot remember too much about it. It was a very small and incidental moment in my musical life, so not of any great significance. That's why it's a struggle for me to come up with anything more meaningful than I already have done. It was mainly a rehearsal thing as I remember, for our own amusement. I don't actually have any opinion of this way of writing music. It's not dissimilar in many ways to the way I write music, except there's no chord sequence involved in what I do within composition. I have to say though, that it would be a too introspective way of writing for myself. So although I can appreciate his music as I do Bill Evans' music for instance. It wouldn't be the way I would personally want to do it. I value the originality of thought though".

The finding of these tunes testifies that by now '64 Taylor was interested in composing for small jazz orchestras. In fact, on the frontispiece we can read the four tunes were composed to be played by a septet formed by piano, double-bass, drums and a rich section of reeds (sax tenor and soprano, trumpet and trombone).

Another memory of Burke's shows us Mike's joyful imaginative excitement during these months: "At one of our *soirées*, Mike said he'd come up with some new ideas and he played us a tape of music he'd written, which eventually became the basis for his album *Pendulum*. I was totally over-awed by Mike's new direction in sound. It was totally unlike any other form of jazz that was being played in Britain, or, indeed anywhere else in the world. Completely unique! That same evening I especially remember that we listened to a recording of the Shostakovich *7th Symphony*, as well as records by Ornette Coleman and John Coltrane. A lot of wonderful sounds!"

The event is dated back to between the end of '63 and the beginning of '64. "I only saw Mike one or two times after that", says Burke. "My wife and I had moved to South London, and we'd lost contact with many of our friends. Mike came over a couple of times, but seemed quite distant and perhaps sort of strange. Our friendship seemed to have grown cold..."

3
The wit and the pendulum

*"I say play your own way. Don't play what the public wants -
you play what you want and let the public pick up what you're doing -
even if it does take them 15 or 20 years"*
(Thelonious Monk)

After documented concerts at L.S.E. and at I.C.A. of London, between January and March, and the gig with Ornette Coleman at the Fairfield Hall in Croydon in August, in October 1965 [53] the *Mike Taylor Quartet* went to the Lansdowne studios in London's Holland Park to record an album under the production of Denis Preston, introduced by *Nucleus* trumpet player Ian Carr. At that time Carr was playing in the *Rendell-Carr Quintet*, a band signed by Preston for his company called 'Record Supervision' that recorded a lot of the best British jazz in 1950s and '60s [54], getting the epithet "an impresario of near-genius" by the influential *The Gramophone* magazine.

Preston (who died in 1979) owned the Lansdowne Studios, and Dave Gelly is correct when he states today that the album "wouldn't have been made at all if it hadn't been for Denis Preston".

Hiseman: "We all played together in Lansdowne Studios and each piece was played completely one or two times. The producer, Denis Preston, made the decision which one was best after discussing the take with us. Mike was always very clear which one he preferred but I was never that clear what he was really looking for. I do know that Roland Kirk heard the album *Pendulum* and as a result asked me to play with him at Ronnie Scotts. I was out of town, so I think Phil Seamen did it instead. That was unfortunate for me because I was a great fan of Roland".

Tomlin: "The album was composed of reworked standards and some originals from Mike; one of which was "Leeway", dedicated to my daughter Lee who had been named after Lee Morgan, trumpet player with Art Blakey's Jazz Messengers... There's not much I can say about the recording of "Pendulum" except that there where no second takes as there probably are nowadays, we just went in and played the set once through and left. This was a pity for if we had been able to warm up and play each one a couple of times it would have been a better LP. Still we still seem to have got away with it".

"We made the album in a couple of days", confirmed Reeves to Martyn Hanson. "I didn't realise it then, but Mike was a depressive. He was smoking a lot and tried to turn *me* onto cannabis, but it had no effect." [55]

According some sources circulated through the years, the tracks were rehearsed during six months at an old photographic studio in Ilford to get confidence in Taylor's ideas. Robert Bolton wrote that "Hiseman admits that after playing on the beat *à la* Philly Jo Jones and co., it took him six months in his early association with Taylor to understand what he was getting at in 'freedom' music". [56]

The drummer, in the same period playing also with the *Group Sounds Five*, years later said to Carr: "I had to get up at 8 am and go to work all day. I'd get home at about 6 pm, have something to eat and then practise till about 8 pm, then go out to play a gig or rehearse. I'd be going to bed after 1 am. Then the next day the whole process would repeat itself. The problem was that *Group Sounds Five* would rehearse three nights a week but only do one actual gig a month. And the *Mike Taylor Quartet* – those albums were made as the result of Mike Taylor, Tony Reeves, Dave Tomlin and myself meeting in a film studio at Ilford twice a week for six months – and that was an hour's drive away from my home!" [57]

Tomlin claims the story of the six months at Ilford is totally distant from the facts: "You must be joking. Six months! We would never have rehearsed something for six months. We were moving through new stuff all the time and never spent six months on any of them, maybe just a couple of evenings and then used on the next gig. We would never go all the way out to Ilford just to do rehearsals. Ilford is a long way out of town and never heard of these film studios. Don't know what these *sources* are but myths and stories of this sort always occur after events and this one is totally untrue".

The only references to Ilford would seem to be a pair of concerts played by the quartet there. Tomlin again: "Have never seen Carr's book, neither did I ever meet him, the only connection with Ilford was we did a gig there *once* at a small jazz club and one other in a public house - *The Greyhound* - and that's it".

Published some months later in May 1966 as *Pendulum* (Columbia SX6042 mono), on the back record cover Taylor affirmed two related concepts attesting to his ideas: "Our music comes out of the innate character and personality of the musicians who play it" and "This is what I want to do." As much as to say that the music was captured at an *hic et nunc* one-shot moment, with no musical superstructures, futile frills, foxy mannerism. An essential statement of Art.

As Hiseman reveals: "We were never conscious of rehearsing an album. In the studio we simply played what would have constituted a gig".

Writing the notes on the back cover, Ian Carr had no doubts about the greatness of Taylor's album, writing: "This record is something of a landmark in British jazz. It is one of the first recordings, perhaps the very first, made by the new generation of musicians who grew up when 'Hard-Bop' and 'Funky' school of playing was already losing its vogue and prophetic voices were learning to pronounce more elegant slogans such as 'The New Thing', or 'The Avant-Garde'". For Carr, this wasn't just a 'promising debut' but "an exquisite performance by a quartet which has created his own music – a whole way of playing which is mature, honest, and fully understood by the four musicians. It must be listened to with an open mind and acute ears, for it is genuinely improvised – there are none of the old clichés on this LP, not a single familiar hot-lick or groovy phrase on the map of this new territory."

And regarding the particular character of Mike's playing, Carr had words totally appreciative of Taylor describing him as "one of the most fertile and original composers/arrangers this side of the Atlantic. It is his compositions which are the basis for the quartet's fresh approach, and even when they play a standard tune (…) the chemistry of Taylor's mind seems to change the piece's whole identity. This is perhaps because he did not begin playing jazz in the usual way; instead of learning standard tunes first and then trying to write his own compositions, he began at the very outset by playing little-known compositions and eventually his own themes. It's only in latter years that he came to learn the standard tunes which are in every jazz musician's repertoire. This also helps to account for his unique development – during the formative years he didn't associate with many others musicians because he had little in common with them. Such a lonely apprenticeship was invaluable, however, for he has emerged at the age of twenty-seven as a mature and highly individual talent". [58]

Carr expressed opinions also about the other musicians of the quartet. About the work of Tony Reeves and Jon Hiseman he wrote it was "outstanding", underlining the fertile artistic friendship between Taylor and Tomlin: "They have been studying and playing together for a long time which perhaps accounts for their almost uncanny rapport".

"At the time of the recording we were not a well known group and none of us were in any way famous", Tomlin admits. "Ian Carr however was quite famous and a very well respected trumpet player and it was great good fortune that he wrote the sleeve notes, which was very helpful".

The album consists of six tracks, three radical reworkings of jazz standards ("A night in Tunisia", "But not for me" and "Exactly like you") and three brand new tunes composed by Taylor himself ("To Segovia", "Leeway" and "Pendulum").

And even if Tony Reeves has manifested some perplexities on the outcome of the three standards ("I thought they didn't work at all", he told to Duncan Heining in 2008. "The original things like "Pendulum" itself were much more effective but "But Not For Me" skirts and wanders around the tune and eventually launches off into hyperspace. You could have played the free form part of it to any head.") listened to it today, as written by Carr, the record sounds fresh and full of ideas, a miraculous interplay of inspired musicians dipped in a magmatic sonic matter.

It's the solid, discreet Hiseman's and Reeves' rhythmic section that guarantees the show of piano and tenor on a landscape that is still hard-bop, but near to breaking apart in a 'temperate' free-jazz.

Taylor's piano, analysed in depth, reveals a clear evolution of its style; from the blues chords of the beginning to the fragmentation in single rhythmic notes, derived clearly from Monk, after the period Mike was charmed by Horace Silver and by the ballad à la Bill Evans.

In "Exactly like you", the theme's exposition follows an improvisation where some untied notes define a rhythmic background, with continuous repetitions, that prepare Tomlin's entry on soprano; in "But not for me", the piano has not even a clear melodic line and the notes amass one on the other, insinuating in the rhythmic structure of bass and drums – they are iterate, percussive, untied and fractioned. They define a minimalist sound landscape adopting a form that is not that used by Monk (Riverside period), in fact nor the one played by Evans, but without pushing in that kind of free atonal improvisation recorded by a Cecil Taylor or a Joe Bonner.

At the beginning of "A Night in Tunisia" Mike plays some sequences of continued notes, that are pure improvisation with untied notes, tangled harmonizations, no melodic lines with chords, until the real blues solos that provide a background for the Tomlin's explosive vaultings and some exquisite Reeves' solos. The tune is characterised by a prolonged solo by Hiseman that shows once more his extraordinary technique and his rare musical taste.

The wonderful "Leeway", dedicated to Tomlin's daughter Lee, with a cryptic wordplay on the title ("Leeway - Ships passing each other needed plenty of room between them (leeway). To be in the lee of the land meant that ships were protected from high winds by the high coastline. Lee - her way. Leeway", Tomlin explains...), to close the album with a perfect interplay wherein Tomlin exposes the theme and repeats it until a melodic disintegration with an almost atonal improvisation, while Taylor obsessively plays supporting the rhythmic pattern of bass and drums with improvisations of untied notes played with the right hand.

A mature record, *Pendulum*, distant from the joyful, hopping up-tempo of a typical hard bop album of that time, and yet not so difficult to listen to as a free-jazz record played by the *Spontaneous Music Ensemble* or Cornelius Cardew's *AMM*.

If it can be a further proof of the strong, empathic, collaborations of the four musicians, the album cover wasn't just the work of a graphic designer chosen by the record company, according to a custom of that time, but it was the graphic transposition of Taylor's musical ideas. Dave Tomlin designed it using a method of composition as personal as innovative.

He has described it to me in this way: "At the time I was also composing music myself using an innovative method: graph-paper instead of conventional music manuscript. This was the method: each vertical square of the graph-paper is equal to one half-tone. Twelve vertical squares equal one octave. Time is horizontal. One square to equal one semi-quaver. Two squares one quaver. Four squares one crotchet etc. Geometrical shapes were then drawn and transposed onto a musical stave. Mike's melody "Pendulum" was transposed in this way onto graph-paper and the squares replaced with coloured dots. The cover of the LP illustrates the last six bars of the piece. The piano is represented in light green, the soprano sax in red and the bass in dark green. The soprano sax is playing the melodic line forwards, the piano is playing the same line backwards. If you listen closely this becomes apparent."

Who had the idea? - I ask him.

"The idea of writing music on graph-paper was just an idea that came to me. The music that emerged was very strange but I used to rehearse it with a small piano-less quartet, with people like Johnny Mumford and Henry Lowther, even did one or two gigs, but then came the sixties - flower power and all the rest - and the whole thing got lost. Mike was not interested as he had his own way of writing using the piano".

Even if not interested to the method of composition conceived by Tomlin it's an undeniable fact that Taylor, having adopted it for the *Pendulum* cover, showed a clear awareness of his musical uniqueness.

After being published, the album got very good reviews. [59]

Melody Maker (May 28th, 1966) wrote: "Taylor has managed to be "progressive" without sounding in the least bit chaotic, no mean feat, and this is one of the outstanding British jazz releases, in any sphere, for some time". .

While *Record Mirror* (May 21st, 1966) admitted the album was "in places inspired", on *Records & Recordings* (July 1966) one tried a more articulate analysis: "The new jazz music is slowly but surely coagulating and from its body we are now getting noises which make positive sense. Where John Coltrane, Ornette Coleman, Charles Mingus and company are concerned this is to be expected, but for an old obscure quartet to walk into the Lansdowne House studios by Notting Hill and, without fuss and ballyhoo, produce such an original, moving album as this one is must be almost in the nature of a minor miracle. The liquid acidity of Dave Tomlin's soprano saxophone is a major part of the success of this album, and, wedded to the progressive sounding piano of leader Mike Taylor, this comes out as intelligent, swinging music – and I was beginning to despair that I would ever be able to say that about the home grown product. They mould their individual talent to the three evergreens on side one with distinction (and I must mention bassist Tony Reeves and drummer Jon Hiseman with their polished, skilful rhythm work) and play three Mike Taylor originals on the reverse. These are musically interesting throughout, the descriptively bizarre "Pendulum", the off-beat tribute to the Spanish guitarist, Segovia, and "Leeway" with Tomlin at the peak of his form. Modernists who have hitherto, with good reason, declined to credit British avant-gardists with sufficient know-how should listen to this".

Also *Jazz Monthly*, that only one year before had criticized Taylor's music at the *Fairfield Hall* concert in Croydon, published an absolutely positive judgement, analysing some relevant technical aspects of the emerging peculiarity of Taylor's touch. Bruce King wrote: "Mike Taylor's quartet must be one of the more advanced groups playing in England. They have taken some of the harmonic and rhythmic ideas explored by Coltrane and others in recent years and developed them in new directions. On first listening the music may seem overly cerebral, but familiarity reveals an unexpected warmth of emotion. (…) Tomlin and Taylor have clearly rehearsed together for some time and have developed an uncanny feel for extending each others' ideas, even in passages of free improvisations. The trouble is that none of the musicians has a strong melodic or rhythmic imagination; consequently the solos tend to be monotonous. Tomlin seems influenced by Coltrane, but lacks the latter's feelings for over-all structure. Taylor is a more interesting musical personality. He plays strange, beautiful harmonies which unfortunately never seem to develop melodically." [60]

For the journalist, a paradigmatic example of the direction was the rendition of "A Night in Tunisia", his favourite of the album: "Tomlin plays a beautiful modification of the theme and Taylor works in some lovely counterpoint in a distant key. There are passages of simultaneous variation and, after an interesting bass solo, instead of a fixed rhythm, an ebbing and flowing pulsation. If the other numbers were as good, I would be a Taylor enthusiast". [61]

Also *Jazz Journal* recognized the value of Taylor ("... he is a composer of real value on the evidence...") and the band ("the quartet work well together... due to the long association and musical compatibility"), describing the music as "avant garde" but "not wildly far out".

"The tracks they move along are logical. Each number of the group is listening to what the others are up to. (…) Taylor and Hiseman would have profited from a better recording balance, but then I suppose we must be grateful to E.M.I. and Denis Preston for having the perspicacity to record a fine group which might otherwise be in perpetual obscurity. I look forward to more from the Mike Taylor Quartet (they'll convert me yet)." [62]

The same month Dave Gelly wrote a very long review about the album for *Jazz Guide* where he refuted some clichés about the Quartet's identity. Because it's probably the best ever written on the record, it is worth reproducing: "It is, I suppose, in the nature of things that a Britain jazz musician should be judged in terms of some revered American model upon when he is presumed to have based his style. But, universal though it may be, the practice is an egregiously unfair one since it denies that musician any real originality or voice of his own. The whole sad business has operated in a particularly witless way in the case of the Mike Taylor Quartet. Because the group appeared at the Ornette Coleman concert and at the Little Theatre Club it was presumed to be a "free form" group (whereas its musical discipline is unusually tight) and, because it contained a soprano saxophone and rhythm section, it was further assumed to be a "pale copy" of the John Coltrane Quartet, which it does not even remotely resemble. Bob Houston, in the *Melody Maker*, realising that Dave Tomlin didn't sound at all like Coltrane, settled on the only handy alternative and declared that his style "owes something to Steve Lacy". It doesn't.

"Having cursed everyone else for being fools and/or knaves I had better try to do better. The trouble is, of course, that originality (particularly, relevant originality) may be easy to feel – it may, as with this record, come and hit amiably on the nose – but it is devilishly difficult to say anything about. The first thing, I think, is the authority of the whole performance. By this I don't just mean that it is well played, which it is, but that one has the impression that here is a sample of a really matured approach; there is a sense of inevitability, that this music is completely natural, understood and integrated.

"The Quartet has a dry, crystalline tone-colour, each voice being equal in weight, and the piano and soprano particularly enact a melodic dialogue rather than providing melody-with-accompaniment. The performance of this kind of thing needs to be razor-sharp if it is to be effective, and to hear how good it is listen to the piano-soprano unison on "Leeway": it really is unison, both in timing and intonation, while on the subject of "Leeway", it would draw your attention to the melody itself. The line evolves continuously, turning corners at the most unexpected places and its springy resilience is never spoiled by blandness. (...) I find that the word "melody" has been cropping up rather a lot in this review: this is because Mike Taylor and Dave Tomlin are both supremely melodic thinkers. Don't look for "harmonic" improvisation of the "line over a ground-bass" type. Just listen to the interplay of voices. I won't say much about the drums and bass except to point out that Tony Reeves is also playing a melodic part and playing it very well indeed. As for Jon Hiseman, if you can find me a more intelligent and expert drummer in Britain I shall be suitably astonished (...) ". [63]

Gelly is enthusiastic about the album even today: "Listen to *Pendulum* and compare it with anything else that was new at the time. Everything is very precise - quite cool for the time. Most other bands were much more loose and impressionistic, following in the steps of Coltrane etc..."

In spite of clearly positive album reviews, however, Taylor's music suffered a substantial incomprehension due to the traditional narrow-mindedness by provincial critics and record companies: difficult to categorize, the *Mike Taylor Quartet* was destined, as Gelly well highlights, to be misconceived, considered just as one of the many American colossus' imitators who were a big success in Europe.

In the absence of specific testimonies, it's very difficult to document the feelings of an artist strenuously interested in playing his *own* music, reluctant as he was to accept the typical session man routine or, even worse, force himself to the inclinations of market with inevitable interviews, TV appearances, radio programmes...

Hiseman confirms today another of Taylor's 'eccentric' beliefs, apparently in conflict with his status of musician: "Mike never gave any interviews - he said 'the music will speak for itself.' I always agreed with that until I found out that only a few top music journalists listen to the music and make good judgements. Most music journalists really want to be political writers or sports journalists, where there really is a big interested audience for what they do. They don't listen to the music and need interviews to have something to write about. I have always used them to get my message across. But in the sixties we didn't understand that. Mike never wanted to talk about the music anyway - not even to his players - he chose his musicians for their strength and originality and then just let them loose on his compositions or arrangements without any guidance or instructions. However his playing was so unique that with very few notes he could dominate the performance, getting the result he wanted without words. He was endlessly surprised and always found great pleasure in what happened collectively during a performance. At the centre of Mike's approach was *happinessence* - he set a piece running with his interpretation of a theme or an original composition and knew that with the players he had chosen something interesting would turn up. It usually did".

An approach to the music not conditioned by the urges of the market, free and 'disinterested', serious and rigorous, just as that characterized by Bill Evans, one of Mike's main references. An idea of absolute aims, uncompromising artistic expression, we could define it as 'romantic', in a period when the record market (above all that relating to popular music) was starting to drastically impose its commercial logic.

If it can be considered further proof of the exclusive character of Taylor's ideas about the music and of the strong determination to realize them, here's another memory by Hiseman, related more or less to the period just after *Pendulum* was recorded. On the stage of the famous *London 100 Club* there was one of the most popular jazz bands of the period, the *Don Rendell-Ian Carr Quintet* and Carr, and knowing Taylor well, they had the idea to ask him to play with them: "An apprehensive Rendell introduced him in the second half, counted in a fast blues and Mike sat at the piano playing nothing through the theme and first solo, then proceeded to play the same single note sporadically throughout his own solo and on to the end of the piece. The crowd applauded wildly… though, looking back, it was probably a case of the *Emperor's New Clothes…* but to me, that took courage and I thought it showed just how special he was – and of course it *was* the right note!" [64]

During the months between the recording of *Pendulum* and its arrival in the shops, Taylor spent his time feeding the flame burning inside him by playing some concerts and, above all, composing his music.

A significant proof of it were the three compositions Taylor offered to the jazz 'supergroup' *Group Sounds Five*, two of them played on air at BBC Third Programme "Jazz Record Requests" on November 15th, 1965: "One of them was called "Thirteen-Note Samba", Lowther told writer John Wickes in 1990, "which was based not on a chord sequence, but on a bass figure which went down the whole chromatic scale, octave to octave, which is thirteen notes. And there was a piece called "Black & White Raga", which is the black notes of the piano and the white notes alternating. You'd play on the black notes – the raga - then you'd use a phrase to switch to the white, and you could alternate like that". [65]

Lyn Dobson: "Black & White Raga was/is a very beautiful piece of music. I enjoyed playing it… Unfortunately now I don't remember anything about that experience…"

It seems that the broadcast caused consternation at the BBC.

Hiseman remembers: "Mike's compositions played with *Group Sounds Five* were exceptional in that they were so different from the conventional jazz of the time. I recount in my book, *Playing the Band*, how GS5 were asked to play on the BBC's *Jazz Club* programme which was recorded in front of a live audience and was compèred by Humphrey Lyttleton. I was acting for the band in dealing with the BBC and was telephoned up by the producer and asked to give him the five jazz standards we would be playing. I told him that we would only probably be able to pay three numbers because one of them is likely to last about 20 minutes. This was Mike's "Black and White Raga". The producer was horrified – he was only interested in conventional jazz. I told him that we wouldn't be able to perform unless we could do our own music because that's what the band did and we didn't know anything else. Not strictly true of course, because we could have played anything, but we didn't want to do anything other than present what GS5 was becoming known for. Finally, the producer gave in and on the broadcast Humphrey Lyttleton actually announces that there will be a departure from the usual procedure in that we would playing something completely different".

Hiseman thinks he may have a recording of the performance and it will be published sooner or later: "Actually I believe I have a copy of that recording and I was in the process of getting all my performance tapes onto CD when I was interrupted by *Colosseum* going back on the road again this year (2014) - which has stopped all my long-term projects dead in their tracks. When you realise that I probably have around 300 tapes of broadcasts and performances and that this particular broadcast is somewhere in that archive you get an idea of the scale of the problem. Maybe in 2015 or 2016 I will get back to this project again. Anyway, the broadcast was a great success with other drummers ringing me up intrigued to know what I was doing. I was actually playing pulse without bar lines which I had first developed with Mike's Quartet inspired by his compositions. At the end of the broadcast a drummer called John Stevens, who was leading the other band on the bill, came up to me and started asking questions about the 'new thing' I was doing. His was an octet playing conventional jazz. Six months later he started a career in advanced free-form jazz...."

"*The Group Sounds Five*", Lyn Dobson says, "grew from the group of me, Henry Lowther, Harry Miller and Don Brown, a Caribbean drummer who had played with Chet Baker. Don Brown died and Alan Jackson was the new drummer, later to be replaced by Jon Hiseman, and Harry Miller was replaced by Jack Bruce. Also Ron Rubin joined the group: Ron was great and was with us for quite a long time. Also Ron Mathewson for a time I think and one special night Dave Holland came around, and he and Ron Mathewson had a cutting contest, that was something! There was also a pianist, Tony Hymas, later Ken McCarthy. We played original compositions from us all, especially Jack Bruce. We played gigs around UK but mostly we were resident in a club in the east end of London owned by the Kray twins, famous gangsters of the time. The Group was voted into "Downbeat" magazine by Charles Fox, a noted British jazz critic...."

Henry Lowther, who had known Taylor through Hiseman, says that "Mike Taylor used to come and listen to the band. (...) He was some strange guy, Mike Taylor. He'd come to the gigs. He'd stay ten minutes, travel all the way across London from Kew where he lived, up to this place where we used to play at Stoke Newington, and go all the way back to Kew. You'd think: he mustn't like it; and the next day he'd say: "I thought it was fantastic!". [66]

And more recently: "At that time, about 1965, Jon was playing in a quartet with Mike, along with Dave Tomlin and Tony Reeves. Around that time I joined the *New Jazz Orchestra* and Jon was the drummer. Mike had written a couple of charts for the band and it's possible that I met him then. However, I do remember him coming along to a club, the Regency in Stoke Newington, that the Group Sounds Five played in regularly two or three times a week. He came all the way over from the other side of London and then only stayed for about ten minutes. I thought that this was strange and it was because he didn't like the music, but later

Jon Hiseman told me that he did indeed like the band and that he wanted to write something for us".

Despite appearances, Taylor so appreciated the band that he proposed three of his compositions, three scores edited in his own way, on drawing paper, as they were little works of art themselves. As Lowther remembers, "the score of these came in a large artist's white paper sketch pad where, rather than using ready printed music manuscript paper, he had drawn the staves himself using a five pointed pen. The scores were a work of art in themselves. We only ever got round to playing one of these pieces. It was called, "Black and White Raga". The "Black" part was written using only the black notes of the piano and the "White" part used only the white notes. The idea was that the improvising would be on one part for a while before a written cue would give the signal to modulate to the other part and then similarly after a while another written cue would be given to take the music back again and so on and on, alternating in this manner until we would play the head again at the end. As I remember it, the black notes corresponded to an Eb Dorian mode and the white notes a D Dorian mode (the same two modes used in Miles Davis's "So What"). The melody alternated between notes of the piano black keys with notes of the white keys. The piece gave us a lot of freedom and on one gig we played it for a whole set, one hour long! All I can remember of the second piece is that it was called "Thirteen Note Samba" and consisted of a descending bass through all twelve notes of the chromatic scale with the octave making it thirteen. We may have tried it, I'm not sure, but certainly never played it in performance..."

"Later Mike asked for the score of these pieces back. I didn't know then that he wanted it back in order to destroy it. He had, however, written us another piece at a later date. We never played it and somewhere in my house I still have his immaculate scores".

Unfortunately Lowther is unable to find them; they are hidden somewhere in his house, and we have lost the opportunity to see how Taylor made it. Another track of Mike Taylor's passage on Earth maybe lost forever.

In those days, Taylor had frequent contacts with the *New Jazz Orchestra*, an 18-piece band under the leadership of composer Neil Ardley, involving such musicians as Jon Hiseman and Dave Gelly, and the 'cream' of English jazz: Barbara Thompson, Trevor Watts, Tony Reeves, John Mumford, Lionel Grigson, Paul Rutherford, Dick Hart, Ian Carr.

Originally set up in 1963 by Ian Bird and Clive Burroughs as a co-operative band, organising itself, and mixing professional and amateur players, in 1964 Neil Ardley became the leader/director with an ambition to play and record the Miles Davis/Gil Evans peculiar sound of late '50's. "He was pretty well qualified, in educational background, music training and social "standing" to be in the position of spokesperson/arranger/conductor, and it was a case of "right Place, right Time, and perhaps right Person," Mumford states. "Also the Band (as do most) needed someone who could do "the talking" to promoters and executives".

NJO was then interested in recording one of Taylor's compositions and the pianist proposed "Pendulum", from his first album, and he arranged a full band score. But, as Gelly admits with a delicate euphemism, "the encounter wasn't a success".

"Devoted though he was", Dave Gelly has written, "Mike had not really mastered the skills of orchestration, and his method of rehearsing consisted simply of waiting until the whole thing came to grinding halt, going back to the beginning and starting again, with the same result. The NJO did eventually play several of Mike's pieces (including "Pendulum"), recorded a few and broadcast several more, but the orchestrations were mainly the work of Neil Ardley". [67]

And on another occasion: "Simply we *couldn't* play it. Mike had never written an orchestration and didn't know about instrumental ranges etc. Neil Ardley helped him re-write it and we played it quite often after that".

Another very different view claims that the *New Jazz Orchestra* wasn't able to play the tune because it was too complex to perform.

Steve Ingless, for example, referring to a comment by Bolton, has written: "(...) Interestingly, Mike wrote a big band version of "Pendulum" for the musicians of The NJO, but sadly the arrangement was too complex, too ahead of its time for them, so they aborted the idea of recording it". [68]

Nevertheless a recollection confirmed by Hiseman, who in 1974 revealed to Bolton: "The section men couldn't play the parts. We put it away because we were always getting into a mess with it. Three years ago – in 1971 – the NJO was brought together again and the men in the band sight read the piece completely. It just shows the change". [69]

How these things truly went, it's difficult to say. The fact remains that "Pendulum" with its harmonic structure and its peculiar evolution will become one of the more distinctive tunes from Taylor's repertoire, impressive enough to raise the unconditional admiration of many colleagues.

Pete Brown, for example, who has always esteemed Mike's music, admits he was inspired during his long career by *Pendulum* and by Taylor's composition work: "After digesting them a bit I really grew to love Mike's compositions. I have always been a very big admirer of originality and I believe he was a true original. Having heard at one time or another big band arrangements of some of his work, by the *New Jazz Orchestra* and Neil Ardley, when I was thinking about something to go with Heckstall-Smith's "Celtic Steppes", which we are doing with a reasonable-sized orchestra, then I thought of Mike's work. Especially "Pendulum", which is stunning in a big band format".

So, rejecting the idea of recording Taylor's tune, the first album of the NJO band titled was *Western Reunion* (Decca LK4690 Vocalion CDSML 8427, today available just only on CD, the first issue in 700 copies having all sold...). Titled from a composition by Gerry Mulligan, it was recorded at London Hampstead's Decca Studio on March 14th, 1965 with ten tracks composed by various musicians (some by Ardley, the most by Miles Davis, Gerry Mulligan and Leonard Bernstein) but nothing by Taylor. When published in the following July it would be been selected by *Melody Maker* as "Jazz album of the month"...

Jazz Journal, judged the recording excellent, although stating that the *New Jazz Orchestra* was "Jazz" more than "New": "Of the avant-garde there is not a trace, merely some swinging big band jazz. The closest American comparison is perhaps the Gerald Wilson band, though there are shades of Woody Herman ("Tiny's Blues") and Gil Evans-Miles Davis collaboration ("Milestones", "So What")". [70]

It's merely speculative now to ask what role it could have had on the record; a tune like "Pendulum", by now anyway very innovative, would have cast the others in comparison as decisively *mainstream*.

So, considering the rewarding collaborations that were establishing him inside the microcosm of dedicated English jazz musicians, at the end of 1965 the band played one of their rare gigs – Saturday 12th December – at London I.C.A. Gallery again, with on the bill also the *Dave Tomlin Sextet*, the *Graham Bond Organisation*, the *John Stevens Trio* and the *Pete Lemer Trio*. The concert programme was edited by Rubin who used for the cover one of Taylor's abstract drawings that fitted very well with the idea of *temperate,* 'New Thing' of the bands involved there. The 'New Thing', which in those days some journalists (such as Mark Gardner and Steve Voce on *Jazz Journal*) had criticised after have listened to the new radical Albert Ayler album, was mainly rated as being 'noisy' and 'uncompromisingly aggressive'.

At this point Reeves left the band to concentrate on his A&R work and involvement with the *New Jazz Orchestra*. His substitute was Rubin, who had returned to London after his time in Mallorca from May to September.

"I didn't exactly leave", Reeves explains me, "I played with a lot of other bands and the gigs for the *Mike Taylor Quartet* just stopped".

In fact the gigs became rare and something seems to have happened to Mike.

During this period Mike, as told by his sister Muriel, "tried to gas himself... due to his inability to be recognised as a musician" Hiseman is dismissive of this when he affirms he never heard anything about it, also because "he never expressed any desire to me to be recognised". Tomlin claims the same saying that he "never heard of that"...

"After some time Mike began having trouble with his wife Ann", Tomlin remembers, "and I too suffered major difficulties with mine as she was becoming very stroppy, the result of which was that we both ended up wifeless. Mike then offered me a room at his flat in Kew Gardens and there we began to write a musical with Mike providing the music and I the lyrics".

Among the songs Tomlin wrote the lyrics to were: 'Timewind', 'Summer sounds, Summer sights' and 'Jumping off the Sun', included years later on the commemorative *Mike Taylor Remembered* album and sung by Norma Winstone.

Another track titled "Cardboard Sky" was never finished but Tomlin remembers the tune's contents and some of the words. "It tells the story of a little girl who is in hospital. While she is there her mother gets an artist who lives in their house to decorate the girl's bedroom. He makes a false cardboard ceiling and paints it blue with white clouds and hangs tinsel stars from it. When the girl comes out of hospital she lies on her bed and gazes each night up at them and imagines herself flying. She then often dreams of this. However, her mother warns her not to try to touch them. But the girl cannot resist and so one day she puts a box on her bed and reaches up to discover that her magical ceiling is only made of cardboard; the magic spell is broken and now she has lost her lovely dreams".

"Painted clouds
tinsel stars
hang from my cardboard sky
touch them my dreams fade away..."

""Jumping off the Sun", was also recorded by *Colosseum*, and certainly sung by Jack Bruce on the BBC", as Tomlin confirms, has frivolous lyrics talking about the song itself (*meta-textual* semiologists would say) and an explicit reference to the house where both musicians were dwelling.

Jumping off the Sun
This song goes up and up down and down and up and down again
These notes are (like) coloured balls
Leaving smoke trails like an aeroplane
Shooting up falling down like a rocket and then
Jumping of the Sun, jumping of the Sun.

This song holds bunches of summer flowers and the smell of rain
Dogs barking, smoke rising
cigarettes in bed with you again
These notes make a necklace that sings like a man
Jumping off the sun, jumping off the sun.

This song is dancing like sunlight on the River Thames at Kew
Tides pull the sound of it
Down to Charing Cross and Waterloo
Well I know that sounds funny, one might as well go
Jumping off the Sun, jumping off the Sun.
This song goes up and up down and down and up and down again
Lemonade kisses I string together like a daisy chain
But these words have no meaning unless they are sung
Jumping off the Sun, Jumping off the Sun.
(©1965 Dave Tomlin)

Another track composed with Tomlin titled "Summer sounds Summer sights", has more sunny lyrics, inspired by a sort of simple bucolic feeling:

Summer sounds summer sights
What is that something like wine the air
When I feel the earth turning
And passing its mood on to me
It's the coming of summer
Why do I walk with a smile on my face
When the rain falls upon me
And blows with the wind through my hair
It's the soft rain of summer
These things are mine and this year it's my summer too.
Summer sounds, summer sights
Summer days, summer nights
(©1965 Dave Tomlin)

"Timewind" is about the time passing inescapably and with it all the experiences of life. The end of a love and the memory of moments of happiness which nothing can cancel out. Autobiographical lyrics, as Tomlin confesses today, partially inspired by the recent loss of his stroppy wife and the end of his marriage.

Timewind
Time passes, the days fall away blown along by the wind
Time brushes the memory I hold.
Hours dying around me
Drift down like a carpet of leaves
I long for the Timewind to blow me a day with you.
Time passes, the years fall away blown along by the wind
Time carries your face from my sight
Days emptying into the past take the sound of your voice
I long for the Timewind to blow me an hour with you.
Time passes, your ghost falls away blown along by the wind
Time soothing the ache in my heart
Years cannot deprive me the love that was born long ago
I hope that the Timewind is blowing good days for you.
(©1965 Dave Tomlin)

The musical remained just a project on paper and never become a real finished work. The tunes composed, unrealised for years, were included on the posthumous album with remakes of Taylor's works recorded by the *New Jazz Orchestra* with Norma Winstone as a singer.

Asking Winstone about the experience of singing these Mike Taylor's tunes, she told me: "Around 1973 I was asked to record Mike's music with Neil Ardley and Barbara Thompson. I was given some compositions of his to learn. The recording was not released (I don't know why) until a few years ago when a company called Dusk Fire released it".

"I find the songs interesting, especially the lyrics which are quite strange! I didn't find any difficulties to sing his songs. I liked the fact that the shape of the compositions was unusual. I always liked "Song of Love" which I recorded on my album *Edge of Time*, also "Timewind" I liked too. This one I found a little more conventional, but brighter and more optimistic than some of the others."

"When I said that they were (some of them) an unusual shape I meant that they didn't follow the shape of 'The Great American Songbook' where you would have mostly 32 bar themes. "Song of Love" for instance has a very different shape; there is an 8 bar section followed by a six bar section and then you will suddenly find a 2/4 bar. I can't spend the time going through them all but if you count through them you will see what I mean. This made them a challenge and quite attractive to me.

"As far as the words are concerned I always assumed (as no-one ever mentioned lyric writers) that Mike had written them. On the sleeve notes of the CD it seems that there are some where we know that someone else wrote the lyrics for instance "Jumping off the Sun" (Dave Tomlin) and these lyrics to me are strange by which I mean that I didn't really understand them but they were somehow enjoyable to sing. I assume that the lyrics to "Song of Love" are by Mike himself and seem like a love song for the world and mankind rather than the usual romantic love song. "Stars go shining, men go mining..." the words felt good to sing even if I was not sure exactly what they were saying. I enjoyed singing these songs because at that time I had not come across any songs like them and I loved to be challenged. The middle section of "I See You" is harmonically static and the melody dissonant which was quite hard to sing accurately. It was a very formative musical period in my life and although I did not realise it at the time seems to have become an important time in British jazz".

Even though a dozen compositions would be reworked and recorded later by his friends as a celebration of his art, we don't know exactly which are the songs Mike Taylor composed (sometimes writing the lyrics by himself) in that period, but there is no doubt that it was a prolific stage in his life, at least at the beginning in the Kew flat at 54 Forest Road (London TW9 3BZ), very near to the wonderful Kew Gardens.

There, in his new two-floored home, a typical red brick Edwardian building, with essential furniture, Mike set up his player piano, a model that plays itself if piano rolls are installed, but would also act as a normal upright piano. As Jon Hiseman recalls, "it was old when Mike owned it and gradually the cost of keeping it in tune and repairing it meant it was no longer possible to keep it going. It went to the great concert hall in the sky at some point in the late 70s..."

Recently watching a short film about French jazz pianist Michel Petrucciani I smiled at the idea that Taylor would also go into a shop to choose a piano he liked after having played some of them as happened to Petrucciani. The pianos in Taylor's time were cheap, often only upright, as those found in the jazz clubs... anything but Steinway or Yamaha grand pianos! And the practice and the sound were conditioned by the quality of the instruments available.

"Pianos in the clubs and pubs of the '60s where much as they are now", Hiseman explains.

"The clubs can rarely afford new ones so get given or a donated a piano which is often in need of serious work. They then don't keep tuned properly. The pianos are played by a wide variety of performers who work with loud rhythm sections often necessitating a rather heavy handed approach. The pianos suffer greatly and Mike who was never a great technician, always lived in hope of a great piano. He was usually disappointed".

Nothing to do with Keith Jarrett's mania to have a grand piano backstage at any gig.

Dave Tomlin has fleeting memories of that period at Kew: "I think he took the flat alone and afterwards offered me a room when I simultaneously broke up with my wife. At the flat the kitchen was on the same floor as my room and late at night I would hear him come down to eat. When he went up again I would go out and do the same. We mostly ate eggs and bacon, Mike had his own bacon and eggs and I had mine and only very rarely did we meet in the kitchen. But the washing up had to be done immediately so the kitchen was always very clean, to see a dirty plate would have been distressing to Mike".

Another anecdote, this, that confirms the controlled nature of the pianist, who as we have seen was little inclined, in the typically English tradition, to talk about himself and reluctant to reveal his private world.

Tomlin again: "Mike never talked about his personal relationship with Ann which was very harmonious as far as I could see, although apparently she had a lover towards the end, this also must have been an important factor in his breakdown. He never spoke of his work, like his wife these things belonged to our private worlds and music was our only topic".

So life at the Kew flat was passing seemingly quietly, with few unforgettable facts to remember. During the day Mike and Dave were busy with their day jobs, the nights spent playing in clubs. Just very rarely, as Tomlin recalls, "we played together at Kew, only sometimes tried out a new piece, but not often..."

And as for visitors, "I think Ann may have come there once but don't remember seeing her much then. Other people never came there".

One of the few to visit the flat in those days was Hiseman, who reveals: "A tape recorder, which I still have, was to be used for recording the Mike Taylor gigs. I remember going to Forest Road, Kew, and listening to the replays with Mike. By the time I got there he was usually already out of his head on cannabis but he seemed to enjoy listening to the gigs very much indeed, laughing a lot. I would smoke a little too but, conscious that I was always going to have to drive home and since I was always affected by either cannabis or alcohol after only consuming very small quantities, I guess I was never as happy as Mike was".

From the beginning of his career, Mike used to record his rehearsals and gigs, an attitude considered in retrospect by some journalists as a warning sign of his madness. Hiseman does not agree with this interpretation and wryly reacts in this way: "Mike used to record most of his gigs. I also recorded them using a tape recorder borrowed from Barbara's stepfather. I listened with Mike to most of the ones I recorded. He would light a joint and listen with eyes closed and with a look of quiet ecstasy on his face, smiling and laughing at the parts where the improvisations came together as if composed. If some journalists consider a musician recording and listening to his/her performances as the first sign of madness, you have to ask who is really mad here. I would suggest it is the journalists... I have been recording my performances for 40 years and have 24 track multitrack recordings of all my tours since 1999. Multiply my madness by 24!"

In the beginning things between Mike and Tomlin at Kew seemed to be going very well, but quite soon they changed rapidly, as Tomlin remembers, when "Graham Bond and his girlfriend came to stay at the flat, but they had to leave since no one else in the flat could get any sleep owing to the extremely loud copulations which the couple engaged in at night".

"At the time Graham Bond was looking for somewhere to live and Mike offered him a room. Graham was a heroin addict but Mike, being very straight, told him he must promise never to take it in the flat. One evening Graham was going up the stairs in front of me and he stumbled and dropped a syringe. He saw that I had seen it and was worried that I would tell Mike. However, Graham was also a friend of mine so I said nothing to Mike who was very suspicious of his addiction. After a while Graham moved his girlfriend in which was fine except that they indulged in very loud copulation several times a night and his girlfriend's voice was very penetrating. Mike lost a lot of sleep over this and since he had to get up early for work each morning it was very stressful for him and he began to be very tired and irritable. He said to me that he wouldn't have minded if she had a voice like Billie Holiday or Ella Fitzgerald, but he complained that she sounded like the siren of a fire-engine rushing to a fire..."

There are mentions of the period when Bond went on to share the flat in Kew with Taylor; they are in a biography Harry Shapiro published in 1992, even though this part is characterised by some questionable psychological statements, to say the least.

Shapiro wrote that "Mike was an orphan, so once again Graham found common ground with a musician who needed to express pain through music. Similarly, they both had to combat external pressures pulling them away from the music scene; in Mike's case he was expected to run the family newsagents' business. He too, took up a job and entered the slick world of advertising. But the core of his creative being was saved for the time spent sitting at the piano composing over three hundred pieces in almost every musical form".[71]

It's not easy to prove that these were the real motivations of the meeting of Bond with Taylor. More logically it seems journalist Richard Morton Jack's opinion that Bond "became close friends with Taylor at this time, partly because both were so recklessly experimental with drugs". [72] Tomlin, cannot say now how Mike met Bond. He's sure, anyway, they had very little harmony.

He says: "Graham Bond was quite a popular musician at the time but moved in completely different circles from me so he wasn't a friend of mine, we only nodded our heads if we passed. It was more or less the same with him and Mike. I don't know how he met Bond, probably heard that he needed a place to stay and offered him a room but he didn't relate to him on a personal level and neither did I".

Also Hiseman admits he has no idea about how Mike and Bond became friends: "Graham was a musical maverick like Mike and on the small local avant-garde scene in London at that time, I guess it was inevitable that they should meet. But who introduced who to whom, I have no idea. And I am surprised to hear they ever shared a flat - I don't remember them sharing a flat officially but for sure they spent some long nights smoking and jamming in other peoples pads".

This is an idea that Pete Brown, who spent time with both of them for brief periods, has agreed with. "I suppose Mike and Graham must have been aware of each other, the modern jazz scene in London was very small. They also had Hiseman in common. And they both liked hallucinogenics".

Anyway, losing the tranquillity of the house, Taylor was soon forced to turn Bond and his girlfriend out. But the calmness was just temporary, because the next to leave was Tomlin...

"The whole situation became unstable", he remembers, "when I was asked to do some arranging and a little recording with *Manfred Mann*, a popular group at the time. I was working a boring day job as a messenger in the City and getting paid peanuts so was glad for an opportunity to do something a little more creative. Mike, however, was disturbed by this. He told me that if I wanted to continue living in his flat I must keep a proper day job or leave. He was working as a salesman for his grandparents' business and they would have disapproved of him becoming a professional musician, so he was stuck and may have been annoyed that I had this chance to stop working. But I could not accept these terms as they restricted my freedom, and we fell out over this when I left the flat. At the time we had no work as a group and so we gradually drifted apart and although I saw him from time to time his manner was extremely frosty towards me".

It's a very interesting recollection, because it lights up a perhaps significant dimension of Taylor's background and its effect on his personality.

This may have been a key-moment in Taylor's attempt to become an established musician and the beginning of his rapid mental decline.

Maybe other motivations were the background differences between them, which may have compromised their relationship. Tomlin tries here to give an explication about how the things went: "Although Mike and I got on quite well we had such different backgrounds that we only had music in common. Mike came straight into modern jazz, whereas I had quite a different route. I started on clarinet years before playing archaic New Orleans Jazz - Bunk Johnson - George Lewis stuff - then moved slowly into more mainstream jazz - going to Germany and taking bands there to play contracts in clubs which was how I got into tenor sax. I was playing in a band in Wuppertal and the bass-player was a modernist. One day I went to a music shop and bought a tenor sax and that evening before we started I tried it out in the toilet. Then, when we were about to start I couldn't find my clarinet; the bass-player had hidden it and I was forced to play the sax so that's how I got started. There was of course a lot of drinking and smoking and we were quite wild. Mike had missed all that sort of wildness and disapproved of such things so that was the difference between us. Also I think you discovered that he had been an officer in the Air Force (I didn't know that) which would also have made him a bit formal, I had been in the Scots Guards for five years, but as a corporal so there was also a touch of class involved".

For Richard Morton Jack, "his commercial failure may have accelerated Taylor's decline, but things had already started to go frighteningly awry in his personal life. He'd always been withdrawn, but friends started to notice radical changes in his persona and appearance. In place of the smart young man in tweeds and tie who would talk eloquently about his music, was an unkempt bohemian who'd embraced LSD and cannabis, and communicated largely in hand gestures". [73]

Rubin: "Earlier in the decade I used to call him 'the 3 o'clock man' because every Saturday he'd arrive at my house absolutely dead on time to rehearse and improvise. He was that precise. But by 1966 he'd become absolutely bedraggled and incoherent." [74]

Also Gelly admits: "I didn't even recognise him the first time I saw him after he cracked up. When I'd first known him he was so smart he even wore a tie-pin. Now he looked like a hippie-come-tramp."

A "hippie-come-tramp" is a very incisive expression if one wants to clarify the turning point in the Taylor's life, but it risks generating a stigma and thus avoids understanding the real nature of things.

The problems with his wife Ann, culminating in a painful split when she began a relationship with someone else; [75] could these have generated a sense of emptiness in him, a space to be filled by a reckless use of drugs, especially hashish? Or maybe to the contrary, it was the abuse of drugs that gradually separated Ann from him and induced her to hang out with another man.

From any point of view one cares to consider, the end of this relationship with his wife, leaves little doubt that the separation had some role in fragmenting Taylor's personality. More than the supposed disappointment of a commercial flop, which must be an unlikely consideration as plausible reason.

"Ann and Mike, when we knew them were inseparable", Burke remembers. "They were almost always together. She was a beautiful girl, and we liked her as much as we liked Mike. It wasn't until 1965, when Mike came over to our flat in Clapham, that we heard that he and Ann had separated. Then we moved to New York, and we completely lost touch".

Regarding Ann and Mike being inseparable and in a harmonious relationship, it can be confirmed by two other photographs, again thanks to Burke. While in one picture Ann and Diane, Burke's wife, are cheerfully posing emerging from behind a marble fountain (the inscription says: "The fear of the Lord is a fountain of life"), on the other one Mike is beyond the statue with the two women at his side. His head is reclined on the right shoulder, his eyes looking to the camera, the look of one posing relaxed, with a calm mind. He wears glasses, the same black-framed glasses taken on the pictures at the Richmond's Jazz Cellar. He wears also a long winter coat, with shirt and tie, the trousers are slightly short and he wears gloves. On both photographs Ann looks intelligent, and bright; her eyes are shining, she seems happy to be there.

It's Sunday March 17th 1962, and the sky is grey; spring is still far off. The place is Hampstead Heath, and the four friends decide to stop at Whitestone Pond. Mike and Ann had been married just a few months before.

Noting in his journal, found at the end of 2013, Burke says: "It was the Sunday morning after we stayed all night at Dave Tomlin's (where I smoked grass for the very first time!). On the way home, Mike, who was driving, stopped and parked the car at the Whitestone Pond on Hampstead Heath, north-west London, and we all (Mike, Ann, Dianne and myself) got out and took the photos at the memorial fountain there. It was the climax of what had been a very exciting weekend which began on Friday night when we went down to The Jazz Cellar, which was the club in Richmond, West London, where Mike was playing with his quintet. The following evening we met at Dave's flat and smoked the grass. As I said, it was the first time for me, and quite an experience. We listened to *The Big Beat* by Art Blakey and the Messengers, *Monk at Town Hall*, *Someday My Prince Will Come* by Miles, and *My Favourite Things* by Coltrane. Three of those albums were mine, and the Monk belonged to Dave. It was an exciting evening, for sure!"

Burke again: "Mike and Ann were already married when we knew them, and I have no idea of when they got married. They never mentioned any dates or anniversaries. I always thought Mike and Ann seemed very close and loving. Ann was always present at the clubs that Michael and his groups played, so I think she loved to listen and dance to his music. I wasn't even aware that they had any marital problems, until perhaps the last time I saw Mike shortly before we left England. Ann frequently spoke of a guy who designed her clothing, but I don't recall that he was anything more than a friend".

Also Mark Petersen, frequenting them in the first years of the '60s, has some memories of the couple: "Mike and Ann and me and my wife Diana got on well and we'd meet socially on some weekends, either at his place in Twickenham or at mine in North London. Ann was a pretty woman who had been a photographic model modelling clothes for sales catalogues and brochures. Some time after we had lost touch I heard that Ann was having an affair and that Mike was minded to do nothing about it - possibly this situation led to their break up?"

Tomlin suggests a possible interpretation about the causes of the separation: "Ann was very beautiful although not overtly sexy. She was, like Mike, very proper and always well-dressed. She had the features and complexion of a Dresden china shepherdess, but also a good sense of humour. I think she fell out with Mike because he was so obsessed with music that he didn't give her much attention, so she was forced to look elsewhere for love, (Mike may have been too cool, considering 'love' sentimental)".

What were the deep feelings of Mike Taylor in those days at the end of 1965? Who can say anything about it? Again, we don't have a single photo, a recording, a letter or anything written that might reveal something of the ideas that were building up inside him during those days at Kew.

And it's not easy pursuing the logic of a trouble mind of the tortured artist to explain the facts with a chronological, rational sequence of little things happening, photos, and memories and paint a true portrait to understand everything.

No, we don't know the real connection of facts; the few witnesses are now old and their memories unreliable, and so this is an impossible exercise.

How many biographies have we read where all things seemed perfectly framed as a puzzle, with nothing obscure or inexplicable left out?

This is the picture I have of him; a very talented young musician, totally absorbed in his music, totally committed to playing his own compositions, and feeling the pressure to give in with compromises of his reality.

Is it true? Is it false? Is it too romantic an attempt to give an assured explanation?

I don't know. We don't know. All in all we can't know.

Are you sure the artist is really a clandestine?

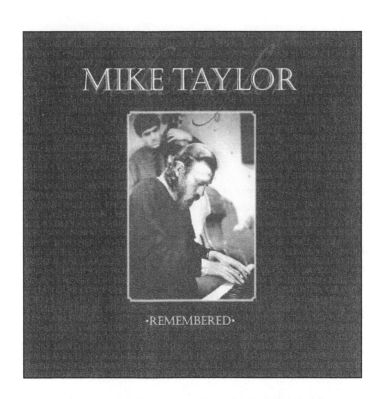

CD cover above, LP cover below

PENDULUM

mike taylor quartet

PENDULUM
THE
MIKE TAYLOR
QUARTET

Personnel:
Mike Taylor (piano);
Dave Tomlin (sop. sax);
Tony Reeves (bass);
John Hiseman (drums)

Side One
1. BUT NOT FOR ME *(Gershwin)*
2. EXACTLY LIKE YOU *(McHugh-Fields)*
3. A NIGHT IN TUNISIA *(Gillespie-Paparelli)*

Side Two
1. PENDULUM *(Taylor)*
2. TO SEGOVIA *(Taylor)*
3. LEEWAY *(Taylor)*

Production
Supervision: David Heelis
Sleeve Design: Dave Tomlin
Sleeve Layout: Denis Preston
Sleeve Notes: Ian Carr
Engineer: David Heelis

This record is something of a landmark in British jazz. It is one of the first recordings, perhaps the very first, made by the new generation of musicians who grew up when the 'Hard-Bop' or 'Funky' school of playing was already losing its vogue, and prophetic voices were beginning to pronounce more elegant slogans such as 'The New Thing', or 'The Avant-Garde'. (The French will have a lot to answer for on Judgement Day.) Against the troubling confusion and hubbub, this virtually unknown group, The Mike Taylor Quartet, has quietly produced an excellent LP. "PENDULUM" is not merely a 'promising début'; it is an exquisite performance by a quartet which has created its own music—a whole way of playing which is mature, honest, and fully understood by the four musicians. It must be listened to with an open mind and acute ears, for it is genuinely improvised—there are none of the old clichés on this LP, not a single familiar hot-lick or groovy phrase on the map of this new territory. Mike Taylor comments: "Our music comes out of the innate character and personality of the musicians who play it".

Pianist Mike Taylor is one of the most fertile and original composer/arrangers this side of the Atlantic. It is his compositions which are the basis for the quartet's fresh approach, and even when they play a standard tune—A Night in Tunisia or But Not For Me—the chemistry of Taylor's mind seems to change the piece's whole identity. This is perhaps because he did not begin playing jazz in the usual way; instead of learning standard tunes first and then trying to write his own compositions, he began at the very outset by playing little-known compositions and constantly his own themes. It's only in latter years that he came to learn the standard tunes which are in every jazz musician's repertoire. This also helps to account for his unique development—during the formative years he didn't associate with many other musicians because he had little in common with them. Such a lonely apprenticeship was invaluable, however, for he has emerged at the age of twenty-seven as a mature and highly individual talent.

Since the quartet was formed, at the beginning of 1964, they have worked very intermittently, playing the occasional concert and appearing spasmodically at various clubs in the London area. They had the honour of playing the first set at Ornette Coleman's London concert last year. But work is scarce and recognition is slow in coming. Mike Taylor sees no financial future in the mind he has chosen, yet he says with simple finality: "This is what I want to do".

The Mike Taylor Quartet bases its improvisations on sequences of chords or scales, but there are passages where the improvisation is free—not tied down to any particular scale or chord. Sometimes there is a definite solo voice, and sometimes, as in Leeway, the improvisation is collective throughout the piece.

The work of bassist Tony Reeves and drummer John Hiseman is outstanding. They seem to be completely at ease with these difficult compositions and Hiseman handles each delicacy in acceleration or deceleration of the pulse with great sureness.

Taylor's association with soprano-saxophonist Dave Tomlin has been particularly fruitful. They have been studying and playing together for a long time which perhaps accounts for their almost uncanny rapport. Although Tomlin's beginnings were along much more conventional lines than Mike Taylor's (he once played clarinet and tenor saxophone with Bob Wallis's traditional band), he has a highly original style. He's also evolved a most unusual method of composition—for he, too, is an indefatigable writer. He composes pictorially, by attempting to express the pattern of a picture in musical terms. The cover design of this record is by Dave Tomlin and he used as its basis the last eight bars of the composition *Pendulum*.

© 1966

LONG PLAY 33⅓ R.P.M

E.M.I. RECORDS
(The Gramophone Company Ltd.)
HAYES · MIDDLESEX · ENGLAND
Made and Printed in Great Britain

TRIO mike taylor

TRIO

The MIKE TAYLOR TRIO

Side One
1. ALL THE THINGS YOU ARE (Hammerstein-Kern)
2. JUST A BLUES (Taylor)
3. WHILE MY LADY SLEEPS (Kahn-Kaper)
4. THE END OF A LOVE AFFAIR (Redding)

Side Two
1. TWO AUTUMNS (Taylor)
2. GURU (Taylor)
3. STELLA BY STARLIGHT (Young)
4. ARENA (Taylor)

(STEREO)

Personnel:
MIKE TAYLOR—Piano
Jack Bruce and/or Ron Rubin—Bass
John Hiseman—Drums

Production:
Supervision: Denis Preston
Engineer: Dave Heelis
Sleeve Design: Denis Preston
Engraving: Jim Ritchie

Once upon a time jazz pianists were self-sufficient and self-contained, using their own left hands to spread the music forward. But conventions changed and by the 1940s hardly any pianist ventured out unaccompanied by a bassist and drummer. Yet the balance of this trinity, built upon the notion that Marshall McLuhan might put it) that bass and drums were extensions of the pianist's minstrel side, has drifted once again. In advanced circles, anyway. The music in this album, for instance, is centred around the pianist, Mike Taylor, but his companions are not so much help-mates as colleagues—indeed equals—making their own individual contributions.

On some tracks two bass players can be heard. This idea goes back to the mid-Thirties, when Duke Ellington used Wellman Braud and Billy Taylor. But Jack Bruce thinks its appearance here has come about through one of those fruitful accidents that sometimes happen. "I turned up at a club by mistake", says Bruce. "I'd got my drum mixed up and Ron Rubin was already there. Anyway, we played together and Mike probably got the idea from hearing us then."

Both bassists are men who were reared in more traditional pastures. Jack Bruce started playing after he heard Humphrey Lyttelton's record of Bad Penny Blues; he wanted to make the same sound in Johnny Parker's left hand. He gigged around Scotland, worked with Jim McGregor's Storyville Jazzband, joined Alexis Korner's "Blues Incorporated" in London, then played with Graham Bond and Manfred Mann before becoming one-third of "The Cream". Ron Rubin was actually a banjo player with a trad band in Liverpool and hated people who blew through saxophones. Later he worked with Sandy Brown. His first venture into avant-garde jazz was made in Paris. "Woody Shaw and Nathan Davis were at the Chat Qui Pêche", says Rubin, "And I filled in with them. But I'd already been listening to Ornette records, and—just like every bass player—I'd been devastated by Scott La Faro." On the tracks where both bassists can be heard it is Jack Bruce who sounds more percussive, a bit closer to Charlie Mingus; Ron Rubin has a slightly lighter, more delicate style.

It, in recent years, the bassist has been liberated from just sounding the root (or the fifth) of the chord, the drummer, too, has also moved into new territory. "I'm not interested in freedom for its own

sake", says Johnny Hiseman. "I just don't want to go tick-tock all the time. Actually, I keep time—in my head, anyway—even in what sound like completely free bars. But the point is that time is too limited in its emotional range. And I like to communicate emotion. I can do this by building tension and relaxation, by making some bits edgy and getting others to float along. You can produce tensions that either sharpen the music or (to the limit). Hiseman has played frequently with Mike Taylor; he has also worked with the New Jazz Orchestra and is the drummer with the Graham Bond Organisation.

These, then, were the musicians who joined Mike Taylor for this album. Sometimes they back up the pianist, swinging along in rhythmic unison as traditionally supposed to do. At other points they become individuals, making unique musical comments. Of the four original themes Just A Blues and Two Autumns are based on the twelve-bar blues; Arena is a very beautiful ballad, and Guru, as its title suggests, has Oriental affinities. There are undertones of Indian music elsewhere; for example, several tracks conclude with a drone rather like that produced by a tamboura.

The man responsible, the impresario of all this activity, is, of course, Mike Taylor, whose own playing sounds remarkably self-contained, as pianistic as the music of Chopin or Lennie Tristano. British musicians—those with taste and imagination, at any rate—are pretty unanimous in admiration of this highly individual musician. They look on him as one of the most original solo artists to appear in this country. This album should add yet more weight to that claim.

Other recommended Jazz Albums
in the Lansdowne Series:

JAZZ SUITE—STAN TRACEY QUARTET   SX 1774
IN PERSON—STAN TRACEY QUARTET
   SX/SCX 6126
INDO-JAZZ SUITE—JOE HARRIOTT DOUBLE QUINTET
   SX/SCX 6025
INDO-JAZZ FUSIONS—JOE HARRIOTT/JOHN MAYER
DOUBLE QUINTET   SX/SCX 6122
DUSK FIRE—DON RENDELL/IAN CARR QUINTET
   SX 6064

E.M.I RECORDS (THE GRAMOPHONE COMPANY LTD)
HAYES · MIDDLESEX · ENGLAND
Made and Printed in Great Britain

THIS HIGH FIDELITY STEREO RECORDING MAY ALSO BE PLAYED AS MONO. Any modern lightweight pickup with a playing weight of not more than 5 grams may be used with this record, but for best results we recommend the use of a stereo pickup cartridge. For atmospheric reproduction sell, of course, be obtained only from a complete stereo reproducer. To keep this record clean and dust free we recommend the regular use of NEW EMITEX.

Jazz Explosion

A PANORAMA OF CONTEMPORARY BRITISH JAZZ

Ian Carr
Joe Harriott
John Mayer
Don Rendell
William Russo
Amancio d'Silva
Mike Taylor
Stan Tracey
Guy Warren of Ghana

WWW.LONDONJAZZCOLLECTOR.WORDPRESS.COM

Le Déjeuner Sur L'herbe with

THE NEW JAZZ ORCHESTRA

Dave Tomlin at The Jazz Cellar, Richmond (London), November 1962
(courtesy of Michael Burke)

**Dave Tomlin at Richmond (London), November 1962
(courtesy of Michael Burke)**

Dave Tomlin and Chris Bateson at Richmond (London), November 1962
(courtesy of Michael Burke)

Chris Bateson, Mike Taylor and Martin Gail at Richmond (London), November
1962 (courtesy of Michael Burke)

ABOVE: Martin Gail, Chris Bateson, and Dave Tomlin at Richmond (London), November 1962   (courtesy of Michael Burke)
BELOW: Martin Gale and Randy Jones at Richmond (London), November 1962 (courtesy of Michael Burke)

ABOVE: Ann and Diane, Hampstead Heath (London) March 17th 1962
BELOW: Diane, Mike and Ann, Hampstead Heath (London)
March 17th 1962

ABOVE: Chris Bateson and Ron Rubin at Modern Jazz Workshop, Herne
Bay, July 1st, 1962 (photo by Terry Taylor)
BELOW: Mike Taylor and Ron Rubin

**ABOVE: Ron Rubin at Modern Jazz Workshop, Herne Bay, July 1st, 1962
(photo by Terry Taylor)
BELOW: Mike Taylor and Ron Rubin**

ABOVE: Mike Taylor, Ron Rubin, Dave Tomlin and Randy Jones at Modern Jazz Workshop, Herne Bay, July 1st, 1962 (photo by Terry Taylor)
BELOW: Ron Rubin and Randy Jones

Barbara Thompson in Mike Taylor's Kew flat, April 12th, 1967
(photo by Norman Potter)

Mike Taylor painting a little picture in c.a. 1964 (photo by Terry Taylor)

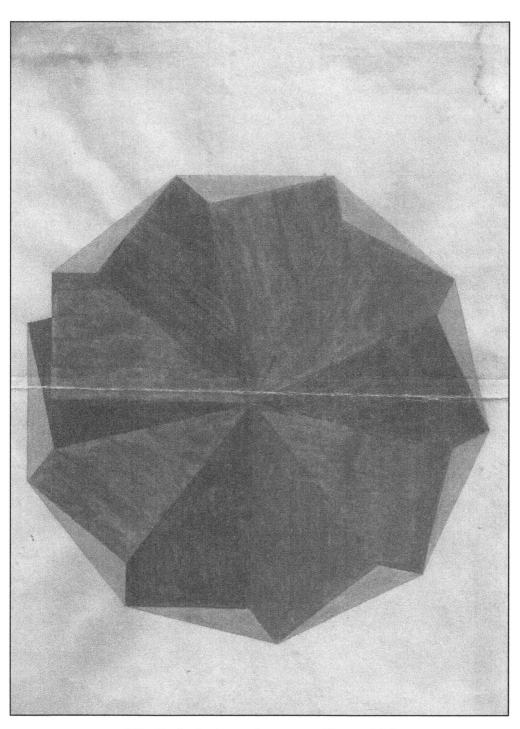

Mike Taylor's picture (courtesy of Ron Rubin)

WARNING: A CERTIFICATE IS NOT EVIDENCE OF IDENTITY.

CERTIFIED COPY OF AN ENTRY OF BIRTH

GIVEN AT THE GENERAL REGISTER OFFICE

Application Number 5892398-1

	REGISTRATION DISTRICT				Brentford				
1938	BIRTH in the Sub-district of Ealing				in the County of Middlesex				

Columns:-	1	2	3	4	5	6	7	8	9	10
No.	When and where born	Name, if any	Sex	Name and surname of father	Name, surname and maiden surname of mother	Occupation of father	Signature, description and residence of informant	When registered	Signature of registrar	Name entered after registration
461	First June 1938 26 Mount Park Road Ealing U.D.	Ronald Michael	Boy	Ronald Harry Frank Taylor	Joan Mary Taylor formerly Miff	Company Lieutenant of 5 Park Hill Court Ealing U.D.	Joan Mary Taylor mother 5 Park Hill Court Ealing	Twelfth July 1938	E.A.Hopkins Interim Registrar	"adopted" J. Charlton Deputy Superintendent Registrar

CERTIFIED to be a true copy of an entry in the certified copy of a Register of Births in the District above mentioned.

Given at the GENERAL REGISTER OFFICE, under the Seal of the said Office, the 26th day of August 2014

BXCG 271183

CAUTION: THERE ARE OFFENCES RELATING TO FALSIFYING OR ALTERING A CERTIFICATE AND USING OR POSSESSING A FALSE CERTIFICATE ©CROWN COPYRIGHT

WARNING: A CERTIFICATE IS NOT EVIDENCE OF IDENTITY.

CERTIFIED COPY OF AN ENTRY OF DEATH

GIVEN AT THE GENERAL REGISTER OFFICE

Application Number 5802823-1

	REGISTRATION DISTRICT			Southend-on-Sea				
1969	DEATH in the Sub-district of Southend-on-Sea Second			in the County Borough of Southend on Sea				

Columns:-	1	2	3	4	5	6	7	8	9
No.	When and where died	Name and surname	Sex	Age	Occupation	Cause of death	Signature, description and residence of informant	When registered	Signature of registrar
216.	15th January, 1969, Leigh Creek, opposite Lady Saville, one quarter of mile from the shore.	Ronald Michael TAYLOR.	Male.	30 years	Home address; 12, Fairlawn Grove, London, W.14. Musician.	Drowning in the sea. Open Verdict.	Certificate received from G.T.Jarmon, Coroner for Southend-on-Sea,Q.B. Inquest held 6th February,1969.	Seventh February, 1969.	D.C.Belsham, Registrar

CERTIFIED to be a true copy of an entry in the certified copy of a Register of Deaths in the District above mentioned.

Given at the GENERAL REGISTER OFFICE, under the Seal of the said Office, the 16th day of July 2014

DYD 723133

See note overleaf

CAUTION: THERE ARE OFFENCES RELATING TO FALSIFYING OR ALTERING A CERTIFICATE AND USING OR POSSESSING A FALSE CERTIFICATE ©CROWN COPYRIGHT

WARNING: A CERTIFICATE IS NOT EVIDENCE OF IDENTITY.

GIVEN AT THE GENERAL REGISTER OFFICE

Application Number 5926640-1

19 61. Marriage solemnized at *The Register Office* in the

District of *Ealing* in the *County of Middlesex*

No.	When married	Name and surname	Age	Condition	Rank or profession	Residence at the time of marriage	Father's name and surname	Rank or profession of father
98	Thirtieth September 1961	Ronald Michael Taylor	23 years	Bachelor	Salesman (Wallpaper and Paints)	The Common Ealing W5	Ronald Harry Taylor (deceased)	Accountant (Wallpaper & Paints)
		Ann Summersby	22 years	Spinster	Receptionist (Wholesale Textiles)	Ryder House Wenton SW19	Ernest John Summersby	

Married in the *Register Office* by *Certificate before* me,

| This marriage was solemnized between us, | R. M. Taylor, A. Summersby | in the presence of us, | R. Hall, R. A. Hall | |

Superintendent Registrar
Deputy Registrar

CERTIFIED to be a true copy of an entry in the certified copy of a register of Marriages in the Registration District of Ealing

Given at the General Register Office, under the Seal of the said Office, the 11th day of September 2014

MXG 344223

CAUTION: THERE ARE OFFENCES RELATING TO FALSIFYING OR ALTERING A CERTIFICATE AND USING OR POSSESSING A FALSE CERTIFICATE © CROWN COPYRIGHT

WARNING: A CERTIFICATE IS NOT EVIDENCE OF IDENTITY.

GMB

DUPLICATE

ORIGINAL

No.	Rank	NAME				CLASPS ENTITLED TO UNDER ARMY Army Order	Record of Despatch	REMARKS
27/193	T/Capt.	Bunting E	T/Capt. R.E. 9 Bomb Disposal Squadron			G.S.M. & CLASP BOMB & MINE CLEARANCE 1945-49		Service Confirmed Award approved Bac 3949/48 MG O(as) THE WAR OFFICE A.G.4 (MEDALS) 18 November 1949
323381	LT	COTTON N	22 BD Coy RE	NO		BOMB		
113496	Maj	BLACKWELL R	21 BD Coy RE (HQ)	NO				
371633	LT	WEBB PRW	2/LT 16 BD Sqn RE	NO				
304970	LT	ARMSTRONG W	LT 21 BD Coy RE	NO	DECEASED			
96820	CAPT	TAYLOR	RM CAPT 58 D Coy RE	NO				
353140	Capt	DALBY DJW	CAPT RE	YES & CLASP				
126305	Maj	ARCHER (G.C.) B.S.T	MAT RE	NO				
233407	LT	BAYS GM	PA LT RE	NO				

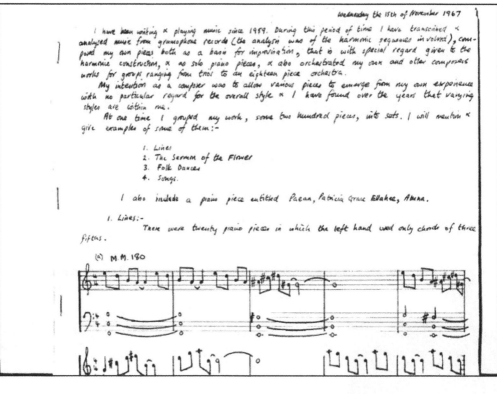

Wednesday the 15th of November 1967

I have been writing & playing music since 1959. During this period of time I have transcribed & analysed music from gramophone records (the analysis was of the harmonic sequences involved), composed my own pieces both as a basis for improvisation, that is with special regard given to the harmonic construction, & as solo piano pieces, & also orchestrated my own and other composers works for groups ranging from trios to an eighteen piece orchestra.

My intention as a composer was to allow various pieces to emerge from my own experience with no particular regard for the overall style & I have found over the years that varying styles are within me.

At one time I grouped my work, some two hundred pieces, into sets. I will mention & give examples of some of them:-

1. Lines
2. The Sermon of the Flower
3. Folk Dances
4. Songs.

I also include a piano piece entitled Paean, Patricia Grace Blakee, Amna.

1. Lines:-

There were twenty piano pieces in which the left hand used only chords of three fifths.

(a) M.M. 180

Mike Taylor's CV November 15th 1967

JAZZ IS ALIVE & WELL

A SERIES OF 6 CONCERTS
AT CONWAY HALL RED LION SQUARE WC1
(HOLBORN KINGSWAY TUBE, BUS)

Presented by LONDON JAZZ CENTRE
in association with ARTS COUNCIL OF GREAT BRITAIN
Tickets 5s 7/6d 10s 12/6d from Dobells, Colletts, Chris Wellards,
or by post from London Jazz Centre, 6, Lewisham Way SE14

OCT 11	DON RENDELL/IAN CARR QUINTET JOHN SURMAN TRIO
NOV 8	NEW JAZZ ORCHESTRA MIKE TAYLOR TRIO
DEC 13	AN EVENING with MIKE WESTBROOK
JAN 10	RONNIE SCOTT AND THE BAND DAVE GELLY GROUP
FEB 14	CHRIS McGREGOR GROUP SPONTANEOUS MUSIC ENSEMBLE
MAR 14	GRAHAM COLLIER SEXTET, (GUEST STAR: SANDY BROWN) HOWARD RILEY TRIO

2/6d OFF 12/6d and 10s TICKETS, FOR STUDENTS AND JAZZ CENTRE MEMBERS

JAZZ IS ALIVE AND WELL

A SERIES OF SIX CONCERTS AT THE CONWAY HALL

Red Lion Square, W.C.1.   (Chancery Lane Tube, Bus)

Presented by The London Jazz Centre Society
In Association with - The Arts Council of Great Britain

October 11th,   7-30 p.m.
DON RENDELL / IAN CARR QUINTET
JOHN SURMAN TRIO

November 8th,   7-30 p.m.
NEW JAZZ ORCHESTRA
MIKE TAYLOR TRIO

December 13th, 7-30 p.m.
AN EVENING with MIKE WESTBROOK

January 10th,   7-30 p.m.
RONNIE SCOTT AND THE BAND
DAVE GELLY / FRANK RICOTTI GROUP

February 14th,   7-30 p.m.
CHRIS McGREGOR BAND
SPONTANEOUS MUSIC ENSEMBLE

March 14th,   7-30 p.m.
GRAHAM COLLIER BAND
Guest Star **SANDY BROWN. 'MUSIC'**

TICKETS: 5/-, 7/6, 10/-, 12/6
Available from Dobell's, Colletts or by Post from 6 Lewisham Way, S.E.14

2/6 off all 12/6 - 10/6 Tickets for Students & Jazz Centre Members
(On Production of Membership Card)

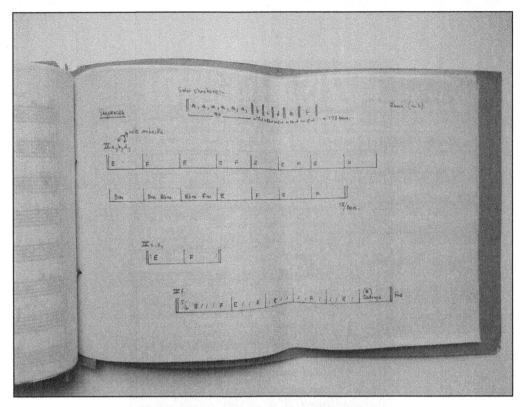

Mike Taylor's original handmade scores (courtesy of Trevor Watts)

Mike Taylor, Ronnie Scott's Old Place, London, October 27th, 1967
(photo by Jak Kilby)

**Mike Taylor, Ronnie Scott's Old Place, London, October 27th, 1967
(photo by Jak Kilby)**

Mike Taylor, Ronnie Scott's Old Place, London, October 27th, 1967
(photo by Jak Kilby)

**Mike Taylor, Ronnie Scott's Old Place, London, October 27th, 1967
(photo by Jak Kilby)**

Mike Taylor's grave (Courtesy of Tony Tomlin)

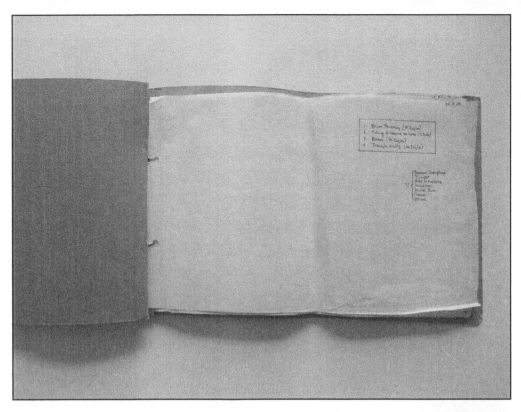

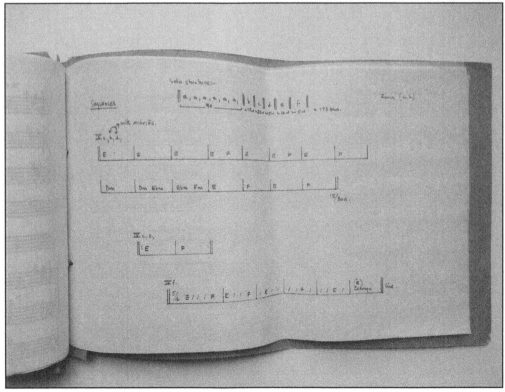

Mike Taylor's original handmade scores (courtesy of Trevor Watts)

4

Full of magnetic currents

"Mike Taylor's Trio on Columbia must be
the most exciting event in jazz for a long time –
and it's BRITISH! Congratulations!"
(L. C. Spratt, Eltham, London SE9 –
on a letter to *Melody Maker*, May 1967)

There now began a radical change in Taylor's personality and behaviour that soon became irreversible, although in spite of his collapsed marriage, he tried to reorganise his work with the quartet.

At this point, bassist Reeves' split and Tomlin's imminent departure induced Mike on 29th December to arrange a meeting at the Kew flat, probably with the idea of forming a new band.

It was a "summit meeting", to use the expression Rubin noted down in his journal. To the two words, significantly, he followed with a question mark in parenthesis, which reveals his scepticism.

Involved that day was Tomlin (maybe for a last attempt at agreement) and the pianist Peter Lerner, while Steve Stollman, brother of well-known Bernard (the founder of ESP Records), didn't show. At the time Rubin wrote, he was "probably stoned" We don't know what was decided that evening, Rubin doesn't remember anything more than the brief note in his diary, but a few days later (it's January 3rd 1966) Taylor was on stage with his quartet (Rubin, Tomlin and Hiseman) at the inauguration of the *Little Theatre Club* in Garrick Yard, St. Martin's Lane (London, just off Trafalgar Square), "a small theatre type club, which I think normally put on fringe plays to 50 or 60 people...", Jon Hiseman remembers. "They decided to try *fringe* jazz if I remember correctly..."

Born from the ashes of the *Hovenden Theatre Club*, the building dated back to the Edwardian age. Drummer John Stevens had discovered it and soon he became the manager with the proposal "to give the opportunity to known or little-known musicians to present their music in public", as he proclaimed to the press.

From 10.30 pm to 1.00 am, six nights a week, on the little stage with black and white cartoons pinned to the wall behind, it'll host regular avant-garde musicians such as Evan Parker, Howard Riley, Paul Rutherford, Derek Bailey, Trevor Watts, *Group Sounds Five* and the *Spontaneous Music Ensemble* (SME), founded by Stevens and Watts, one of the most radical experiences of jazz developments in those years.

As Ian Carr wrote, the club "rapidly established itself as the platform and crucible for the ideas and experiments of the rising generations of musicians. Apart from providing a regular weekly playing spot for numerous little-known musicians and groups, it also became the place where all kinds of musicians, known and unknown, dropped in to listen or to sit-in when there was a loosely organised blowing session – which happened most nights. *When the Ronnie Scott Club* moved to new premises in Frith Street, and the Old Place became vacant, the centre of gravity of the scene shifted". [76]

At the *Little Theatre*, as John Wickes writes, "for the first time the implications of black American free jazz were thoroughly explored, and affinities with the 'classical' avant-garde investigated, so that by the end of the decade, a powerful range of experimental approaches had become established, with collaborative links forged with leading exponents of radical new developments in Europe and the United States". [77]

Anyway, according the *Melody Maker*'s account, even if great musicians as Trevor Watts, Peter Lemer, Jeff Clyne, and Kenny Wheeler played that night, the opening concerts were not so memorable: "It was a swinging evening – for drinking and talking - because none of the music swung in the slightest".

The headline of the famous magazine was clear: "Is the New Wave just a passing fad? Or has 'jazz' become another meaningless word?" Bob Dawbarn, usually very acute, was very explicit when writing of his perplexity about the project: "No one can question the right of musicians to experiment. But we do have the right to ask whether their chosen path is worth following..."

"Odd mixture of musicians and actors present, like creatures from two different planets", Rubin wrote in the pages of his journal with his usual irony. "No money, of course – free jazz in both senses".

After the double-bass player made his début on the same stage with his 'free trio' (Keith Thompson on alto sax and Laurie Allen on drums) he confided again in his diary, "I've already nagging doubts about the whole 'new thing'".

After Tomlin's definitive exit, the following concerts was played as a trio with Rubin and Hiseman, the first one at the prestigious Marquee Club in London Wardour Street – a promotional happening to launch Stollman's E.S.P. Records, a gig where confusion ruled the roost.

Rubin: "As anything is apparently allowed at a happening, I just happened to make myself scarce when things started getting very silly." - Bob Dawbarn's harsh criticism in *Melody Maker* about the event tended to confirm this opinion.

Then, after another gig at the Little Theatre on 14th February, the trio played two dates in May (one at Regency Club in Stoke Newington, on 18th, the other one again at Little Theatre on 25th) and one in June (at Little Theatre on 29th), before Mike was involved in a new recording project, on the basis of producer Denis Preston's esteem and confidence, and the positive reactions given to *Pendulum* by the jazz commentators and critics.

Confirming his appreciation of the pianist, Preston told Robert Bolton: "He is one of the handful of talented jazzmen I have dealt with in this country. Individually, although he was not a musical director, he was one of the outstanding talents - an original". [78]

The sessions for the new album, again with the assistance of the sound engineer David Heelis, held over two days, on Tuesday 12th and Wednesday 13th July, 1966 he played with a band composed of old friends Jon Hiseman, Ron Rubin and Jack Bruce, who had formed *Cream* just some days before.

Mike soon established his well-known attitude to work in the studio: "He never expressed any views, he didn't say "let's do that again"", Preston remembered. [79] Despite the excellent final results, at one stage the producer was seriously concerned that the album might never be completed.

This was a memory confirmed by Rubin: "Because his take on standards was unrecognisable, I asked him to jot down the changes for me on "The end of a love affair". He refused, telling me he preferred a random approach – and, for some reason, it worked". [80]

An anecdote that refers to other legendary experiences on the music scene: during the sessions for his solo albums (1969-1970), even Pink Floyd founder Syd Barrett didn't say anything about ideas he had and let the producers (especially Dave Gilmour) interpret them. Similarly, folk hero Nick Drake at the end of his short career, when he recorded his enigmatic, *Pink Moon* (1972) spoke just few words during the recording sessions and a conclusive sentence became a rock legend, when the producer John Wood lamented the record's extreme shortness: "I don't want them arranged, no *frills*", the guitarist replied.

In the case of Mike, was the increasing use of drugs beginning to isolate him from studio work? Or was it the conscious idea of an art based on aleatory and improvisation, on which, speaking for the avant garde, John Cage had described?

Of the eight tracks recorded, four are standards ("All the things you are", "While my lady sleeps", "The end of a love affair" and "Stella by starlight") and four original compositions by Taylor ("Just a Blues", "Two Autumns", "Guru" and "Abena").

One of the new things in these sessions was the involvement of two bass players simultaneously, a rare event in jazz circles. It has been considered as evidence of Taylor's mental confusion in that he had invited both double-bassists to the studio by error, a conjecture contradicted by Jon Hiseman who explains: "I know that it is said that Mike confused the booking of musicians so both Jack Bruce and Ron Rubin turned up, but at the time I assumed that that had been designed by Mike, who, as I remember, always thought that calling a jazz album *Trio* with four musicians was an inspired idea. In some ways of course it did capture the essence of Mike".

In fact, from the sleeve notes compiled by journalist Charles Fox for the back cover, things are explained clearly as a "fruitful accident": "On some tracks two bass players can be heard. That idea goes back to the mid-Thirties, when Duke Ellington used Wellman Braud and Billy Taylor. But Jack Bruce thinks its appearance here has come about through one of those fruitful accidents that sometimes happen: "I turned up at a club by mistake", Bruce says. "I'd got my dates mixed up and Ron Rubin was already there. Anyway, we played together and Mike probably got the idea from hearing us then".

About the question of who the bass players were who played on the tracks, after reiterated errors generated by Robert Bolton's articles (in *Jazz Journal* in 1974 and 1975), the things were definitely cleared by Ron Rubin in December 2004 with an ironic letter sent to *Jazz Journal* that had reviewed the Universal CD edition of the album published that year:

> *"One bass miss!*
>
> *Sir,*
>
> *With regard to Simon Adam's review of the Mike Taylor Trio CD recorded in 1966, (...) allow me to clear up the matter of which bass player is featured on which of the eight tracks:*
> *I am playing on tracks 1, 2, 4 & 8*
> *Jack Bruce is on track 7*
> *We both play on tracks 3, 5 & 6.*
>
> *On another track, I fear that my old Liverpool chum Stev Voce must have had a senior moment when he associated Isaac Newton with the past time of fishing (JJI October 2004). Steve obviously meant Izaak Walton, author of The Compleat Angler.*
>
> *As far as I know, Sir Isaac was more interested in matters gravitational than piscatorial.*
>
> *Ron Rubin, London".*

So, Newton and Walton permitting, Rubin played on four tracks ("All the things you are", "Just a Blues", "The end of a love affair" and "Abena"), Jack Bruce on "Stella by starlight" and both on the rest "While my lady sleeps", "Two autumns" and "Guru".

On the back cover notes, analysing the record, jazz critic Charles Fox wrote that "the music in this album is centred around the pianist, Mike Taylor, but his companions are not so much help-mates as colleagues - indeed equals – making their own individual contributions". And about this, he underlined sometimes the musicians "back up the pianist, swinging along as rhythm sections are traditionally supposed to do. At other points they become individuals, making unique musical comments".

His conclusion was that "the man responsible, the inspiration of all the activity, is, of course, Mike Taylor, whose own playing sounds remarkably self-contained, as pianistic as the music of Chopin or Lennie Tristano. British musicians – those with taste and imagination, at any rate – are pretty unanimous in admiration of this highly individual musician. They look on him as one of the most original jazz artists to appear in this country. This album should add yet more weight to that claim".

Indisputable words, for nothing else were suited to the occasion or stands up as an authentic masterpiece in the contemporary jazz panorama, and not only for its evident music value.

The suspended time suggested from the very first chords of "All the things you are" cause the indifferent listener to wake up: there are just five seconds where Hiseman's cymbals and a minor chord played by Rubin define sense of wait that gives vertigo and seems to draw one into an abyss; Taylor's right hand chord followed by some untied notes with the left hand that fall to the next chord.

Stayed from falling into the abyss, the listener's time has been suspended for around fifty seconds by cymbals and double-bass while Taylor plays improvised chords and single notes to prepare the entry of a melody that makes "All the things you are" the unforgettable tune that is.

Comparing any other version of this tune is a useless exercise: there's no other arrangement so extraordinarily perturbing from the very first beat, so absolute and conclusive it traces a sharp demarcation between the original interpretation and a (new) creation.

Lennie Tristano, for example, on one of his more complete albums (*Lennie Tristano*, Atlantic 1955), re-reads this standard with the exposition of the theme and Lee Konitz's sax alto is a good example which offers a rhythmic improvisation on the piano that barely equates with the positive mood desired by the tune's author. In this remake there is also a great solo, sustained by drums and double-bass, but even if clearly futuristic it's quite consistent with the whole piece.

Also Bill Evans, who played the tune many times; his wonderful remakes never get the incredible intensity captured by Taylor. That feeling of 'emotional confusion' for something that is about to happen; a distressing fear to not find that joyful certainty that makes her "all the things"? Or is it the feeling of dismay about a meeting which will not go as one hopes? Or, more simply, is it a hesitation before discovering what we know of being, that every time of meeting becomes a form of bliss?

When in 1939 he composed it for the musical *Very Warm For May*, Jerome Kern couldn't imagine that this tune would be become one of the most popular jazz standards, above all because its harmonic structure was so unusual and complex if compared to other popular songs. Besides, Oscar Hammerstein III's lyrics, so sentimental and flat ("You are the angel glow that lights a star"...), when compared to other great lyricist of the time (as Ira Gershwin, one of the best), doesn't seem to help the song. But the 32 beats of the chorus, so bright and joyful, immediately made it a strong hit, above all thanks to the interpretations of the *Tommy Dorsey Band* and *The Artie Shaw Orchestra* (its version got to the top of the charts in the U.S.A.), before the tune was recast by the foremost singers and musicians of the age - from Ella Fitzgerald to Frank Sinatra, from Charlie Parker to Clifford Brown, from Chet Baker to Joe Pass – to become immortal. [81]

Also "While my lady sleeps" was a well-known sentimental ballad played on the jazz scene in those years: interpretations by John Coltrane, Chet Baker, Zoot Sims were circulating for a long time, both instrumental and vocal (with Gus Khan's lyrics) and it might seem an easy choice by Taylor to include on his album a well-known tune like this.

Yet also this new arrangement was destined to surprise the listener, used to the sentimental range utilised by Bronislau Kaper and here obliged to confront from the very first beats a very different mood: an anxious, even gloomy feeling accompanied Taylor's take on "his lady while she sleeps". So nothing relaxed and pacified, nothing that might reassure sight, or a mind oppressed by negative thoughts.

And how to interpret the choice of another standard as "The end of a love affair"? How much personal feeling was contained in the choice of this tune after the painful ending of his short marriage with Ann?

Here, as in the other standards recorded, the looming feeling is anything but resolved, or well-balanced, in fact the heart of the tune bursts out with a strong improvised free sequence of drums, double-bass and piano, with Taylor compulsively beating the keys in a haphazard manner. Nothing of that affected sentimentalism of Nat King Cole or Frank Sinatra, the disillusioned resignation of Billie Holiday, who made the tune immortal during the 1958 *Lady in Satin* recording sessions, or the sparkling hard bop by Dexter Gordon and Art Blakey who had accented its rhythmic, purely melodious form.

In Taylor's version of "end of a love affair" there's no place for nostalgia, regret, or self-indulgence. And even if this tune is arranged and played as an instrumental, the lyrics written by its author Edward C. Redding in 1950 couldn't be far distant from the furious feelings of Taylor. What could he have to do with such lyrics as:

"So I walk a little too fast and I drive a little too fast
And I'm reckless it's true, but what else can you do at the
End of a love affair?"?

In the same way, in "Stella by the starlight", composed in '41 by Victor Young for the creepy Paramount ghost movie *The Uninvited* and performed (with lyrics by Ned Washington, written in 1946) by many jazz musicians, Taylor's new interpretation resets the major key, cleanses the melody, making it a painful and restless ballad, where some few references to the original version float.

It would be really inconceivable, unlike how it happens in the movie, that one could dedicate a rendering such as this to Stella [82]. The tension is so tangible, the tune's progression is inconclusive, disarranging that feeling of tenderness that the listener finds in the original version.

Also the four tunes composed by the pianist are pervaded by an anxious and pensive spirit: if "Guru" is that angular free jazz, scanned by a shamanic beating on the background of a deep meditation that seems erupting from the bowels of the Earth, "Just a blues" has a surprisingly classical style where the blues is rethought inside a tradition that is entirely European; to the nervous hard bop of "Two Autumns", a rhythmic gallop always on the verge on collapsing, with Rubin's and Bruce's double-basses improvising suggestive harmonic twists, it follows the interior dialogue of "Abena" ("Tuesday" in an African dialect), a stripped-back, claustrophobic, sublime composition. Maybe it's the apex of the band's interplay.

As Rubin wrote in his journal commenting on the tune: "Hiseman plays beautifully. For me the best track is the hauntingly lovely "Abena"".

Trio is Taylor's masterpiece, the mature evolution of *Pendulum*, a prodigious synthesis of a jazz aesthetic that didn't exist and will not exist again, above and beyond stereotypical labels: in a few words, neither hard bop, or cool jazz, nor free jazz, but a new music, *never heard before*, because a synthesis of the jazz avant-garde and European classical music (Chopin? Debussy? Satie? Ravel?), filtered by a mind in the throes of an inner revolution.

And because paraphrasing Duchamp, "it's the listener who plays the record", this album recorded by Taylor has become for me, the very essence of jazz music, a '900's artwork that, happens rarely, and in circumstances unique, it fixes a point of no return in the evolution of the musical medium, lifting the threshold of perception of the listener. An iconoclastic work, it breaks habits, it shakes the labels, it subverts the rules. As *Pink Moon* by Nick Drake or *Lorca* by Tim Buckley; as *Apres midi d'un faune* by Debussy or *The Rite of Spring* by Stravinsky; as *The Goldberg Variations* by Bach played by Glen Gould in 1981 or *In A Silent Way* by Miles Davis. As the *Pierrot Lunaire* by Schoenberg and *Arcana* by Varèse...

After *Trio*, many jazz records will look repetitive, and pedantic. Lacking in that rare intensity, that irrepressible drive, that arcane obscure charm of *Trio*, an artwork out of nowhere just as its author... Unexpected and unique.

As for his début album, *Trio* would be published just one year after, in June 1967, with an intriguing and enigmatic cover designed by Canadian sculptor Jim Ritchie, friend of producer Dennis Preston. [83]

An interval, that even for that age, illustrated the impossibility of getting the fruits of the undeniable success bestowed by the critics, though the concept of 'success', in the jazz field, had to be related to the period and the context, absolutely subordinate to other forms of mainstream music (pop, first of all, but also the classical music...). [84]

Nevertheless the specialised press played tribute to the unique value of Taylor's new record...

Ian Breach from *The Guardian* (June 1967) wrote that the record was "another way of stating the Tristano-Monk-Evans progression without actually sounding like any of those three pianists". And added: "Taylor is one of a handful of British players (Michael Garrick and Stan Tracey among them) who are breaking new ground without abandoning too many precepts. His method of fragmenting the chords (…) and the use of two bassists (Ron Rubin and Jack Bruce) are forthright, but I should like to hear more before prosecuting all the claims that have been laid for him...". And if Derek Jewell on the jazz review page of the *Sundays Time* (October the 1st, 1967) abruptly admitted that "Taylor is another Briton whose reputation has remained strangely muted. His ability to swing as well as to play sonata-style ought soon to remedy that. This is a very impressive trio record, marred only by an excess of scuffle-type drumming...", *Melody Maker* (June 10th, 1967) dedicated a more extended analysis of the record by Bob Dawbarn, literally bound by the quality of the music.

"This is one of those rare jazz albums which repay continuous playing. I've been listening to it for nearly a month now and each new playing throws up entirely new facets. It is, in fact, a thoroughly rewarding LP, deserving the highest praise for the four young British musicians involved. Almost all the reservations I had on first hearing have now disappeared. My only two minor complaints are that Taylor could make a more effective use of dynamics and I feel that the music is almost too concentrated with no passages of comparative light relief to give contrast. However, these are tiny blemishes on an otherwise excellent performance. Taylor is obviously familiar with the work of Lenny Tristano, but his ideas are entirely original and he is at his best building to a threatening climax of almost unbearable intensity on his own compositions (...). The trio in fact becomes a quartet on some tracks with the use of two bass players but all four musicians are so disciplined that this never becomes a mere gimmick. Hiseman's drumming deserves special praise. This really is thinking drumming which gives extra depth to the piano lines".

Alan Morgan, on *Gramophone Magazine*, recognizing that Taylor was "one of the new school of young British jazz musicians who seem to have reached maturity at a very early stage", stated that the album was "one of most refreshing piano records to have been made in this country for some time". Talking about Taylor's style he wrote: "Taylor's style is free, flowing and graceful, a compound of elements to be found in the work of men such as Lennie Tristano and Bill Evans. But he makes greater use of his accompanists than either Tristano (who tends to use bass and drums simply to mark time) or Evans, and for that reason the LP is almost as much a triumph for drummer John Hiseman, certainly one of the very finest small band drummers this side of the Atlantic".

The journalist recognized the album's structure (four standards and four original compositions) was "ideal, while the choice of musicians could hardly be bettered. I am not, as readers have probably guessed, an advocate of *avant-garde* jazz (surely the most predictably obsolescent term since "progressive jazz", incidentally). Taylor and his men show that there are paths for jazz development to follow which are logical extensions of what has gone before, without necessarily being radical simply for the sake of being radical".

Jazz Journal's Mark Gardner wrote Mike Taylor "is one of Britain's most original young pianist. That last record was good; this one is very good. His playing has clearly developed and is much freer without sacrificing form. His sense of construction is quite striking. Nice too to hear a really pianistic touch, the Bill Evans influence in Taylor's approach".

And closing his review, talking about the tunes: "These are sometimes avant garde, sometimes conventional but always exciting sounds. Taylor could cut a lot of his American contemporaries and fox those blindfold test experts."

So, as the first album was issued, with the press enthusiastic, Mike was severely increasing his drugs consumption, exacerbating his behaviour, 'out of his head'.

Leaving the job with his grandfather, now presumably in retirement, the pianist worked as a dishwasher in a Lyons Tea Shop.

His embarrassment is obvious, when Preston, realizing the economic difficulties he had (what's more, *Trio*, sold at the equivalent of €15 nowadays, and it didn't sell too well...), during a break in the recording sessions asked him how he was earning a living. "When I asked him how he was earning for a living, he said: "Working". I asked what sort of work and he said: "Just work, washing up and things". [85]

This work, entirely separate from *his music*, had always been a way to take one day at a time, and that vague reply - "washing up and things" - said it all. It's evident he was striving to do something, because the favourable conditions he had had until then was finished.

Anyway now his mind was elsewhere, more and more the victim of drugs, and even if his universe was shrinking he was still associating with his close circle of friends - Jon Hiseman, Graham Bond, Ron Rubin – if it's true that at the end of '66 he took part in a jam session at Barbara Thompson's home, (she was a musician in the NJO and future wife of Hiseman.)

The drummer recounts: "Barbara lived in a very big house in Wimbledon. Both her mother and step-father worked long hours in central London - and while the cats were away, the mice would play. Barbara used to invite players she met at the Royal Collage of Music (where she was studying Piano, Flute, Clarinet and Composition - there was no course for saxophone - it was not a recognised instrument in those days) to play big band jazz in the large sitting room at the house. I was there, but not as a player - I never played at those sessions. I taped it on Barbara's step-father's Grundig mono tape recorder. When I first met Barbara in a New Jazz Orchestra rehearsal towards the end of 1964 I talked to her about borrowing her father's tape recorder in return for me giving her driving lessons..."

In Thompson's parents' home, where musicians of the Royal College of Music often used to play, sometimes there were more limited sessions where Hiseman played his drums and Barbara played reeds. On one of these occasions, with Bond (alto sax), Tony Reeves (bass) and Louie (congas), Mike was playing the piano. Hiseman activated the father-in-law's Grundig and recorded something.

"I may indeed have a tape of part of it", he says, "I started a project getting all my 2-track tapes into the digital domain last year. I came across a tape with Graham Bond/Mike Tayor and others - and it said "GB & MT" on the box, but with no details. I could not tell who it was. However I am sure this is *the* tape, but Barbara and I have no recollection of the session. The tape recorder did not record for very long because the tapes were on small reel..."

"It was in this kind of informal gathering that Mike was able to perform ever greater things than were put into the two albums", Robert Bolton wrote in 1975. "That afternoon some music was taped and I've been able to hear one track, the "Improvisation" which demonstrates how far Taylor had gone into free ideas. This was a free-blowing session without any organisation yet the music produced by Taylor, Reeves, Bond, and a congas drummer named Louie has a complete telepathy. There is an intense slow-burning feeling with Taylor in scintillating form, leading, nudging and supporting the group and soloists in this very open ended improvised piece". [86]

Unfortunately Reeves remembers little of those circumstances, even if he's intrigued by the tape's existence. He says: "Sorry, I remember very little about this, other than going to Barbara's place and doing it. I sort of remember the conga player. It may have been a rehearsal of new tunes from Mike but I think it must have been 90% improvised. I'd love to hear the tape."

Another possible tune recorded that day was "Pipes", described by Bolton as "a freely improvised piece with Mike and Barbara Thompson on recorders and Hiseman on drums. (…) We find him concerned entirely with improvised music, and with colours and textures within a narrow tonality. There is a great deal of free interplay here, the music having so few rough edges that again one is inclined to think the work has been rehearsed when it is really the meeting of musical minds".

According to the journalist it was one of the last compositions of the pianist.

There was a similar event on Mike's calendar leading toward the dissolution. It was a session played in a house at Ladbroke Grove (but where and with whom exactly?) again with Bond (alto sax), Jon Hiseman (drums), Tony Reeves (bass) and Jack Masserik (alto sax), but there's no memory about this, nor recordings.

It's the circumstance where Bond was trying to record a new album also involving Pete Brown's lyrics? Brown doesn't recall precise facts or dates when he reveals that "my main recollections of Mike were when he was beginning to lose it and was hanging around with Graham, who had also lost it to some extent. He then had very long hair and was quite changed from his earlier smart appearance. Graham wanted both of us to contribute to an album that was never made, with some pretty far out ideas including sound poetry..."

Bolton reported about this an opinion of Bond's on Taylor revealing the deep esteem for him: "It was extremely *avant garde* music for the period, but also very melodic. With Taylor it was another Bach coming into existence", [87] while Masserik, playing at the jam, said: "Mike had an increasing re-occupation with effect, tonal richness. These sessions set the stage for a great deal of experimental work". [88]

On another occasion Brown told me that "I was together with them once in Kew. Graham liked my sound poems and wanted Mike to help incorporate something like that into some music they were working on. I seem to remember that Mike had changed his appearance by then and was also in love with a pair of ceramic bongo drums which he took everywhere. I recall it was a strange meeting and I don't think Mike spoke very much..."

After Bond and Tomlin left the Forest Road flat, for some weeks Taylor was host to his brother Terry, but the cohabitation became difficult, as Mike was wandering around London and often didn't come home. At this point Mike asked Hiseman to move into the flat.

"When I got to the flat", the drummer recalls, "Terry lived in one room. After Mike left Terry stayed as my flatmate, but I was responsible for paying. Terry was a photographer, though whether he had a day job as well, I don't remember. Barbara moved in with me sometime in late 1966 and I think Terry was still there but I don't remember seeing him a lot...". [89]

Then things began to fall apart and his old friend Tomlin was witness to a meeting with Taylor which was, to say the least, disquieting; and could be seen as the beginning of the end. It was more or less half-way through 1966, he says: "The opportunity to join the Manfred Mann's band led to nothing, mostly because their amplification was so loud that I couldn't hear myself at all and I began to go a little dotty myself. I felt my life was going nowhere and as a consequence gave away all my possessions and left the room I was renting. I was at the time teaching music at the London Free School in Notting Hill and therefore had a key to the school premises, so was able to sleep there at night and after some time, and the arrival of a few other musicians and artists, managed to establish a living situation there".

It was while he was living at the London Free School, a community action adult education project inspired by American free universities (and the Victorian Jewish Free School in Spitalfields) founded in March by John 'Hoppy' Hopkins and Rhaune Laslett, that Tomlin bumped into Taylor again. But the man who just few months before seemed a bright pianist destined to a long jazz career was transformed into a totally different person: "The school was very open to visitors offering soup and tea to any who knocked the door; the soup was made from vegetables collected in the evening from the gutters in the nearby Portobello Road market. One day there came a knock at the door and standing on the doorstep was what I took to be a tramp of some sort. His hair and beard were long and he was dirty and barefoot with a small drum under his arm. I invited him in for tea since the school was always ready to help people down on their luck. I put a kettle on and when the tea was made poured out two cups and handed him one. We sat down and I looked at him properly for the first time. He seemed familiar in some way and after a moment or two I realised with a shock that it was Mike Taylor. I said: 'Mike is it really you?' He wouldn't answer but glared angrily at me as if I were his worst enemy. Nevertheless he stayed for the night and it was then that I saw him in action for the first time, which illustrated to me where he was coming from. He wasn't angry at me; he was angry at the whole world!"

The next morning they took a walk down Portobello Road when they met a woman with a child of about three years old in a perambulator. The child was crying and the woman was screaming at it to shut up and threatening to give it a good smack if it did not stop.

"Mike walked up close and began banging his drum furiously while glaring angrily at her and the woman was terrified. It was then that I understood Mike's psychological position. LSD in many cases causes the delusions under which we live to fall away and reveal the real world beneath, and this is what had happened to him since his acid taking. Having been brought up in a straight middle class and protected environment, what he saw now was a demonic world; a small helpless being with little knowledge or experience, being terrorised by the person who one might have expected to grant it limitless love and understanding. Mike then became the 'Truth Shaman' bringing reality to the woman's ignorance, and this was the world he now found himself in and no wonder he wanted to put an end to it".

There's surely great affection and indulgence in Tomlin's memories of these events, with the inclination to bestow mystic motivations to an undeniable expression of psychic disadvantage. The world revealed to Taylor by the LSD became the hell painted by Hieronymus Bosch in *The Garden of Earthly Delights*, the effective result of a serious sociopathy that would eventually isolate him from the real world. A real daydream nightmare confusing his reality, a far cry from that self-freedom experienced some years before by Leary, Metzner and Alpert in their fascinating pop psychedelic re-reading of the *Tibetan Book of Dead*. [90]

In these following months one of the few persons to visit Mike was Ron Rubin, who tried to persuade Taylor to play a few gigs, occasionally sometimes reported in his personal journal, a testimony that helps us to put some order in this elusive and disorienting period of pianist's life.

Rubin noted, on January 3rd 1967 about a session played at the Kew flat – consisting of Mike (piano), Jon Hiseman (drums/percussions), Barbara Thompson (flutes) "and a bloke called Fizz (on pipes)". Unfortunately, none of the people involved remember anything about that circumstance.

On Saturday 18th February 1967 he wrote: "Mike spent the entire evening lying comatose, rigid and immobile in the middle of the floor below the bandstand, his hands crossed on his chest with the dancers gyrating around him. We played without him".

At the UFO Club in Tottenham Court Road there was a typical underground happening titled *Festival of Love* (10.30 till dawn), with *Soft Machine*, Indian music, Mark Boyle projections and "movies, food, erogenous 3+4".

Among the bands involved was Dave Tomlin's *Giant Sun Trolley* with drummer Glen Sweeney. Tomlin remembers the appearance of Taylor, after the disquieting meeting which happened some time before at the London Free School: "The floor was filled with dancers and Mike walked right out into the middle of it all and laid down on his back and stayed there throughout the evening. At some point around then he disappeared and I never saw him again..."

That evening Steve Pank, musician who will become the tour manager of the *Third Ear Band*, a group founded by Sweeney from the ashes of the *Giant Sun Trolley*, got to know Mike.

He says: "I first met Mike Taylor in the UFO Club when he came down with Dave Tomlin. He had a hand drum with him; it was when the Sun Trolley was playing at UFO. They used to play a set in the early morning before the club closed. At the time the Sun Trolley was Dave and Glen, and Glen was playing a side drum. Occasionally when the group was playing Mike would bang this hand drum, I remember Glen grumbling about the fact that when the money was shared out Mike Taylor got as much as Glen".

So, according to Pank's memory, Taylor would play his hand drums occasionally with the *Giant Sun Trolley*, even if Tomlin reduces this to a couple of casual episodes: "Actually it was my group Sun Trolley which had a gig at UFO on Friday nights. Once or twice Mike turned up there, he wasn't officially part of the group." [91]

Anyway Pank has another memory about Taylor: "I remember one time I was wearing this button badge that I bought from Mike Lesser's badge shop. It seemed to be a facetious comment that summed up the philosophy of the Vietnam War. It said: "Kill a Commie for Christ". Mike looked at this badge and said: "Do you mean that"? I was shocked that anybody should think I meant it literally and took the badge off and threw it away..."

On June 15th Mike handed Rubin "a strange painting" but "without a word": it's a sort of primitive, childish windmill with three colours (green, violet and blue) made of ten rectangles inserted on a coloured paper octagon. Remaining for over forty years on Rubin's wall in his flat in London, it's one more mystery of Mike's secret and enigmatic life.

Ron says today that "knowing Mike, I'd guess it's an 'aid to contemplation'", but conjectures aside it's difficult to understand the real reason and meaning of it.

It's easier to interpret the drawing as a product of a mind derailed from the tracks of reason; even if it is fascinating to suppose that the pianist wished to communicate something cryptic to his friend.

Anyway Rubin noted in his journal a very significant thing when he wrote that Mike "must be the only person who's not aware of the Israel/Arab war which is screaming in the headlines. I suspect that the world outside his mind is of no interest to him".

Again it was Rubin, a well-known musician on the London jazz scene, who introduced Taylor to Ronnie Scott's Old Place, one of the few venues in those days where local bands can play on stage. A typical ad printed in London magazines announced:

"all night every night jazz, food, warm-sit down
8.00 pm till 4 am
Admissions 5/-, members & students (bring card)
7/6 guests
After 10.45 free admission
(except Saturdays)"

As we have seen, the club was founded in 1959 by tenor saxophonist Ronnie Scott and his fellow alto saxophonist Peter King and set at 39 Gerrard Street, in Soho, where rooms had been used before as a kind of rest room for taxi drivers and as a tea-bar.

The plan was to have a place where English jazz musicians could play and, in fact, the first concerts saw on stage such artists as the *Tubby Hayes Quartet*, and soon the Old Place became one of the most famous jazz club in Europe, the so-called "Mintons of British jazz". As documented before, Mike Taylor never played there...

After Scott and King transferred the club at to Frith Street in November 1965, and the attempt to convince John Stevens to become the manager, the direction of the 'Old Place' was committed to John Jack, who describes it in this way: "The club was just a cellar down some stairs... which in fact a few years previously, during either a Stan Getz or Bill Evans engagement the stairs broke and I and Dougie Rouse had to work all through the night under the light of a street lamp to try to build a replacement; unfortunately we made a mistake about how many steps there should be, made them too close together and when the club opened next evening people kept falling on them. Money was very short so that night Doug and I had to spend another night very carefully taking them out and re-positioning the steps; we had no money to buy fresh wood so had to be very careful in preserving the existing timber... luckily it worked ok! Anyway what I am trying to explain is that all our operations were improvised... no tickets, no posters or any such mementoes... only memories!!!"

Mike's first appearance, in duo with Rubin, was on August 23th. "Unusual gig with Mike Taylor", the bassist reported. "He was booked to play piano but all he did was play a broken Indian tabla/drum and pipe. *Indo-Jazz confusions*? Mind you, it was fun to be playing virtually solo bass all evening".

On August 28th Ron Rubin wrote in his diary about the gig with Taylor which failed at Ronnie Scott's, maybe the very first symptom of the pianist's psychic deterioration: "Mike turned up bearded and barefooted and had a job getting past the doorman. Played no piano at all, just a broken tabla drum and pipes, an astonished American couple on front row goggling at the burning fag Mike was holding between his toes. At one point Mike seemed to be talking gibberish. When I said I couldn't understand what he was saying, he said: "It's okay, Ron – I was talking to the loudspeaker". Manager John Jack gaping at all this from the back of the club. But he did pay us".

"I took over the management of the club on May 8th, 1967", John Jack remembers, "and presented music six and occasionally seven nights a week, with Saturday opening at 8pm and closing about 6 am Sunday morning! The first date I can find in the account book of the Old Place for Mike Taylor was on 23rd August sharing the evening with Trevor Watts... I do not remember what sized groups either had, but 27 people paid to see them but we lost about £2.00 on the evening."

Luckily, the manager doesn't remember Taylor's embarrassing performance (as with Trevor Watts, there with his trio Amalgam - John Stevens on drums and Jeff Clyne on bass...) nor that surreal, alarming 'conversation' of the pianist with the speakers.

A tragic expression of psychic disruption similar to the last years in the life of the great Italian poet Dino Campana, sectioned at the Castel Pulci (Florence)'s insane asylum, who confided to the doctor Carlo Pariani: "I'm not alive. I live in a state of continuous suggestion, I'm hypnotic at the maximum grade, I'm all full of magnetic currents, I do the magnetic medium..." Or: "I've a very strong extrasensory power. Now I work in the suggestive broadcast, they have put broadcasts in the towns of Italy". And again: "Sometimes I've got special communications with some agents of electricity, who give me some ideas about the news; policy, newspapers releases, they communicate a lot of things. Ideas and thoughts are transmitted to me". (...) "They are unusual thoughts and ideas which are communicated. They are waves received directly from thought, without words, with no special receivers: forms of energy transmitted from a distance". [92]

A few months after the studio recordings of his second album Taylor seemed another person entirely. Despite all the very good reviews on *Trio* published in the press, he had increased his consumption of drugs, most of all LSD.

Hiseman: "Towards the end of my year with Graham Bond, during the summer of 1967, Mike was high on cannabis and/or LSD for most of the time. His mind was in another place completely, divorced from reality. From here on it would be downhill all the way until his untimely death."

Created in 1943 almost by chance at the Swiss laboratories of Sandoz by chemist Albert Hofman, after five years of experiments with alkaloids contained in rye and finally to synthesize a sort of pacemaker for the flow of blood, LSD-25 would become one of the most common drugs in the USA and Great Britain throughout the Sixties and Seventies. It would be destined to open the "doors of perception" which Aldous Huxley had written in 1954.

Initially developed in Holland and England for the cure of psychic diseases; therapy against mental pain and the easing of life's ending, the substance was the subject of research with intensive military tests by the American government directed to produce new chemical weapons. By the time Sandoz decided to stop its production in 1966, the drug was widely popular in the underground, above all in the USA and England.

Before the English government would declare it illegal in September 1966, there were at least five places in London to get it. Among these was a flat in Cromwell Road, where Syd Barrett, guitarist and founder of the *Pink Floyd* lived; a flat often frequented by Mick Jagger, Paul McCartney and Donovan. [93]

It's meaningful that one of the first scientific studies about the psychedelic drug published in England at the beginning of '70's [94] still expresses some caution on the effects of the substance. "However, regrettably we don't know much about the way LSD acts..." Brian Wells writes. "Unfortunately more refined chemical techniques cannot follow the path of LSD and of its metabolism throughout the body. Biochemical modifications that appear are so various and complex that probably we have to wait for some time before it is possible to fill out a complete technical description".

In a paragraph specifically dedicated to the analysis of relations between LSD and psychosis, the author admits that even if "LSD had a close connection with a lot of psychiatric attacks (…) for setting a relation between cause and effect it's not enough to observe only some associations".

Then Wells lists a sequence of clinical case (among them, the story of a twenty year old female student who had taken LSD thirty-one times then, after relating the experience of becoming a swan, she dived from a window and crashed to the ground). "Sadly, most of the news about LSD's tragedies excite our emotions but can weaken our analytic capabilities".

"Our sympathetic reactions to such a tragic event is the feeling that it must never have to happen, and that immediate measures should be taken to make sure it does not".

So, according to Wells, who in this essay quotes from the previous *Report on public healthcare and patients*, issued in England in 1970, there are no irrefutable proofs about the danger of LSD inducing lasting psychotic behaviour.

Therefore when Mike started to take it regularly, no one around him was conscious of its devastating nature. His friends saw discordant manners, but they didn't link them with the use of acid.

Years after, Albert Hofmann, father of the substance, will deny LSD's negative effects during an interview, and stated he had "lived with them for half century" and explained that LSD, compared with other kinds of drugs doesn't induce any form of dependence. "With absolute certainty, acid doesn't produce dependence, and it doesn't destroy cells. The only problem is to be ready for the shock of the first revelation. There have been cases of young men who were unable to recover." And again: "Taken too frequently and too close together it simply loses its effect. Over many years of experimentations I have decided that at least a week's interval is needed between one dose and the other". [95]

This maybe explains the variations in Mike's periods of instability.

"It was much more an elite thing", Tomlin explains. "People didn't know about LSD. There were all kind of happenings in private flats and everyone would take acid. It was much later that it became a commoner sort of things. Round about '64 there were Americans coming over here and bringing this new kind of energy, if you like. The English thing was very polite but they would cut through all that. So, that was very attractive to a lot of musicians". [96]

Around the last months of that year it became known on the English jazz scene that Taylor had apparently given in to his desire to become a full time musician playing only his own music.

Hiseman again: "I had taken over the flat in Kew, where he was living when I first met him. Returning home in the early hours of the morning from a gig in the north of England, I noticed papers sticking out of the top of the trash bin which was always at the front of the house. The lid had been pushed on but there was so much paper inside it didn't close properly. When I investigated I discovered that it was most of his music. Without saying anything to him, because talk was useless by now, I retrieved it all and I believe much of it finished up with Neil Ardley who used some of it for the *New Jazz Orchestra*. I expect that his estate has it now, since Neil passed away several years ago..."

This gesture to get rid of all his scores could be interpreted as the effect of a typical maniacal outburst if Henry Lowther hadn't witnessed a similar request by Taylor, who asked him to give back the three scores he had offered some time before for the *Group Sounds Five*. "I did have scores for three pieces of Mike's and after two or three years he did ask for them back", he says. "I didn't know then that he wanted them back in order to destroy them. I believe that he destroyed quite a bit of his music at this time".

So, not a burst of madness, easily labelled as the sphere of schizophrenic behaviour induced by LSD abuse, but a premeditated act that seems to confirm his decision to give up his musician/composer vocation.

Anyway, among the scores recovered by Hiseman that in '73 will end up on the tribute album dedicated to Taylor, along with compositions for the never realised musical, was work, in collaboration with Tomlin, for which the pianist had written the lyrics.

"I see you", later arranged for orchestra by the pianist Howard Riley, was characterized by melody and sung in unison, with a dissonant section in the middle. Mike's lyrics, inspired by a love affair, expressed clear sensibility towards nature with a particular attention to the contrasts - light-darkness, silence-rumour - and an undeniable faith in reality. Some lines leave no doubts: "the world has no keys/just answers and pleas", "it is a world that cannot be blind", "You only need ask/and men drop their mask/they think and then speak/they're strong and not weak".

The inclination to deal with existence in a confident spirit ("And you may venture far away"), open to the world and addressed to the loved one ("And you will be the soul of my mind") culminates in a really poetic final verse where the line "the elephant's call" is the only incoherent, very surreal element:

"Shimmering you dance through the days
reflecting the sights, around you magic plays

*and you hear and see the beauty of all
the clay and the wall, the jump and the fall
the elephant's call... are you".*

Another composition which avoided destruction was "Song of Love", that some years later would be recorded by Norma Winstone on her inspired first album: a tune with a languid, indolent but bright melody, speaking of summer days lived within a lazy slowness of static time.

These lyrics, a pantheistic hymn to the greatness of Nature, of Sun and Moon, to the metronomic recurrence of dawns and sunsets that give a sense to human existence, could well lie in *Romancero Gitano* ("The Gypsy Ballads") of Spanish poet Federico Garcia Lorca, or among John Keats and Percy Shelley's poems:

*"When the moon arises we will see it shine
say that it's good, moon shines in wood
Night has come today..."
When the sun arises we will feel it's warmth
what it goes its way
Moon and sun combine to make a sign that it's two stars away"*

The last verse surprisingly quotes "men and their mothers walk to work today", a line that could refer to the past which Mike was always reluctant to talk about, with a finale of universalistic references and a deep empathy with humankind:

*"Flying through the air are insects and their brothers,
Dust, fire and others,
Men and their mothers walk to work today.
We can feel the change that comes with care and that is here to stay.
As we move the earth goes round the world in a song,
a song of love".*

Among the other tunes Hiseman preserved, one never recorded was a composition of a suite for three drummers, apparently written for Hiseman, Ginger Baker and Phil Seaman, titled "Horn, Gut and Skin", which was inspired by the Great Pyramids at Giza.

Journalist Robert Bolton, who defined the composition "an amazing work", described it in this way: "It was based on the mathematics involved in building the pyramids and their mystical significance. This was a large ensemble work for three drums (...) together with horn players galore". [97]

Unfortunately, even if Bolton hoped the tune would be recorded sooner or later, it would remain unrealised. Anyway, Baker and Seamen played an excerpt of it during a brief show (around thirty minutes) at the "National Jazz and Blues Festival" in Kempton Park (Sunbury) on August 10th 1968. No traces of this performance survive.

On Tuesday, 5th September fate put the Horace Silver Quintet on BBC 2 TV, and in a new appearance at 43 Greek Street's folk club Les Cousins for *A Spontaneous Music Evening* a duo with Rubin performed (other musicians involved were Derek Bailey, *Amalgam* and *The Spontaneous Music Ensemble*). Even if Rubin doesn't remember anything now, we have some notes from his diary: "Mike, without telling me, sent along a deputy. A very strange character who played African marimba and Chinese flute (no piano)..."

Just a few days later at Ronnie Scotts, on Wednesday 20th September, in trio with the same Rubin and drummer John Stevens, Taylor shared the stage with a drummer called Benny Goodman (who was working with Sandy Brown's group at times) this time only 18 people turned up for a "somewhat chaotic gig" (Rubin again).

On 20th September, faithful friend and bassist Ron Rubin noted in his diary another disquieting fact, after an attempt at rehearsing with Mike at his flat to prepare for the evening concert: "Mike Taylor came around, still barefoot and hirsute. Said he'd walked all the way from Richmond Park where he's been living rough. Says he likes chatting with the deer there. He's been in jail, though it's not clear whether for vagrancy or for possession of something – he actually wrote to me from prison asking if I could get him some hashish... He sat on our sofa picking stones and debris out of his feet. Showed me his poems, songs and paintings. I think he's going crazy".

In the meanwhile, after the controversial cohabitation with Tomlin and Graham Bond, about which he spoke to Rubin, Taylor became homeless, though he sometimes found someone to stay with for one or two nights. Jon Hiseman, who used to visit him in those vague days, remembers: "I used to visit him and rehearse there long before I became a professional musician (when I joined the *Graham Bond Organisation*). By the time I joined Graham, I had moved into the flat, but not sharing it. As Mike began to smoke most of the time, becoming increasingly divorced from reality, he wanted to shed all his worldly possessions including the flat he was renting. So I, needing to leave my family home, took over the lease on the flat, and in turn sub-let a room to Mike's brother Terry Taylor, who was a photographer. At that point Mike had nowhere to live and used to turn up and sleep with us sometimes, spending other times with other friends and of course sometimes, I thought, with his estranged wife. There was a piano in the flat which Mike had left there and which he used to tune up and play from time to time. When I finally married Barbara [Thompson] in 1967 and left that flat to buy our own house, the piano came with us, and was used by Barbara to compose for many years."

At this time Mike hung around "a druggy bunch of alternative lifestyle people, 'tripping' on LSD much of the time, who frankly I did not have much time for", as Hiseman remembers.

During Mike's wandering around London, Richmond Park became one of his favourite refuges. John Jack, manager of Ronnie Scott's Old Place, confirms it: "He lived in West London and used to like spending time in Richmond Park meditating and talking with the beautiful herd of deer that wander free there."

Those who don't know Richmond Park, and who have never tried at least once to pass through it, cannot have an idea of the exceptional nature of the place. The term 'park' is surely incorrect, limited, and misleading.

Created by Charles I in 1634, it is a vast wild area of almost 1,000 hectares (2,500 acres), where around 650 roaming red and fallow deer live free. A place apart, it could be anywhere, an Elsewhere in the timeless chaotic majesty of London.

There, among ancient oaks and small lakes, Mike found a refuge, his burrow if you will, as a dropout – but now music is a very distant memory.

Even if memory can allow a suggestion, it's difficult to support the picture of Mike as a person who was *really* "meditating and talking" with the deer. Easier, even if less literal to imagine the pianist's intention to cruise Richmond Park chasing the vivid and contrasting images that fill his mind due to the acid.

That controversial year: 1967, culminated in the London underground scene with the so-called "Summer of Love" - the explosion of the psychedelic fashion gravitating around the UFO Club and the Roundhouse, for Mike closed anyway with a few other gigs at Ronnie Scott's: in front of an audience of just 13 customers, on Monday October 9th he played with a trio (Rubin and Hiseman) sharing the evening with altoist Ray Warleight's trio; a gig for the quartet (this time with Rubin, Hiseman and Lowther) on October 27th (another group involved was the house-band *Chris McGregor Group*) and Mike by now seemed in an unrecoverable condition.

Lowther: "I can only remember playing one gig with Mike but it is possible I did at least one or two others. The gig I do remember was at Ronnie Scott's Old Place, and as well as Mike, there was Jon Hiseman and Ron Rubin. Mike was showing distinct and alarming signs of mental instability. By this stage in his life he had become unkempt with old ragged clothes, long hair and beard and he was no longer wearing shoes. He leapt about the stage, played very little piano of any kind preferring to play a small broken clay drum whilst sitting on the floor. Alarmingly he would quite often scream loudly and he seemed to me to being seriously and dangerously unwell".

During that afternoon of rehearsals, as we have seen at the beginning of this story, photographer Jak Kilby offered by chance a crucial proof of Taylor's condition, describing him as a "tramp".

And it's significant that while Taylor seems derailing from the tracks of normality and taking an irreversible steep slope, that evening in London Thelonious Monk played at the Hammersmith Odeon, and the day after, Sarah Vaughan and her Trio were on the bill for a concert where also great names of jazz such as Gary Burton, Jim Hall, Barney Kessel and George Benson. And what about the 29th where at Hammersmith the triumphant *Miles Davis Quintet* and the band of Archie Shepp.

While on a minor stage (but not so minor in the end) Mike's disjointed state inexorably marked the end of a true talent, which could have branded the jazz scene with fire with his extraordinary, peculiar alternative to the American forms.

Taylor now preferred small percussion instruments and a flute to the piano, as if he were released from the conditions of form, scores and music stands that had characterized his entry into the jazz scene. A need for freedom, the feeling of having the chance to play music without barriers, an alternative to the traditional established structures of controlled music, tours, gigs, agents and managers. Or even an unconscious political statement; a refusal to be a canonical, normal musician as required by the establishment.

Trevor Watts: "I think you are quite close to the heart of the matter, though this guy had problems also not to do with music I am sure, the music he made is a manifestation of this in some ways. After all, music came first in all our lives, managers and promoters later unfortunately. First the creative force, and then the destruction of it, aided and abetted by the musicians themselves.

"I have been playing Tarabuka for quite a few years now, though I never gave up sax of course, and there's a directness and freedom to the art of drumming. You don't need to think about notes at all. You do sometimes need to think about hands, but once you've mastered which hand to do which task in a more tricky rhythmic passage, then it's still exhilarating to do because it's a physical thing, more like movement/dancing thing or whatever. Sure, sax is physical, but not in that way, more to do with diaphragm and breathing. I even recorded my drumming on CD's such as "Ancestry" and "Live in Sao Paulo"... But for me it was also the study of rhythm I have been into for years, and what I learn on the drum, unencumbered by notes, I can then transfer to the saxophone. Gives me more a feeling of freedom somehow. So I do have a real insight into that area..."

It was with the percussion instruments that Mike sometimes unpredictably showed up at the Little Theatre, where he had played with his quartet in the first half of '66.

Jak Kilby, one of the more regular *clubbers*, remembers: "I used to be around the Little Theatre a lot at that time. My association with it started in April 1967 after I met John Stevens. Over a period of time I was involved with the Jazz Club as a photographer, photographing many of the groupings of musicians playing there, plus becoming friends with a core of the musicians, sometimes running the door and even driving the musicians home after. I also became involved with the theatre productions doing the front of house photography".

Unlike other interviewees, Kilby doesn't remember having seen Taylor there: "I cannot remember ever seeing Mike Taylor play at the club. That's not to say he did not. He might have before my time, or when I was not around..."

Evan Parker, on the contrary, has clear memories: "I remember him coming to the Little Theatre Club to sit in but he didn't play piano, just a little clay drum, and sat in a chair and sometimes spoke as part of the music. I think that may have been just a few times".

According to Trevor Watts, often on stage at the Little Theatre, "he jammed with us". He adds: "I am fairly sure that Mike went up there with Ron Rubin, the bass player. He used to sit on the floor, and just play his drums. It seemed to me he felt more liberated doing that than when he was organising his music in what seemed a very particular and specific way. The Little Theatre Club was a place where musicians could just play and experiment, so Mike didn't come up to do performances with a band, but joined in with us, and I fairly sure along with Ron. Just improvising whatever came up. Must have been about 1967, something like this. He was definitely a very different Mike Taylor than the one I'd met and played with in more formal circumstances. It's like his "alter ego" had come out. Very strange, but then when he was really straight, that was strange too to me. The human balance seemed to be missing a little if you know what I mean. Quite tragic, as he was a talented player". [98]

Anyway, a documented concert, the only real gig Mike undertook in 1967 at the Little Theatre, claims that he played in duo with Rubin on August 31st. It's the double-bassist's diary which again reported the event: "Mike on tabla and pipe again. Says he's given up the piano. He gets weirder and weirder – wish I knew how to help him".

With these words Rubin verified the undeniable mental decline of his pianist friend, the tragedy was evident to everyone, but no one was able to help him.

Old Place's manager John Jack was one of the eye witnesses of Mike's painful decline: "Whenever I gave him a gig at the Old Place it was usually with Ron Rubin, a fine pianist and bassist who had a very good rapport with him. I usually hoped he would feel like playing piano but some times he would just sit on the stage with a little-hand drum and/or a reed flute. Ron, I and any audience that we might have would patiently sit and wait for whatever spell he chose to wave that evening. Of course there were occasions when the magic did not happen, or only slightly, but to most of us our regard for Mike's artistry gave him license to explore any and every direction he wished. I always felt privileged to be in his presence..."

And on another occasion, interviewed by Bob Dawbarn for *Melody Maker* about the 'disasters which happened at the club': "One that sticks in my memory was the first time I booked the late, and much lamented, Mike Taylor. I thought I'd booked a pianist but for the first set he sat on stage in his sheepskin coat with a saucer beside him and tin of tobacco and occasionally played a few sounds on a broken, pottery hand drum and an old wooden flute. The other half of the duo, Ron Rubin, just leaned on his bass looking as baffled as I was". [99]

We don't know now if that concert on November 4th at the Old Place that Taylor played with his quartet can be included among the evenings where, according to Jack, the magic of the interplay showed itself in all its fullness. Anyway as things went, that evening just a few lucky people (precisely 25, according to Jack's annotation) attended one of the last of Mike Taylor's appearances.

5
The Man of God

"I think it's necessary for a man to rise up against himself
and that he can't recognise himself
nor love deeply himself
if he isn't the object of a condemnation"
(George Bataille)

An exceptional document, one of the few in existence, is thanks to the meticulous custodianship of Dave Gelly. It's a sort of *curriculum vitae,* hand written by Mike on November 15th, 1967 as part of a job reference from Gelly`s sister. He had tried to sign on the dole and having told the official at the Department of Health and Social Security he was a "composer", the official asked for proof of it.

Gelly writes about it: "In an effort to escape from the drudgery of 'just work', Mike applied for unemployment benefit as an out-of-work composer. It says something about the gulf between then and now that he wasn't simply thrown out of the office. Indeed, he was given a serious interview and advised that, since he had no formal musical qualifications, his first move should be to get a reference, signed by a *bona fide*, qualified musician, stating that he was in fact a competent composer." [100]

Casting about for a suitable referee, Taylor discovered that Gelly's sister Marion had recently graduated from the London's Royal College of Music.

"Handing me a 15-page, hand-written document" - says Gelly - "a kind of cross between a prospectus and a *catalogue raisonné* with examples of his work, he asked me to show it to her and arrange a meeting. This I did. Marion read his document, listened to him play, they chatted for a while and she wrote him a reference. I understand that it proved sufficient to get him a few weeks' dole". [101]

Here's the transcript of the beginning:

> *"I have been writing and playing music since 1959. During this period of time I have transcribed and analysed music from gramophone records (the analysis was of the harmonic sequences involved), composed my own pieces both as a basis for improvisation, that is with special regard given to the harmonic construction, and as solo piano pieces, and also orchestrated my own and other composers works for groups ranging from trios to an eighteen piece orchestra. My intention as a composer was to allow various pieces to emerge from my own experience with no particular regard for the overall style and I have found over the years that varying styles are within me.*
>
> *At one time I grouped my work, some two hundred pieces, into sets. I will mention and give examples of some of them:*
>
> *1. Lines*
>
> *2. The Sermon of the Flower*
>
> *3. Folk Dances*
>
> *4. Songs*
>
> *I also include a piano piece untitled Paean, Patricia Grace Ellahee, Anna."*

Regarding the manuscript, one is really amazed at the precise control of the handwriting, the slightly unusual order and grace, the mildness of tone, as well as the frankness and lucidity of contents, produced by a man usually described in those days as being totally out of his mind because of his LSD intake.

These contents reveal a high level of consciousness and a remarkable awareness of the focused aim of his artistic research: "My intention as a composer", he wrote, "was to allow various pieces to emerge from my own experience with no particular regard for the overall style...": it's a clear statement, really unequivocal, about how he was determined to put the form before the substance of an expression which tended to show his inner feeling. We can't ignore the well-aware use of the past at the time of this project. He uses "was", and maybe it's no accident, showing his awareness that the project is now defunct, at any rate in this phase of his life. [102]

From the end of '67, after the attempt to regain a career that seems lost, Taylor's appearance in public became scarce, and the accidental sightings, due more to the legend than the reality, made him an elusive, even sinister figure, by now out of control, "often spotted in London's West End, sitting on the ground with his broken clay drum. If anybody spoke to him he would reply, "I'm a Man of God!" - as Henry Lowther says.

That curriculum, so carefully compiled, had no significant effect (he got only a few week's dole). Now with no job or home, and no ongoing relationships he can count on, the few friends left, had started to be wary of him because he seemed to have become very aggressive. At this point it was doubtful if he composed any more...

Again it is Rubin's journal which fixes another tragic moment of his fall. The day is Saturday 13th January 1968. The short observation is really terrible to read: "Henry Lowther says Mike is going completely potty. He attacked his wife Ann because she wasn't treating the man she now lives with properly, and he is now almost certifiable and perhaps even dangerous. Marie is scared for the children and Dick Heckstall-Smith's wife won't let him into the house. Mike thinks that Dave Tomlin wants to kill him. He seems to be sinking fast".

As an evident sign of a mind adrift, Mike might have imagined that Tomlin wanted to kill him as an aftermath to the end of their cohabitation at Kew. Tomlin, who ignored this thing for years, today explains: "Why would I have wanted to kill him? It's a nasty story and Rubin is the only one saying it. Whether Mike said this to him or not I've no idea, but if he did it could only have been because he was mad, I respected Mike as a man and for his music and had no bad feelings towards him at all, although he may have had some towards me at the end, but I never knew why. I think it may have been because I went for audition with the Manfred Mann group which he may have considered a betrayal (he had to keep his day-job because it was family business, but I was free to take professional work and he may not have liked that)".

This difficult time for Taylor is testified also by Lowther: "The last time I saw him was on the gig at the Old Place and he certainly seemed to be dangerously unstable..."

Anyway, some days later at the beginning of 1968, Taylor was on stage at Ronnie Scott's, this time with a trio (again Rubin and the drummer Laurie Allen): "On Friday 19th January Mike shared the evening (I am not sure if solo) with the group led by trumpeter Frank Powell, quite a big night - 42 customers...", Jack remembers. "Looking at what I paid the musicians I think Mike probably had a trio...".

That evening Lowther was due to play but he didn't turn up, "perhaps because of the state Mike is in", Rubin wrote in his journal.

Murial also, surprisingly, attended the gig. She knew about her brother's condition and was trying to help him? Rubin noted: "Mike's sister was there being kind and gentle with him. I didn't enjoy the gig and Laurie's dodgy timekeeping didn't help".

Unfortunately today he doesn't remember anything of that evening and he seems sure he had never met or known Mike's sister. Someone told him she was there and he's convinced that it was just an occasional event, one of a kind.

Then, two other shows followed, according the Old Place's managers archive: "On the 4th

March we had a gig by the *New Jazz Orchestra*, but I do not recollect if Mike still played with them. The last entry I can find is 11th April when he was opposite Adrian Patton's group..." [103] In duo with Rubin, Mike was on the piano, but he also played the flute and percussion, alternating the sounds with his "weird chanting" (Rubin's words).

It's the last time the double-bassist played with Taylor; most likely also the very last one 'played' by Mike Taylor.

At this point playing with him had become too difficult and Hiseman (he was, anyway, now busy full time with *John Mayall's Bluesbreakers* after the end of his experience with the *Graham Bond Organisation* and brief collaborations with *Georgie Fame and the Blue Flames* and Arthur Brown...) Rubin also now accepted work with other musicians, leaving his friend to his fate: on March 18th Rubin played with his new quartet at the *Poetry & Jazz Festival* in Holborn, and Hiseman played with John McLaughlin at the Old Place on March 20th.

That year, owing to the inscrutable shifts of fate, could well have been the occasion too for re-launching himself as a musician and composer.

In fact it's on August 1968 when one of the most famous records of rock was recorded by the most popular group of those times, *Cream.*

Wheels of Fire, a double album published by Polydor, in a few weeks rose to third position in the English charts (the first in the American). These two records were initially published separately: one contains live recordings from their American tour at Fillmore West and Winterland in San Francisco in March 1968; the other is a studio recording; nine tracks with three composed by Mike Taylor.

During July and August of '67 Eric Clapton (guitar), Ginger Baker (drums) and Jack Bruce (bass) had laid down four tracks at IBC Studios in London. Then, in September and October they returned to Atlantic Studios in New York to continue work on the album, and then again in January and February of '68.

As soon as these sessions were complete, *Cream* started out on their second American tour, which began in Santa Monica, February 23rd, returning to the studio in June for the final overdubs on the album.

Maybe it's significant that none of the main characters involved, at least officially [104], have ever mentioned the involvement of Taylor in the project. The musician and record's producer Felix Pappalardi (murdered by his wife in 1983) in a concise reconstruction of the album's genesis he wrote a quick, shallow mention of Mike's contribution.

He wrote: "There are a lot of guys that work with *Cream*, like Pete Brown who collaborates on almost all of Jack Bruce's songs. Mike Taylor is an ex-British jazz pianist with a strong classical background", [105] and apart from the reference to Taylor's "classical background", it's quite significant that he uses the phrase "ex-British jazz pianist".

Anyway, in a quite heavy harvest, where such evergreen hits as "White Room" stand out, and 'heavy' blues as "Sitting on the top of the world" (Willie Dixon), "Politician" (composed by Bruce and Pete Brown) and "Born under bad sign" (Booker T. Jones – William Bell), the three tracks composed by Taylor (with lyrics by Ginger Baker) are very different fruits, and not totally ripe.

Here, quite surprisingly, Taylor's jazz experience is, as it were, removed, to engender a dimension nearer to art-pop (as in the first two verses of "Passing the time", characterized by a simple melodic sequence of glockenspiel and Calliope, or in that little minuet theme played by Pappalardi's trumpet on "Pressed Rat and Warthog", or in "Those were the days" chorus...) even if hidden by the band's solid and experienced rock-blues, surely more congenial with a hard blues such as "White Room" or "Politician". As journalist Dave Thompson has rightly commented, "with his emphasis firmly in a rock/pop toned territory, Taylor's union with Baker had little in common with the unerring purity of his own solo efforts. But it certainly worked in the context of Cream, producing no less than three of group's more distinctive latter-day numbers...". [106]

"Pressed Rat & Warthog", musically based on the traditional English tune titled "The Cutty Wren" (1776), in just three verses tells the surreal story of Pressed Rat and Warthog who are obliged to close their little shop of "atonal apples", "amplified heat" and "pressed rat's collection of dog legs and feet" due to the bad "Captain Madman".

Very opportunely, its composer Ginger Baker, on a rare occasion described the tune as "a silly goon inside joke". [107]

Yet, on balance, we don't know Taylor's real contribution to the composition, because it's unlikely the record's tunes were recorded in the same form as they were composed. After all, as we know, the album's genesis was rather vague and anyway it's more plausible that on Taylor's original compositions (probably composed at the piano), the band had arranged the tunes in rock style on vinyl.

Even with prevailing positive opinions (above all a posteriori), the album caused controversial reactions. Memorable was the strong stance of *Rolling Stone* in a piece written by editor Jann S. Wenner, in which he launched an out-and-out attack, at least for the section recorded in the studio.

Wenner wrote: "*Cream* is good at a number of things; unfortunately song-writing and recording are not among them. However, they are fantastic performers and excellent musicians. Their latest recording, *Wheels of Fire,* a two-record set inside a silver jacket, proves all this". [108] It's a more than explicit synthesis of the very long, articulated assessment of the album, with just two tracks played live. No quotations concerning Taylor's contribution, but a clear demolition of his compositions. Wenner described "Passing the Time" as "a soft sad-circus tune with various instrumental paraphernalia thrown in, is a stone bore. The transition from verse to chorus is absolutely absurd", and got rid of "Pressed Rat and Warthog", as "a Ginger Baker poem recited to a background of drum rolls and Clapton's chording". "It's nice, but not what you want to buy the album for. The trumpet solos spoil whatever mood was trying to be evoked by their superfluousness and obviousness". Instead, no hint was indicated of "These were the days".

In an opposite tone, representative of the gratifying reviews published in those days, John Ford's synthetic 'reading' from the pages of *Beat Instrumental*: "(...) It's lovely; the most experimental and most emotional work they've ever put on record, with a combination of unbelievable musical guts and genuine innovation in structure, sound and lyrics. Buy this or live in misery for the rest of your days". [109]

That that year *could* have been the year of Taylor's public emergence was testified to by the recording in September (sessions of 17th and 18th at the big Pye studio, near Marble Arch in London) of the *New Jazz Orchestra's* second album, *Le Dejeuner sur l'Herbe* (Verve SVLP 9236) where, besides re-arrangements of some famous pieces by John Coltrane ("Naima") and Miles Davis ("Nardis"), and compositions by Neil Ardley, Mike Gibbs and Howard Riley, two tunes was included by the pianist, "Ballad" and "Study".

It had taken a year to rebuild the *New Jazz Orchestra* after the issue in '65 of *Western Reunion* and the following split. Ardley had developed the ambitious project to widen the orchestra from eight to sixteen members to obtain a more hefty sound, working on compositions and arrangements more complex and structured, with sections of reeds with rich timbre and a stronger rhythmic approach.

Christopher Bird, sent by *Melody Maker* to the Pye Studios while the band was mixing the album, had collected Ardley's rashly enthusiastic impressions. He wrote: "Fifteen of Britain's best, but not so often recorded, jazz musicians, such as Henry Lowther, Harry Beckett, Frank Ricotti, John Mumford and Derek Wadsworth, are crammed into the control room listening intently to the play-back of Neil Ardley's composition "Dejeuner Sur L'Herbe" (…). There is a feeling of something special taking place; the hope that, with a bit of luck, this one is going to make a mark and draw attention internationally to a whole batch of musicians and composers on the British jazz scene".

The last word was left to Ardley who declared: "I think at last we've captured almost exactly what the *New Jazz Orchestra* is about. There are eight tracks on the album and that means that, apart from two of my own things, you can hear the work of Mike Gibbs, Alan Cohen, Mike Taylor, Howard Riley and, of course, Michael Garrick...".

And again: "Then there are the soloists that are not heard too often, if ever, on record: Dave Gelly for example, on Taylor's "Ballad" and Jimmy Philip in Alan's arrangement of "Naima". I'm sure that this is something like their best work."

Ardley recognised the essential role of Hiseman in having brought all the musicians together, booked the sessions, and organised the gigs with the Orchestra. "But apart from the one we did at the Old Place", he admitted, "they fell through. We just could never get all the chaps together. So we said 'well let's at least do a broadcast if we can', and we did. We called Derek Watkins and really that was it. What a fantastic player - it lifted the whole band on to a new level. Bassist Tony Reeves took the tape of the broadcast to MGM and they liked it so much they booked three days of studio time. It was almost too good to be true. That is why Tony, who is a recording engineer, has produced the whole album and is not on bass while Jack Bruce is". [110]

On the record, "Ballad", an original composition by Taylor, is a heart rending, wonderful ballad à la Bill Evans of 5:24, that, from the painful slow theme played by a trumpet à la Chet Baker by a very inspired Carr, develops through relaxed variations of a tenor solo by Gelly, then the reeds in unison, with the reprise of the trumpet to finish.

"Study", instead, is the arrangement made by Taylor of Polish composer Alexandre Tansman's *Berceuse d' Orient*, based on a Segovia's guitar adaptation published in 1959 on the album *Andres Segovia: Music for the Guitar* (Decca DL710046) under the title "Three pieces for guitar" (the first two, composed by Tansman, are "Canzonetta" and "Alla Polacca"). As we have seen, the guitarist had already inspired Taylor in a composition for his *Pendulum*, with an explicit, even if didactic title "To Segovia".

"It oscillates continually, between two scales", reports the cover album notes, "Henry Lowther and Barbara Thompson are heard on trumpet and soprano respectively, both solo and in sympathetic duet, not least in the improvised ending".

Resuming the Polish composer's tune, while Segovia makes a 3:30 mid-tempo piece for guitar, characterised by arpeggios with a virtuoso technique according with the style that made him a legend, Taylor, for Ardley's 18-piece *New Jazz Orchestra*, composed it as a solemn hymn theme (of 6:33) with a slow, strongly evocative and dreaming stride, based on the reeds played chorally and the transparent colours of the glockenspiel; a small masterpiece of sensitivity and imagination that seems to go beyond the limits of a typical jazz composition, striving for a more classical dimension. It was Taylor's continuous listening to Dmitry Shostakovich's symphonies, as Tomlin and Burke remember, to have bestowed on this composition a seductive solemn character, a painful slowness... and influenced him to make a piece so allusively anguished, with a so severe profile. Today it's difficult to say; also because the Russian composer's *7th Symphony*, that surely Mike knew well, having listened to it many times [111], doesn't seem to be related with elements in "Study", that is more similar, in cadence and mood, to a requiem.

Anyway it's curious and quite ironic, yet impossible to know why, that Taylor had titled his tune just "Study", according to a practice used among classical musicians and by Segovia himself, who composed and recorded several 'studies' for guitar.

Was it a study for a requiem, perhaps? The section of an unrealised wider symphonic composition?

Where did these two wonderful compositions come from?

It's impossible get a clear picture that comes within the pianist's creative mindset, disclosing the motivations and the process of creation. Also Tomlin is sure that "they were written and arranged after we split. He wasn't working on orchestral arrangements of this sort when we were working together", Hiseman is inclined to refer to when Mike got to know the *New Jazz Orchestra* for the first time, in '65. He says: "Mike came to hear the NJO because Ian Carr and I played in it. He was impressed and wanted to contribute scores. Neil was desperate to find writers because he had a serious career as a book author. So Mike wrote the pieces for NJO specifically and they were received very well as being really new material - just what the band wanted to play".

Gelly's memories seem more precise and circumstantial: "The orchestration on the record sounds to me like Neil Ardley. Mike composed "Ballad" and Neil arranged it for me to play on the same album. That was recorded in September 1968. I think we first saw the parts earlier in that year. Mike's *Pendulum* album was recorded in 1965, and I'm pretty sure "Ballad" came along after that. I don't know if this clears anything up. I'm not at all certain about when Mike actually wrote things. I know that we worked on "Study" and "Ballad" after the band was re-formed, which was 1967".

Whatever the tune's origin, when the record was published (in the middle of '69) press reaction was discordant. While the monthly magazine of classic music *Gramophone* reviewed the album in more than gratifying terms (it defined it "a masterly piece of work, and much of the credit must go to arranger and director Neil Ardley "...), exalting the bright work of the band, "one of the most advanced and adventurous orchestras now operating in Europe", and appraising Taylor's contribution judging "Ballad" as "beautiful" [112], while a review signed by Barry McRae, *Jazz Journal*, harshly criticized Ardley's arrangements.

"This album raises one of the oldest questions in jazz", the journalist wrote. "How much power should be given to the arranger? On the strength of the music heard here, I am tempted to side with the faction that maintain he should be given the very minimum. On an album that has good solo work by Carr, Philip, Lowther and Mumford, it is his controlling arm that renders the NJO a pedestrian and somewhat an uninspired unit. This is in spite of Hiseman's often brilliant drumming and the obvious enthusiasm of the sideman".

"Naima", "a beautiful rendering of Trane's fine composition", according to the journalist the NJO had huge potentiality, although frustrated "in a meaningless finished product".

It's undeniable the effect of the hand of Ardley, and his personality, on the New Jazz Orchestra's work, was able to help him achieve his dream of a big orchestra with excellent musicians, it's also true that today's specialized critics and jazz fans will no doubt have opinion regarding his role as composer and arranger.

Just one year later, in *Jazz Journal*, an article dedicated to the arranger, Martin C. King stated that "by using varied techniques of composition (several of which are more usually associated with classical music) but never losing the essential jazz feel, Neil is evolving a personal style which could be indicative of the direction in which jazz writing is going in the next few years". And commenting on the results of *Le Dejeuner*, judged better than the debut album, the journalist wrote: "This method of composition is nearer to the techniques of classical music than of jazz, yet the listener's first impression of the piece is that of a full-blooded jazz performance – fiercely swinging rhythm, first-class solo work and brilliant ensemble passages. Much of the Third Stream music of the 1950s was a failure because of the unnatural forcing together of two opposed styles: it was not so much a fusion of jazz and classical music as a juxtaposition of them. The success of Ardley's music is due to the assimilation of classical techniques within a jazz framework – a true fusion". [113]

Dave Gelly had very kind words about *Le Dejeuner* and the period when it was recorded. He told *Jazz Journal* in 2012: "We knew it was going to be special while we were making it, and there are moments - such as Dick Heckstall-Smith's entry in the title piece, blowing tenor and soprano simultaneously - that are still goose-bump raisers. We were all pretty young at the time, and few of us had received much in the way of formal musical education, with the result that we all sounded different. Neil Ardley had a wonderful flair for writing with our personal quirks and oddities in mind (something that came from his love of Duke Ellington) and that, I'm convinced, is what made the NJO unique. It's also why we could never revive it now. So many of us have since died, Neil included. The last time we played together (not exactly the same line-up, but close) was for a 60s weekend at the Barbican, back in 1991. Some of us became very excited and said we ought to get a tour organised. Neil said we'd better ask Jon Hiseman, because he knew all about things like that. In due course Jon sent back a "realistic" costing, roughly equal to the national debt of Luxembourg, so we abandoned the idea. The label is Verve, which now means Universal. Maybe, if we all ask nicely they'll reissue it on CD". [114]

Many years later, in 2015 the record at last became available on CD (in a limited edition of 1000 copies) thanks to the resourceful Peter Muir's Dusk Fire Records, in a pretty *digipack* edition edited by Gelly with an essay by Roger Farbey taken from *Jazz Journal* of February 2012.

An initiative by Muir who says: "We've just licensed the album from the Neil Ardley Estate. I was surprised no other label had done this! I am looking at more projects of this kind..." Ballad" and above all "Study" suggest that what could become Taylor's field of research, when that kind of strictly jazz composition culminated with the definitive abandonment of the hard bop with *Trio*. An aspiration to composition that seems to have seduced the pianist for all of his short life, revealed through one of the rare reflections on himself granted to his friends. Hiseman remembered it in 1970: "He always said to me that if he could find someone to play his tunes properly he wouldn't bother to play at all. He would rather have been known as a composer, I'm sure of that". [115]

Giving up the instrument with which he had chosen early in his life to express himself with devoting heart and soul to the writing of music: a process of abstraction that would have reduced to the minimum the physical aspect and his relations with the material world. Was it a mystical delirium induced by LSD, or the conscious, painful admission of the insurmountable difficulty to translate inner feelings and ideas in sounds?

Today Hiseman is more pragmatic when he explains: "This is not uncommon amongst composers who are also players. Mike did not like anything about the business of travelling to a gig, having to be there at a certain time, remembering to tell everybody where the gig was, how to get there, the timing etc. etc. - all the normal stuff a bandleader has to do. And of course the big problems for Mike were the pianos he had to play - often their action was poor and not so in tune. This problem haunts all piano players except the ones who can afford to take theirs with them. Mike never rehearsed - every performance, whether rehearsal or gig was the real thing to Mike. So it was the original thought that went into the concept of a composition or arrangement that interested Mike. But he always needed money, everybody does - so he had to do gigs..."

In spite of the undeniable success of *Wheels of Fire* (and the New Jazz Orchestra's album, even if the pianist did not know about it...), at this point, days, weeks, months of *Pendulum*'s composer seemed to flow fast, Mike cruising from place to place, from one a flat to another, occasionally hanging around with squatters, reappearing barefoot in the street, with bongos and a bamboo flute. He showed up suddenly, unexpectedly at the Little Theatre where there's an ongoing jam.

On August 20th Rubin received a letter sent by him with a cheque of £6.(pounds)2 (shillings).and 7 (pence)-half penny as royalties for *Trio* (2/7/ 1/2p) and £6 as payment in full of an old debt. The double-bassist was clearly surprised and with irony noted in his journal: "Well, I always hoped to hit the big time before I was 40. (Just tell him you can't write halfpennies on cheques)".

Then he revealed: "He says he's about to make another LP with a Portuguese Indian called Amancio da Silva (all Portuguese Indians seem to be called 'da Silva') and he'll probably ask Tony Reeves to play bass on the recording, unless I'll reconsider my decision to give up playing bass".

Rubin's irony aside, Amancio d'Silva, who passed away at 60 in 1996, was a great, though little-known Indian jazz guitarist who grew up listening to Charlie Christian, Wes Montgomery and Jim Hall records. He went to London in '67 from Bombay for a cure for his son who had been born with a serious medical condition. He was introduced to the jazz circuit by Denis Preston, Taylor's producer, and played with some of the main musicians on the scene (Harriot, Carr, Rendell, Garrick). He realised a few interesting records, expressions of a technique and musical idea absolutely personal to himself (critics consider his masterpiece *Integration*, published by Columbia in 1969). A vegan of few words just as Mike, he devoted his life to music and teaching guitar.

Although there are no recordings of that announced collaboration with Taylor confirmed by Reeves ("I do very vaguely remember a couple of conversations about doing another album with a guitarist. I can't remember the name, but I think he was Indian, not Portuguese") exist, if it's suggestive to think that this meeting, even with Mike's proverbial unreliability could have originated some interesting results.

Reeves remembers very little about what they said that day: "Just some talk about funding, I said something like it should be fairly easy to sell the idea to Dennis Preston as he already knew Amancio, and his name plus Mike's on the same album might make for better sales. Also the combination of guitar and soprano would make some interesting colours..."

Around the end of that year, in one of the flats he occupied, maybe the last of his verified residences gleaned from documents (12 Fairlawn Grove, in the Chiswick area, again very close to Kew), Hiseman met him.

He says: "I don't remember anything about the squat other than that it was typical - broken used furniture, bare boards, generally uncomfortable - but then I may have got the place confused with another of the places Mike stayed - he was paying no rent anywhere and just moving around...".

There, the drummer, in the jumbled confusion of the 'squat', saw in a corner a strange 'sound machine', the last creative act of Taylor. Hiseman's biographer Martyn Hanson was to describe it years later: "Jon remembers the last time they played together. He had visited him at his 'squat', where he had seen a strange looking 'music machine' which Mike had constructed. It consisted of two circular upright columns attached to a long board, with a roll of 'music' wound around them – the 'notes' on the score consisted of intermittent coloured lines. Vertical bamboo canes of matching colours were placed at intervals round the roll and each musician was assigned a colour. The score was then moved round by turning a handle on one of the columns and when your coloured line on the score appeared behind your cane, you started playing and when that line ended, you stopped. What you played, or what instrument you used, was left entirely open. It was a clever way to direct free improvisation and Jon always thought this system could have been used to great advantage with young children. He also recalls, however, that Mike was as 'high as a kite' at the time and laughing a little too much!" [116]

I asked Hiseman to be more precise about the object: "I can tell you no more about it than is described in the book. It was not a sound machine but a machine to enable some control over when performers played, without using conventional music notation. However, the whole idea was that it did not control *what* the performer played".

A statement of musical anarchism, in line with John Cage's—the author of many influential works—revolutionary concepts of aleatory and improvisation. [117] But had Mike read or listened to John Cage?

It's probably the last time Hiseman met Mike, just before the gig the pianist had to play; a trio at the Conway Hall, in Red Lion Square, on November 8th at a *Jazz is alive and well* festival as the backing band to the *New Jazz Orchestra* (starting at 7.30 pm, tickets from 5s). It was promoted by the London Jazz Centre in association with the Arts Council of Great Britain.

It was more importantly an act of friendship, which Hiseman and Rubin felt towards Taylor, because they were conscious of the difficulties he now had coming to terms with reality.

Dave Gelly, on stage with the *New Jazz Orchestra,* was a witness to the evening: "These, I'm fairly sure, were the first jazz events in Britain to be subsidised through the Arts Council and a great deal hung on their success. As far as I remember, the plan for the evening of Friday 8th November was for the NJO to play the opening and closing sets (to include `Ballad` and `Study`) and for Mike to have a spot in the middle. Come the first interval Mike had not appeared. Howard Riley and Barry Guy, who happened to be in the audience, played the middle set instead. Mike, looking completely out of it, turned up about ten minutes before the end". [118]

"Mike didn't turn up till just before the end, looking dreadful, so we didn't play", Rubin confirmed in his diary. It will be the last time he will see Mike alive.

At this point it was no surprise that *Jazz Journal*, reporting the evening, wrote: "The supporting group, the *Mike Taylor Trio*, failed to appear due to a misunderstanding". [119] Gelly will bump into Taylor one last time, a few days later, just before one of the most promising jazz musicians of his generation was found dead in the water at the mouth of the Thames: "I saw him once more, a week or so later, somewhere in West London. He was barefoot and ragged and carrying a small drum. He didn't speak, preferring to communicate by gestures..."

Why had he gone there? Taking a train from Fenchurch Street to Southend-on-Sea, walking along the coast, then going into the water fully dressed, and thus returning to the nowhere from whence he came; never again to return.

So that my life is more than my action... (a short interlude).

The epigraph on Mike Taylor's gravestone; obscure, and "rather lovely from his mind" Ron Rubin says. Maybe a message, left to posterity, probably implemented by his sister Muriel, who looked after all the material aspects of her brother's death.

"I dive from a springboard
into cool clear water
and yet I furnish my springboard
with my experience
so that my life is more than my action".

MT

The "MT" affirms that these words were written by Mike (even if journalist Richard Morton Jack suggests the idea the "MT" could be 'Muriel Taylor' instead of 'Mike Taylor'...). Probably written, or maybe discovered in the last of his flats at Fairlawn Grove. Anyway they were remembered by his sister when she arranged for the inscription on his grave. The grave, in red granite, stands out among others grey and worn, which I saw after a short trip from London through the countryside towards to the sea, following the Thames, I thought about what Mike wanted to say at the end of his too brief life; a life ending tragically alone, far from

Ealing and West London where he was born and grew up.

The images that his writing evokes, at fist sight, simple, direct, and without doubt metaphorical: a dive from a trampoline into the clear cold water. Just that.

As an epigraph, it risks to appearing sinister. Because Mike's death was by drowning, although it's not sure he intended such a thing.

Anyway, these words, likened to a haiku, seem complicated. "And yet..." a conjunction subverting the simpler meaning.

Nevertheless it's me, Mike writes, that I've build my trampoline thanks to my experience, so that my life is more than my act.

So, more than the act of entering the water. More than all the things done before. More than the gigs played, the albums recorded, more than all the people met, the projects realised. More than desires, the ideas, the things owned.

His life, Mike seems to tell us, is more than relationships, memories, loves.

If to live is to dive into the water through the experience, so my life is more than all I've lived.

These few enigmatic words, confusing the meaning of an existence burned out too soon, remain a mystery.

From this cryptic combination of words, other interpretations can emerge: I dive into the future from my past (the trampoline as his roots), having shaped it with experience for not being victim of it, for being a protagonist in the realization of myself.

So it's the experience, Mike seems to suggest, that led to the transcending of the conditions of a life founded in its origins, in the family, in habits, in the ethical obligations, in the expectations.

His parents' death which he suffered as a child, the duty of having a job that he hadn't chosen, the opportunity to express himself with his music, and the difficult conditions (no promotion, no compromises with the market), falling to the lure of drugs (Compensatory? Recreational?) and finally to end as a victim.

A too short life, sure, but worthy to be lived in such a way, accompanied hand-in-hand by his fate.

6
Mike Taylor Remembered?

"Human beings are too important to be treated as mere symptoms of the past.
They have a value which is independent of any temporal process
which is eternal, and must be felt for its own sake."
(Lytton Strachey)

t's understandable that there is such confusion that given such a drama of human and artistic sequences; of facts so controversial and dramatic, the friends, musicians and journalists who attempt to give an interpretation to minimise the upset, and to explain with a definitive cause all the questions which have no answers, the doubts, the elusive sense of a dissipated life.

The most mistaken view one can give to so powerful a story and its dramatic nature is to immerse it in a pathetic, rhetorical regret about how Taylor would have offered such bounty to jazz if he were still alive. Stale rhetoric that tastes of mould.

Because Taylor in an artistic sense had been absent for a long time, a victim of LSD and of circumstances beyond his control, in an environment within the throes of a deep transformation, which has little inclination to look after those who, for whatever reasons, fall behind.

Between '67 and '68 he did just a handful of gigs, no recordings, no records produced. An end already announced by the tendencies of his current life.

Little was known at the time of the possible destructive effects of the use of LSD which led to an underestimation of the psychic effects on some users. It was not easy, even though being aware of what was happening to Mike (as Rubin wrote it in his diary), to realize how to help him.

The history of art records several cases, similar to Taylor, on the English jazz scene in that period. The consumption of drugs and alcohol was a very common experience, there had been so many deaths of young musicians and a list here would be an embarrassing and useless exercise [120]. In the case of Taylor it wouldn't prove anything more than the known facts already suggest.

And if everyone now agrees that the Ealing pianist was a real talent with boundless potentiality, unfortunately most of which remained unexpressed, the dramatic epilogue of his life, the circumstances of which have never been fully explained, ending inconclusively with a coroner's open verdict, for Taylor this was the natural effect of an inescapable destiny, as if it were embodied in the nature of the musician's personality.

Tomlin is categorical when he affirms that Mike's fall had been "the effect of acid on a conventional mindset". More or less the same as Dave Gelly's words: "I think Mike's mental decline was entirely due to drugs, especially LSD. Some managed to survive the experience. He didn't".

An opinion with which Pete Brown also agrees, even if with some further implications: "I believe the use of acid actually did Mike, as with many other people, tremendous damage. I think he liked a joint before that but that never did anyone much harm. I'm not saying that he should have stayed in commercial art and in his family, but I never knew acid do anyone any good really. It makes me very angry that we lost him so early on. We should try to keep his work and memory alive".

A closer examination by Jon Hiseman who observed the radical changes in Taylor's personality: "I never got the impression that there was any external reason for his fall into purgatory. I saw him descend into his own world, first of all as a result of incessant cannabis smoking and then prolonged use of LSD. With nobody outside himself to be responsible for – with all his real relationships having broken down and with him not actually playing music with other people in any meaningful way - he must've been very alone, although maybe not realising it himself. I guess his disappearance and death was inevitable – one of those casualties, typical of people who step outside the system, who can make a real forward-looking contribution to whatever they're doing simply because they have isolated themselves from the mainstream. He had no reason to conform in any way with the normality going on around him and nobody put any pressure on him to do so. It was a time of hippies and flower-power and doing your own thing - and in the end for those left after him, he simply reaffirms our belief that maybe, just maybe, we are better off being ordinary".

Tony Reeves, warily, observes that he was "a troubled man", alluding to psychological causes maybe already latent, while Burke, who spent lot of time with Mike in those years of his first entry into the jazz scene, claims that "he had so much talent, but, I understand he was over-powered by LSD, which I know can be a very dangerous substance, having had a very frightening trip on it myself". Old Place's manager John Jack, where Taylor plainly showed his psychic problems, gives a benevolent vision justifying his vagrancy and the conversations with deer in Richmond Park as a form of meditation. He says: "Poor Mike Taylor, a lovely, if at times a little difficult, man. A great artist who deserved to have been living in more sympathetic times. He lived in West London and used to like spending time in Richmond Park meditating and talking with the beautiful herd of deer that wander free there".

Also producer Denis Preston, in a rare interview with Bolton, was inclined to give a psychological interpretation of Taylor's decline: "He was a strange sort of person, guided by emotion. He was interested in playing music for himself. He was not prepared to expose his talent to a wider public, although he had obviously thought deeply about his music. In the time I knew him there was a complete change of personality. He became sloppy. His hair and appearance changed: he stopped wearing shoes. And he no longer talked. He used hands to communicate". [121]

According to Trevor Watts, on the other hand, who considers the use of these substances an effect more than a cause, the last years of Taylor's life had more to do with the constraints imposed by middle-class roles: "Mike transformed himself before his death from someone who almost could pass for working in a bank, very neat and tidy, to coming up the Theatre club and being like a hippy playing hand drums only and no piano. It's a real shame. I am not sure what made him flip. Something maybe to do with him being very retrained as a person and wanting to break out of that and maybe finally not handling the "other" self. But I am only surmising".

A well-structured analysis by Digby Fairweather concerns a recurring topic in biographies of Sixties and Seventies' artists: "I don't know if Mike was really a 'genius' - it's an overworked term! - but he was certainly well ahead of his time at the period! There are others who could certainly advance more informed and reliable opinions. But either way there's no doubt that the romantics amongst jazz followers tend to bestow the title on any musician of note who is unlucky enough to die early. I think the reason for his 'decline' was - at least in part - bound up with the dramatic change in popular fashions in music at the time. This after all was at the very point of the 'Beatles Invasion' which drove jazz once and for all into an intellectual byway - where it still remains. And the kind of jazz that Mike chose to play would have stood little chance of any widespread popularity as the 'baby-boomer' generation took the Beatles, the Stones and rock music to their hearts".

An interpretation by Burke that includes another precious memory complicates this thesis since Mike would seem to have appreciated The Beatles and the fashionable Twist. He remembers: "Things in England were changing radically at the time I knew Mike, though being in the thick of it, it wasn't altogether evident to us. The main thing, I think, was the emergence of The Beatles, and how young people were now beginning to have more importance in the general consciousness of British life; up to then Britain was still having a hard time recovering from World War II, which had left the country in a state of depression.

Now music was heard for the younger generation. People were Twisting all over the place. I remember being at a party full of people, and Mike and Ann showed up, and we were listening to "Twist and Shout" and loving it. Up till then all we listened to was Jazz, to the exclusion of any other kinds of music, and Rock and Roll was considered beneath us, but the joy and energy of *The Beatles* changed that for everybody, and even the older generation started to accept them. And when Motown was introduced to Britain in 1964, everything *really* changed. *The Rolling Stones* made us really aware of the Blues, and black music. Life was broader. We were no longer confined by the British Establishment. Young people were free to speak their minds and make a difference. It was a most exciting time".

This change of social, artistic and musical scenario may have nipped many talents in the bud, obliging them to confront the new fashions and *ipso facto* put them 'offside'.

John Mumford's doubt, certainly interesting, is that more than *The Beatles*, it was his experiences in hard bop that pushed him to imagine a new expressive direction related to European classical music, and also the sudden rise of 'Free Jazz': "Perhaps the rise to popularity, for whatever reasons, of 'Free-Form' was, for him as a composer, a negative and possibly unhelpful phenomenon?"

And after the Miles Davis' *Bitches Brew* electric revolution, perhaps Taylor would have been keen to renew himself?

Henry Lowther thinks that commercial flop and missed artistic recognition was just an excuse: "I think most musicians working in jazz are more or less commercial flops and we just keep on doing it for love and, at least speaking for myself and many of my colleagues, expect nothing more than what we get. I've no reason to believe that Mike would have been any different in this respect to the rest of us, and I seriously suspect that other factors played a role in Mike's fate. However, I'm sure Mike was very traumatised by his experience with LSD. Whether his problems were latent before that I don't know".

"I described Mike Taylor at the time of the album's release as the 'Syd Barrett of Jazz'", Pete Muir, who in recent years edited Taylor's tribute record and some reissues of his albums relates: "and while they worked in very different worlds, both of these men forged individual creative paths that set them apart from the crowd. Both also succumbed to using narcotics to enhance their minds at a time when little was known of the terrible damage this course of action might inflict on users. Mike's music burned bright but burned short - his death is a warning to the curious..."

Opinions apart, it's a fact that those who had known Taylor and his sparse works make an effort to keep alive his memory.

A few months after his death, on May 17th 1969, Dave Gelly and Jack Bruce promoted a tribute concert at the Jazz Workshop, recorded and aired by BBC Radio 3 on June 4th.

The New Jazz Orchestra played live Taylor's two jewels, composed and arranged for the *Le*

Dejeuner sur l'Herbe album. An extraordinary example of it has luckily survived thanks to Pete Muir's Dusk Fire Records that in 2008 published on CD the complete concert played by the Orchestra at Jeanetta Cochrane Theatre of London on May 26th 1970. These are twelve tunes from the NJO's repertoire with Taylor's "Study" and "Ballad" with excellent performances directed by Ardley, with Gelly, Hiseman, Henry Lowther, Barbara Thompson, and Tony Reeves among the others.

As Gelly writes in the CD booklet enclosed, the version of "Study" was even better that the original studio recording for *Le Dejeuner*: "It is cast in the form of a duet between soprano saxophone (Barbara Thompson) and trumpet (Harry Beckett) and this version is, I think, superior to the one on the *Dejeuner* album – because the interplay between the two of them is so intense". [122]

About the other tune composed by Taylor, "Ballad", he says: "Neil Ardley arranged Mike Taylor's Ballad as a feature for me, partly because I kept nagging on about wanting at least one solo that wasn't a stomping, up-tempo affair. It was my own fault in the first place, for letting myself get typecast in the NJO's early days. In the event he did me proud. I must say it's a spooky experience to listen to something you played 38 years ago, and to follow your own train of thought through a solo you'd completely forgotten..." [123]

That year, in April, Jon Hiseman's Colosseum (formed after the experience of Hiseman with John Mayall and a trip to Rome with his wife Barbara) published *The Grass is Greener* with a 'rock psychedelic' arrangement of Taylor's "Jumping Off The Sun" (lyrics by Tomlin). The track, that opens the first side of the album, was recorded between summer and winter 1968, almost surely Mike didn't know of it.

In January 1970 the NJO played a concert with Colosseum at the Lanchester Arts Festival including, in its repertoire, two Taylor's compositions. Enthusiastic reviews by *Melody Maker* and *The Guardian* welcomed the event.

"This NJO gig", Martyn Hanson has written, "was also something of a milestone for Barbara Thompson, as she got her first chance to play a major solo in public, in a stunning duet with Henry Lowther. Jon recalls: "She played on Mike Taylor's "Study", a very hypnotic slow ballad and it brought the house down. I learned the big lesson that night that you didn't have to go in with a sharp stick to get an audience reaction. I was seldom able to apply it with Colosseum, but I applied it later to Barbara's career. She was fantastic that night, I was so proud of her". [124]

Other NJO's concerts with some Taylor's tunes were aired on radio by the BBC on October 19th 1970 (Radio Three's *Jazz in Britain*) and on February 14th 1971 (Radio Two's *Jazz Scene*), as a further confirmation of the clear will to commemorate his work.

On December 4th 1970 the London Jazz Society promoted a concert dedicated to his memory (*Mike Taylor Memorial Concert*) at the London School of Economics with the cryptic announcement: "A special memorial concert for Mike Taylor will be given by "A group of His

Friends". Though no names are being revealed it is expected many of the top jazz musicians in the country will attend and play tributes". A track archived at the British Library of London ("Son of red blues", arranged by Howard Riley) establishes who played at the concert: Dave Gelly (tenor sax), Ian Carr (trumpet), Barbara Thompson (soprano sax), Howard Riley (piano), Frank Ricotti (vibraphone), Mike Travis (drums) and Daryl Runswick (double bass).

Christopher Bird of *Melody Maker*, present that evening was impressed by the music's quality, he wrote: "The ensemble was led by Dave Gelly, who, in addition to playing well, conceived the whole idea and mapped out the general strategy of the evening. Humanity without sentimentality, musical intelligence without intellectual aridity; these were the hallmarks of Taylor's music. I hadn't realised before just what a loss to the scene his death has been."

Launching the event, *Melody Maker* dedicated a short article to the pianist titled "In memory of Mike Taylor". Referring to Taylor's death, the journalist commented: "His death was ironical, as so many are, because after two or three years existence in very straitened circumstances, he was at the time of his death on the verge of receiving massive royalties for three songs he wrote which were included on Cream's best-selling *Wheels of Fire* album".

In the article there were also some considerations by Jon Hiseman and Henry Lowther.

"In a way he was well before his time", the drummer affirmed. "If he had been alive now, and as fit as he was four or five years ago, he would be having a great impact. He always said to me that if he could find someone to play his tunes properly he wouldn't bother to play at all. He would rather have been known as a composer, I'm sure of that. He started off as a fairly ordinary pianist, influenced by people such as Horace Silver, but he gradually became probably the most remarkable composer of tunes and chords sequences that this country has produced. There's a great stockpile of his writing left and people are just beginning to realise the potential there. He had a very extreme idea of his own direction, and he was always very positive. His pieces were very complex and sometimes difficult, but he wrote some classical pieces that were quite staggering".

Lowther described the talent of Taylor in this way: "His writing was fantastic: it was so original, and his little compositions were quite perfect and self-contained. Funnily enough when I actually played with him we didn't do any of his tunes".

"I don't remember playing any of Mike's tunes", he explains today, "and, considering his psychotic behaviour, I don't think we played anything but freely improvised music or nothing at all while we waited to see what he would do".

The year after Norma Winstone, who had already interpreted live some of Taylor's tunes, decided to tribute the work on her wonderful first album titled *Edge of time* (ARGO ZDA 148, UK 1972), which has become through the years one of British jazz cult albums (it has been timely reissued again by the meritorious Dusk Fire Records in 2010).

With Alan Skidmore (flute), Art Themen (flute, bass clarinet), Henry Lowther (trumpet),

Frank Ricotti (vibraphone) and Chris Laurence (bass), Winstone sings "Song of Love", one of the tunes composed and never recorded by Taylor, here using Neil Ardley's arrangement. "I guess I thought that that one would be a good piece for Neil Ardley to arrange", she says. "He was involved in the *Mike Taylor Remembered* album I think I just liked the piece also. I didn't have difficulties in singing the piece... I sometimes used to sing "Jumping off the Sun" with John Taylor in concerts, but none of his other pieces".

After having played for years Taylor's tunes with the New Jazz Orchestra (in the band repertoire, "Pendulum", "Ballad" and "Study" also the unrealised "Half Blue"), Ardley and Gelly had the idea to put on record their tribute to the memory of the pianist realised as *Mike Taylor Memorial Album*, a compilation of unrealised tunes recovered by chance by John Hiseman from the dustbin in front of the Kew house.

The story of this album is no less incredible than the recovery of the sources on which it is based: initially planned for being realised on December '72, the project was postponed till the year after, and the recording sessions, directed by Ardley, were arranged in only two sessions in June 1973. [125] After being recorded, the album was shelved and 'lost' for years in the vaults.

Gelly: "Denis Preston recorded the *Mike Taylor Memorial Album*, but couldn't get a record company to take it. It was very expensive to record and he was asking quite a high price. Then there was a recession in the music industry. Then Denis died. His studio carried on for a while, but eventually closed and the master tapes were lost. Fortunately, Neil Ardley had kept a master copy and his widow passed it to Peter Muir at Dusk Fire Records. That copy master had a tape fault on one track, but fortunately Jon Hiseman had another copy and that's how the album finally came to be released".

Thanks to Muir's initiative at last the record was published in a limited edition of 500 copies: issued on August 2007, the album sold out in short order, becoming one of the many cult recordings for jazz fans. A new rendition on CD (this time in 2000 copies) edited by Pete Muir's Dusk Fire Record makes the record available again.

"I discovered Mike through my work with the Neil Ardley Estate", he says. "We had reissued some of Neil's work and I found the masters to *Mike Taylor Remembered* in Neil's archives. We mastered off the original studio tapes performances of Mike's fabulous music by some of modern British jazz's leading performers and the artwork benefited enormously from Tim Gill's sympathetic treatment of the subject and Jak Kilby's wonderful photography".

As far as its importance as a historic and documentary profile, *Mike Taylor Remembered* raises some perplexities, above all, if compared with the original works and with the two small masterpieces published by the *New Jazz Orchestra* in 1969. Dave Tomlin, who didn't take part in the project, is right when he states that "the arrangement of Mike's music was very sloppy and chaotic and lost all of the poignancy of his work".

He adds: "Listen to the saxophone solos which are crap as the player hadn't studied the chord structure and just sounds very amateur. That's the trouble with big bands, the arranger thinks he has to use all of the instruments all of the time, whereas Mike's music has a lot of space in it which too many instruments fill up".

The project itself was complex because the material to arrange was fragmented and sometimes scanty ("simply a melody line, or a sketchy piano part, sometimes just a stray page", Gelly writes on the CD booklet), but the final result, Gelly affirms that, "was likely to give a more rounded impression of Mike's musical personality and the breadth of his talent", doesn't do justice to Taylor's sound minimalism, that careful, almost obsessive research of sounds that characterised his work. Then, it's difficult if not impossible to establish in which measure is effectively music composed by Taylor or, as it is perhaps more plausible, a rendition of it by his friends under Ardley's wise direction.

Again, the heterogeneity of the tracks underlines the limit of a compilation: among genuinely hard bop tunes ("Son of Red Blues/Brown Thursday" [126], "Black and white raga"), where the influence of Silver and Blakey is evident; large-scale orchestrations (as the *kentonian* "Half Blue/"Pendulum"); a waltz for piano and voice, and folk tunes ("Folk Dance No 2"), the listener may lose his orientation, because the rendition is too varied and patchy; nothing like the cohesiveness and coherence of the albums recorded by Taylor in trio and quartet.

Most of the reviews published lack an exploration or an analysis of arrangements and the musical project's quality doesn't get the subtleties of this work, valuing only the more superficial aspects. John Fordham, for example, in *The Guardian* wrote that "Taylor wrote everything from pensive love songs to layered, semi-classical passages, and his melodic sense and wayward reinvention of structural principles hinted at the potential never realised. From the eerie opening sounds, like an orchestra tuning up, through a searing chord, and then into the frantic countermelody under continuous brass on "Brown Thursday", and the baleful march-time of "Land of Rhyme in Time", here, Taylor's audacity is plain. (…) Only the lyrics have dated a bit". [127]

In 1973 Ian Carr, who, as we have seen, had introduced Taylor to Preston, published one of the most essential essays about British jazz to show an inner view of the contemporary scene in that time titled *Music Outside. Contemporary Jazz in Britain*. Among critical profiles dedicated to Hiseman, Westbrook, Evan Parker, John Stevens, Trevor Watts there are just a few mentions of the figure of Taylor, evidently Carr didn't consider him worthy enough for an in-depth analysis, despite the great esteem he had for him since the recording of *Pendulum* (furthermore he had written the notes on the back cover).

Maybe even more surprising is Taylor's exclusion from the afterword edited by Roger Cotterrell on the re-release of the book printed by Northway in 2008 who, analysing the fortune of Carr's first edition, "Thirty years on", remembered the pianist between the premature deaths but with no mention of his works.

Surely it was the journalist Robert Bolton, who wrote an article in two parts printed in *Jazz Journal* the year after (December 1974-January 1975), with the first proper attempt to describe the life and work of the pianist through various accounts by some of the musicians who had known him.

Even if rich in first-hand information (that will be the basis for the next biographic articles), sometimes the text indulges in a romantic vision of the musician showing as a sort of "damned artist" with enormous potentiality never expressed, a 'misunderstood genius', ready to sacrifice his existence on the altar of Art.

In the first part titled "The Innovator", Bolton wrote: "He never quite made enough money as a professional to live entirely off his music. He cared little, seemingly, about popular success. Unhappily, his story turned into one of never having the bread – until near the end of his life – and of lost opportunities leading to a state of total withdrawal. (…) He declined all interviews and the chance to broadcast. Michael was, in some ways, a strange figure".

And if, more recently, the contribution of Steve Ingless on *Record Collector* published in 2005, and the appropriation of wide parts of Bolton's articles, are put to one side it will be thanks to Richard Morton Jack and Duncan Heining's works if – above all on the Web - the interest in the brief artistic and human story of Taylor will be kept alive.

Heining, above all, besides filling some gaps in Taylor's biography, has tried a deep analysis of the possible causes of his death, exploring all the hypotheses circulating throughout the years: "(...) Of course, it is not unusual for people who subsequently commit suicide to experience an improvement in mood before they take their life, what his sister Muriel had noted might have been just a passing phase. LSD use had clearly affected Taylor psychologically. We know that following the making of *Trio* he had slept rough in Richmond Park for a time communing with the deer or otherwise living with Graham Bond, with whom he would consume acid in large quantities. It seems likely that he did have an underlying predisposition for psychosis, but given the volume of drugs he was using - LSD and cannabis - these alone would surely have done him no good. His death by drowning 'under mysterious circumstances' near Southend-on-Sea in 1969 has merely enhanced the myth. A tragic figure, dying romantically for his art?

The evidence, what there is, suggests that it was as an accident, or more likely, a misadventure. The curious aspects of the case are how he was dressed, that he had a reasonable amount of money on him and that he had travelled from London to Leigh-on-Sea. People in distress do strange things but would Taylor really have taken himself all the way to Leigh to kill himself, however disturbed his mind? The additional vests and two pairs of trousers he was wearing might suggest that he had prepared for the cold January weather. In general, individuals actively considering suicide do not tend to worry about such details. As for the money he had on him, back then, this was plenty to buy food and pay for a couple of nights in a reasonable, if cheap hotel. It all suggests a level of preparation and planning that was unnecessary for someone intending to take his own life.

We will never know, of course, and many will no doubt prefer the romanticized version of the tormented artist too emotionally sensitive to survive in so cruel a world. In a way, any mystery is surely exaggerated. Mike Taylor took a lot of psychedelic drugs, which can mess up even the most stable individual. His behaviour, bizarre as it became, stemmed from a psychosis probably brought on by drug use. There's nothing mysterious in that". [128]

Most of the reviews in magazines and articles featured on the Web that debate Taylor's story have preferred to give of the impression of the suicidal artist, so tragically passed away, than try to make a wider careful consideration about his music experiences and music. An effect to raise more interest around the few verified facts, most of them destined to remain obscure, than the real value of his music which remains anyway a privilege for only a few jazz followers.

An important, absolutely relevant initiative of November 2014, although partially, rekindled the attention towards Mike Taylor.

"At the recent concert in the Guildhall School of Music and Drama's new concert hall, Milton Court, Art Themen and myself were guest soloists with the Guildhall student's big band", Henry Lowther has told me. "Three of Mike Taylor's pieces that he originally wrote for the New Jazz Orchestra were played. Art Themen wasn't involved in these and I played in only one of them. This was a flugelhorn feature, a ballad, that used to be played in the '60s by Ian Carr and I'm sad to say that I've already forgotten the title ["Ballad"]. The other two big band pieces were "Pendulum" and Mike's arrangement of a guitar study by Segovia simply called "Study".

Scott Stroman, professor of Jazz at the School, and director of the Guildhall Jazz Band for the concert, has commented: "It's a great opportunity for our terrific students, as they get to experience the excitement of performing classic - and little known - big band music from a really influential group of writers, some no longer with us - Neil Ardley, Mike Taylor, Dick Heckstall-Smith - and some still on the cutting edge today [such as] Mike Gibbs and John Warren. With the detailed rehearsal and youthful exuberance we can provide, the Guildhall Jazz Band can often approach and surpass even the original performers in bringing this great music to life." [129]

The heart of the event was in truth the performance of Dick Heckstall-Smith's opera titled *Celtic Steppes*, co-produced with Pete Brown in 1995, after five years of a work of composition.

In spite of the recurring live events, that have the undeniable value in keeping high the attention on it, the cause of the partial oblivion of Taylor's *ouvre* is due to the record industry, that after Preston's death with the related end of his Lansdowne which didn't keep the original vinyl records in the catalogue, and sold out in few years, nor did they reissue them in CD format.

In June 2004 *Trio* was reissued by Universal (which had meanwhile absorbed the titles from Lansdowne) under the label Impressed Re-pressed, but the printing was in so limited an edition that they disappeared very soon from the shops, paradoxically becoming the umpteenth collector's item of Taylor's catalogue.

Nevertheless, fifty years after, some reviews reaffirmed the importance of his work. John Fordham, for example, writing in *The Guardian* defined the group of *Trio* "a line-up that highlights the close links between 1960s Britain's creative rock and R&B scenes and the jazz of the time", adding: "Taylor is a highly rhythmic pianist whose dense chord clusters often travel in tandem with Hiseman's sensitive and flexible percussion. His handling of standards such as "All the Things You Are" is enigmatically fascinating, while his own rhapsodically wayward "Just a Blues" is a lot more than just a blues. And the improvisation against Hiseman's brushes and Bruce's emphatically voluble bass on "While My Lady Sleeps" is the kind of extended long narrative on a standard that Bill Evans was feted for. A unique and very affecting set". [130]

Equally it was the brave venture of journalist and music writer Richard Morton Jack who, in 2007, after having acquired the title's copyrights, reissued *Pendulum* for his tiny label Sunbeam. Claiming to have the original rights of it, Universal asked him to delete the album from the market.

He says: "I licensed *Pendulum* from Adrian Kerridge at Lansdowne, who prepared a remaster from the original tape. After we'd released it, Universal told us that they owned it and asked us to withdraw it. What seems to have happened is that Denis Preston sold the rights to his Record Supervision/Lansdowne catalogue to Polydor in the late '70s, before Adrian took over the business. Adrian had always assumed that he owned the recordings but in fact that was not the case. I never saw any paperwork from Universal, but was not willing to fight them. Incidentally, the original tapes were still in Lansdowne's possession, while Polydor/Universal had copy-masters".

In spite of the short appearance in the shops and on Web commercial sites, the album caused enthusiastic reactions that attested again to the great value of the work. Clifford Allen on the specialized Web site *All About Jazz* wrote: "*Pendulum* presents some of the most challenging music in the annals of British jazz, a busting-open of group interplay in a standard setting and some of the most interesting pianism in the modern canon. Clearly influenced on the movers and shakers in English free piano (Howard Riley; Peter Lemer), it's a wonder what Mike Taylor could have become".

It was echoed by *Record Collector* that commented: "*Pendulum* is an absolute million dollar, 24-carat masterpiece. Every track stretches both musician and listener to breaking point - why more people never picked up on both this album and the talent of this extraordinary musician must surely rank as one of the disappointments and mysteries of the age".

Other jazz fans' sites and blogs published reviews and analysis equally enthusiastic.

Anyway, even if recommended for years by Universal, today not even *Pendulum* is available in the shops, another bitter twist of fate making Taylor's work unobtainable for jazz fans. A work that someone, somewhere, seems to wish vanished with him in the Leigh-on-Sea waters.

All we can do is to embark on a probably fruitless search for one of the few original vinyl copies still around as some years ago Japanese jazz collector Koro Ito did, who has a collection of more than 18,000 long-playing records.

His demise, which was likely to have been an accident, holds an unexpected *coup de théatre*. It is really an incredible story, in line with the short history of Mike Taylor's life.

Steve Pank says: "It was when I was working at the Middle Earth Club and Mike Taylor was there. I knew that he had made some records. I said to him if you bring a copy of your record in maybe we can get it played on the sound system. Later he came in and handed me a copy of *Trio*. I never did get it played, and the next I heard he had committed suicide, so I could not return it".

So Steve finds a copy of Taylor's album at home, and some years later, in 2013, he finds it again and asks Dave Tomlin if he wishes to have it.

"He replied that he didn't have much storage space and that he had a copy of *Pendulum* but didn't have a record player so he could not play it. His brother had gone to a lot of trouble to get hold of it for him, so he felt obliged to store it. I made the suggestion that he could sell it on eBay. Later he told me that his brother was quite adept at dealing on eBay and that his copy of *Pendulum* had been posted. It turned into a bidding war between two gentlemen; one in France and one in Japan, and eventually the Japanese man bought it for £400-£500".

At this point Steve decides to sell *Trio* on eBay.

"Dave took it and sold it to the same Japanese man for around £200, and Dave offered me half of the proceeds. Part of the deal was that Dave would make me a copy on CD. This was the first time that Dave had heard *Trio*. He was amazed at how good it was..."

So Koro Ito became the owner of the *Trio* which had been Mike's personal copy!

He says, "I nearly fell to the floor in a faint when I realised that Mike Taylor had actually touched it".

Notes:

Quotes are taken from interviews with the author, unless indicated.

[1] My research with the Essex Police didn't produce any results. As Information Officer Laura Mills wrote me, "Unfortunately in accordance with Essex Police retention policies any information that may have been held, in relation the incident as outlined in your letter, would have now been destroyed" - Laura Mills, Essex Police Headquarters – Data Protection and Freedom of Information, Chelmsford, UK. So I've tried to get something through the Southend-on-Sea Borough Council's Library Development, but again nothing. A kind officer Barbara Bridge wrote me: "Unfortunately, Southend Libraries do not hold any records on individuals, and the records we do have are unlikely to yield more than the information already available on the Internet. There is an article on Wikipedia, which I am guessing you have already accessed:

http://en.wikipedia.org/wiki/Mike_Taylor_(musician) which references the article on *All Music* http://www.allmusic.com/artist/mike-taylor-mn0001541189. The only resource we hold that may refer to this event are local newspapers on microfilm, although I suspect these have been used to obtain what little information is included in the above articles".

I've tried with the Essex Coroners Office, but once more nothing. A kind Court Administrator

Denise Hutchings replied me that "I have heard back from our archive team and unfortunately they have no records available in this matter. I am sorry that we are unable to help you with your request".

A curious anecdote about Mike Taylor's death is that told me by musician Digby Fairweather in August 2012: "My later connection with Mike had to do with his demise. My father John Fairweather was a civilian photographer in Southend Police at the time and told me that a jazz musician had ended his life by drowning and was washed up (I believe) on the beach at Leigh on Sea. He also showed me the photographs - very sad". Anyway, photos went missed;

[2] C. Pavese, *Il mestiere di vivere. 1935-1950* [The profession of living. 1935-1950] (Einaudi, Torino 1972 - Nuova Iniziativa Editoriale, Roma, 2008);

[3] Ron Rubin interviewed by R. Morton Jack for "Mike Taylor: the mystic who looked like a bank clerk" in *Galactic Ramble*, October 22th, 2010 at http://galacticramble.com;

[4] Ignored since it was unknown for years where exactly the grave was, but thanks to Tony Tomlin, brother of musician Dave who played with Taylor, he recently found its location and supplied a photograph of same. He told me the story of its discovery: "I only became involved with this challenge when an old, vinyl copy of *Pendulum* came to light generating much worldwide interest from fans of Mike that, together with my brother Dave, we decided that we should really find out where Mike ended up. We put together what we knew of his tragic end and, living locally near Southend on Sea, I was well placed to do the simple task of tracing his final resting place. I'd previously done a little ancestry research and was sure it would be a simple task: "Michael Ronald Taylor, born June 1 1938 in Ealing, died January 19 1969 in Southend on Sea". I'd found from previous searches I'd done that the more information you have at hand the easier it is to find the right record so armed with the date of January 19 1969 I visited all of the Leigh on Sea and Southend on Sea cemetery record offices and as many churchyards as are still in use. Surprisingly there was no trace of a "Michael Ronald Taylor", or of a "Michael R Taylor" with a death on or around that date. So where was he? Back to the drawing board. I checked out his birth record which clearly showed his name as Michael R Taylor but when I dug out some old newspaper reports of his death, they, for some reason, had incorrectly referred to him as Ronald Michael Taylor. However, when I checked his death certificate record it too showed Ronald Michael Taylor. I haven't seen his death certificate so cannot say who the informant was who registered him as Ronald Michael. So, I was now looking for a different name and it took no time at all to trace him to the Sutton Road Cemetery where strangely his headstone reads Michael R Taylor – as all his friends remember him";

[5] A. Bates, *Great London Concert* CD booklet (Arista AL1900 , USA 1975);

[6] Ibid.;

[7] Ibid.;

[8] R. Atkins, *Tribune*, September 10th, 1965;

[9] J. Cooke, *Jazz Monthly*, October 1965 p. 22;

[10] Ibid., p. 23;

[11] B. McRae, *Jazz Journal*, October 1965, p. 8-9;

[12] D. Heining, "The strange life and death of Mike Taylor" in *Jazz Wise* #115, December 2007-January 2008;

[13] Ibid.;

[14] J. Kilby in *Mike Taylor Remembered* CD booklet, edited by Dave Gelly, Dusk Fire Records UK 2007;

[15] According the Polling Register of Electors of the Ealing district Mike's grand-parents were residents there at least from 1929. From 1936, were residents with them also Mike's great-grandparents Philip Taylor and Rose Mary Knowles;

[16] Born in 1912, when Mike's father died he was only 29. According the Death Certificate, the informant was his mother Irene, who attended to the registration of the death. In those years, obscuring the location of place of death, the certificate indicates only the street of the building where he was died – 30, Twickenham Rd (Isleworth). It concurs with the area where, from the end of 20th Century, were build the first Workhouses, these were then converted into public hospitals, sanatoriums or asylums. Thanks to the excellent Web site *The Workhouse. The story of an institution* at http://www.workhouses.org.uk/ run by Peter Higginbotham it has been possible to discover the place where Mike's father was died;

[17] Born in 1913, Joan Mary Kift (Cooper was his mother's surname) died at only 31. In spite of deep researches, it seems that there is no Death Certificate for her in the public archives. She died as some journalistic sources affirm, although never verified, or she married again after having committed the children to her parents-in-law?

[18] These brief historiographic references are taken from *The Oxford Illustrated History of Britain* edited by Kenneth O. Morgan, Oxford University Press, Oxford (UK) 1984;

[19] Research by the Author in April 2014 on the archives of several elementary and middle schools of the Ealing area have produced no useful results; except the first attempts of Robert Bolton in *Jazz Journal* in 1974-1975, the more in-depth biographical reconstruction is without doubt that by Richard Morton Jack and Duncan Heining (see References on the Appendix);

[20] B. Dawbarn, February 15th, 1969, on the obituary published by *Melody Maker*. It's curious that a serious musician such as Henry Lowther could have spoken about Taylor during an interview in 1990 with John Wickes that "he was originally a bank manager or something"

maybe to explain the strong contrast between his original personality and the fall into madness;

[21] They married on September 17th, 1961 at the Ealing Register Office in the presence of R. Hall and R. A. Hall and certified by J. N. Laxby. From the Polling Registers of Electors Mike and Ann were residents at the Twickenham address until 1965;

[22] Hence the rhetorical question asked by journalist Duncan Heining from *The Independent* on January 9th 2013: "Why is British jazz always the Cinderella when it comes to tales of 'Swinging London'"? A question to which Ian Carr had already offered a reply in his fundamental book on English jazz printed in 1973, *Music Outside*. Read about this in the first chapter titled "Perspectives";

[23] Referring to the Nucleus Coffee Bar, John Mumford sent me this elegant piece of prose: "Once you'd negotiated the dodgy wooden stairs to the basement you were in for a pretty interesting all-nighter. Let's say an average of six front-line instruments, five in the rhythm section, about five or six solo choruses each, (including drums) followed by 'eights', then 'fours', with probably a triple repeat ending. We, as 'Professional Musicians', called this last bit 'The Coda'. Numbers would easily last for twenty minutes, featuring personnel changes, arguments and helpfully shouted advice. We needed to hear what we were trying to do, the single battered, bruised microphone couldn't cope, we weren't going to be paid, so this deeply satisfying marathon went on with our rather shabby backs turned to the 'Audience', an odd mix, people who'd missed the last train, bewildered foreign students, Soho layabouts and people like us, everyone a bit humid, kippered in a comforting fog of 'Old Holborn' and Woodbines. Friday and Saturday nights, this went on for a couple of years. Gary, red bearded, sturdy and calm, who ran the place, provided mugs of tea throughout, and at dawn, spaghetti bolognaise. After carefully climbing the dodgy staircase back to street level and daylight, small groups of us trudged away through Covent Garden, Seven Dials, Soho, the streets not yet really awake, the morning air carrying a teasing, financially challenging hint of fresh milk and croissants.";

[24] "For Scott, dealing with, and playing alongside, musicians he had long admired, was the ultimate challenge and justification for being in the music", John Wickes wrote. "From his point of view, it opened him and his colleagues to the realities, sometimes hard, often rewarding, of jazz as created by its true authenticators. In the process, Scott's attitude towards promoting and playing jazz changed subtly but nevertheless qualitatively. He harboured no illusions about the originality of his own playing, but significantly, from this point on, Scott rarely chose mere emulators as members of the house bands which would back the guests. In this way, Scott's was an important contribution to the transformation of British jazz in the sixties" (J. Wickes, *Innovations in British jazz*, Soundworld, 1999 - pag. 6);

[25] E. Pieranunzi, *The pianist as an artist*, Stampa Alternativa, Roma 2001, p. 57-58;

[26] D. Heining, *Jazz Wise* #115, December 2007-January 2008, Op. Cit.;

[27] *Trad Dads, Dirty Boppers and Free Fusioneers. British Jazz 1960-1975* is a CD compilation edited by Michael King and published by English label Reel Recordings. Among rare tracks recorded live by 'monsters' of British jazz as Mike Osborne, Elton Dean, Lol Coxill, Lyn Dobson, John Surman... also this track by Mike Taylor. "Mike's admiration for the styling of American hard bop giant Horace Silver places this piece deep in a Blue Note bag", writes the editor. "By the time of his legendary Columbia EMI records (1965 & 1967) the extrovert swing displayed here were recast, refined and revealed as visionary. Stage recording by Goudie Charles using a mono quarter track reel-to-reel machine at slow-speed";

[28] R. Cook-B. Morton, *The Penguin Guide to Jazz On CD*, Penguin Books, London 2000 – Fifth Edition – p. 1356;

[29] I. Carr, *Music Outside. Contemporary jazz in Britain*, Latimer New Dimension, London 1973 (2nd ed. , Northways Publications, London 2008 *with a postscript by R. Cattarell*), pagg. 149 e 150;

[30] "Terry was Graham's road manager for a while. I knew him very slightly", Brown says. "I seem to remember there was a crash that he was involved in and the band were lucky to escape with their lives, but that's all I can recall...". An absolutely elusive figure, maybe more than his brother Mike, Terry doesn't leave traces...;

[31] Some articles report the presence of Chris Bateson in one of the first Taylor band's line-ups, but the truth is that Bateson couldn't read scores and he would play with Mike on very few occasions. Dave Tomlin confirms it: "Sometimes one comes across the name Chris Bateson having played trumpet with him. This is not so. I remember the night when I first met Mike. It was at The Nucleus where musicians went to jam after finishing other gigs. Chris Bateson and myself used to play a lot together and were playing there when Mike turned up and asked to play with us. When we were finished he said he was forming a group but the musicians had to read music. Chris could not so he was unable to join, but I was so I joined and he didn't". Other names circulating have been Lowther and Mumford, but Tomlin adamant: "Henry Lowther tried out (rehearsal) on trumpet but didn't do any gigs. As far as I know Johnny Mumford did not play with Mike (may have rehearsed but no more) and that's about it while I was with him".

Anyway Ron Rubin also quotes in his diary Chris Bateson as he playing in a session at London's Piedmont Restaurant, Frith Street, (Soho) on June 26th 1962;

[32] P. Brown in *Graham Bond Organization. Wade in the water*, 4CDs box booklet edited by Repertoire Records (REP 5250) in 2012;

[33] D. Heining, *Jazz Wise #115*, December 2007-January 2008, Op. cit.;

[34] D. Gelly in *Mike Taylor Remembered*, 2007 Op. cit.. Gelly, among several articles and books (among them, essays on Stan Getz and Lester Young), has published in 2014 *An Unholy Row. Jazz in Britain and its audience 1945-1960*, a competent, documented and enjoyable

picture of the English post-war jazz;

[35] From the original synopsis published on the British Film Institute official Web site at http://collections-search.bfi.org.uk/web/Details/ChoiceFilmWorks/%20%20%20%20%20% 20%20%20%20%20150262097

In the archive the short movie has the reference number: 253520;

[36] Considering that from 1963 the Marquee started having mainly blues and rock bands, and that the club official Web site (www.themarqueeclub.net) under May 1963 doesn't list the date of 5th, Rubin's and Burke's memory is plausible;

[37] Ron Rubin's diary, Saturday December 21st, 1963: "Mike Taylor, the *Three O'Clock Man* came around, as usual bang on time. A gauche mélange of inspiration and inadequacy, hipness and naïveté. We spent the afternoon doing our way-out free form improvisations. Mike tapes these and listens to them in the night, heat-of-the-moment creations which he transmutes into compositions. There's a lot of dross, but it can be magic, when it gels. Gabbed for an hour about theories of music and new forms of expression." First time published (in a wrong form) by Richard Morton Jack and Steve Ingless on *Pendulum* CD booklet , 2007 Op. cit.;

[38] R. Morton Jack-S. Ingless, *Pendulum* CD booklet , 2007 Op. cit.;

[39] N. Havers on *The Observer*, July 19th, 2014, interviewed by Elizabeth Day. Before 1960 morphine was the most popular drug in London, even if limited to medical environment, to patients and war veterans who had had an health treatment. Used on a individual level, in privacy, it wasn't perceived as a 'social problem'... (see Richard Hartnoll, *Multi-city Study, Drug Misuse Trends in Thirteen European Cities*, UK 1994);

[40] D. Heining, *Jazz Wise* #115, December 2007-January 2008, Op. cit.;

[41] R. Bolton, "In the land of warthogs and rhyming piano. Mike Taylor – Part 1: The Innovator", in *Jazz Journal* Vol. 27, December 1974;

[42] R. Morton Jack-S. Ingless, *Pendulum* CD booklet , 2007 Op. cit.;

[43] R. Bolton, 1974 Op. cit.;

[44] D. Heining, *Jazz Wise* #115, December 2007-January 2008, Op. cit.;

[45] R. Bolton, 1974 Op. cit.;

[46] M. Hanson, *Playing the band. The musical life of Jon Hiseman*, Temple Music UK 2010;

[47] R. Morton Jack-S. Ingless, *Pendulum* CD booklet , 2007 Op. cit.;

[48] Ibidem;

[49] R. Bolton, 1974 Op. Cit.;

[50] Curiously, this poster appears on two b/w photographs taken by Norman Potter on April 12th, 1967 with Barbara Thompson (Jon Hiseman's wife) posing with her sax. Hung on the wall behind her, at the bottom of the "Mike Taylor quintet" we can read: "Modern jazz by the Mike Taylor quintet"... "These are newspaper photos of Barbara taken in Mike Taylor's flat at Kew, but some time after he left, when I was still renting it", Hiseman reveals. "Probably early '67, we think they was taken for the *Daily Mirror* when Barbara was playing with an all Girl Group The She Trinity who had a minor hit...";

[51] D. Gelly, *Mike Taylor Remembered*, 2007 Op. cit.;

[52] W. Benjamin, *The Work of Art in the Age of Mechanical Reproducibility, 1936. First English edition was published in 1968 in Hannah Arendt's English-language selection titled "Illuminations" (translation by Harry Zohn.);*

[53] Some biographers such as Dave Gelly have stated that in this period the band had an half-hour broadcast for the BBC Radio 3 programme *Jazz Record Requests* (but the correct title of the programme was *New Sounds, New Faces*). Even if Dave Gelly writes in the booklet of *Mike Taylor Remembered* that "the reaction was remarkably enthusiastic", sources about this event are discordant. Investigating it, I've asked Alyn Shipton (presenter for BBC Radio 3 and jazz critic for *The Times*), a well-known English jazz expert (he's the author of the monumental *A New History of Jazz*, published first time by Bloomsbury Publishing in 2001 and of various biographies , including one on Ian Carr), but nothing is documented in the archives. So Shipton suggested that I should ask Paul Wilson, curator of radio and a jazz expert at the British Library, and he replied that "I'm pretty sure that Mike Taylor never did any BBC sessions at all and I've never come across any in the course of my jazz radio research. I'm a big fan of his two albums so I'd have noticed and remembered if I'd ever come across anything. I think this assumption arises from the sleeve notes of a memorial album featuring posthumous arrangements of some of his compositions which came out a few years ago. As I recall (I don't have it to hand) that suggested that Taylor had done a radio session about 1965 but I know that Jon Hiseman or Barbara Thompson (who both knew him well) said that Taylor was someone who refused to do radio sessions, for whatever reason. Apparently he was asked by Charles Fox, I think, but declined". In fact, as we'll see, Taylor refused to play at TV and radio programmes;

[54] Denis Preston produced, among the others, records by Chris Barber, Annie Ross, Kenny Graham, Rambling Jack Elliott, Don Rendell-Ian Carr, Tony Coe, Stan Tracey, Josh White, Neil Ardley, Shawn Phillips, Roger Whittaker, Don Harper spacing among jazz, blues, folk, classic and world music;

[55] M. Hanson, 2010 Op. cit.;

[56] R. Bolton, 1974 Op. cit. Tony Reeves confirmed to Richard Morton Jack in 2014 talking about *Pendulum*: "I met Mike through Jon Hiseman in 1964, and we started playing as a

quartet with Dave Tomlin on soprano saxophone, rehearsing in an old photographic studio in Ilford. From the start, Mike was an introvert, and you didn't get a lot out of him. I had no meaningful personal relationship with him, and I'm not sure it was possible to. However, he was absolutely able to communicate what he wanted to achieve musically in a rational, specific way. I suppose he was a very competent pianist, rather than a virtuoso – what was important was his imagination and inventiveness" (Tony Reeves to Richard Morton Jack in *Flashback* vol. 6, Winter 2014);

[57] I. Carr, 1973 Op. cit.;

[58] It's odd that Carr in his original, seminal essay on British Jazz published in '73 with the title *Music Outside* wrote just few words about Taylor, quoted more importantly in an interview with Jon Hiseman... In 1973, before Robert Bolton's retrospective published one year later, it's as if Taylor's star were still blurry in the eyes of his mentor...;

[59] "For *Pendulum*", Tomlin remembers, "we were paid £30 each. With this money I bought myself a little transistor radio. As the music I was writing was geometric and serial rather than lyrical I could listen to it while writing, mostly Radio Luxembourg - at that time, Dionne Warwick, Sandie Shaw etc." According to the Web site *This is Money – Historic inflation calculator* (http://www.thisismoney.co.uk/money/bills/article-1633409/Historic-inflation-calculator-value-money-changed-1900.html) in 1965 £30 was the equivalent of around £415 nowadays;

[60] B. King, *Jazz Monthly*, July 1966;

[61] Ibid.;

[62] M. Gardner, *Jazz Journal*, June 1966;

[63] D. Gelly, *Jazz Guide*, 1965;

[64] M. Hanson, 2010 Op. cit.;

[65] J. Wickes, 1999 Op. cit.;

[66] Ibid.;

[67] D. Gelly, *Mike Taylor Remembered*, 2007 Op cit.;

[68] S. Ingless, "The Pendulum swings" in *Record Collector* # 4, April 2005;

[69] R. Bolton, "In the land of warthogs and rhyming piano. Mike Taylor – Part 2: Composer at Work", in *Jazz Journal* Vol. 28 , January 1975 Op. cit.;

[70] M.S., *Jazz Journal*, July 1965;

[71] H. Shapiro, *Graham Bond. The mighty shadow*, Gullane Children's Books, UK 1992. In the

book Shapiro writes that it was Mike who introduced Bond to Hiseman: "Mike Taylor told me that Graham was looking for a drummer as Ginger was leaving and advised me to go for it, but I said I didn't want to. Graham then rang me at the booking agency [where Hiseman had a day job] and asked me if I wanted to join and I said no, but he was very persuasive";

[72] R. Morton Jack-S. Ingless, *Pendulum*, 2007 Op. cit.;

[73] R. Morton Jack, "Mike Taylor: the mystic who looked like a bank clerk" in *Galactic Ramble*, 2010 Op. cit.;

[74] Ron Rubin in D. Heining, "The strange life and death of Mike Taylor", January 23th, 2013 at *Jazz Internationale* Web site (http://www.jazzinternationale.com/mike-taylor-the-not-so-strange-life-and-death-of-mike-taylor/);

[75] Although separated from the first half of 1965, they divorced only in April 1968, leaving no children;

[76] I. Carr, 1973 Op. cit.;

[77] J. Wickes, 1999 Op. cit.;

[78] R. Bolton, 1975 Op. cit.;

[79] Ibid.;

[80] Ibid.;

[81] Surely accidental, but mockingly significant, this typographic error of the title related to the tune on the album CD version published in 2007 with "All the *tings* you are"... as to say that it is in fact "just another thing" compared to the original version played by everyone more or less in the same way...;

[82] "While Young's composition was written as the film's recurrent theme", specialized *Jazz Standard* Web site reports at www.jazzstandards.com, "the song itself became a dramatic focal point when Milland's character Rod serenades his Stella, played by Russell. Looking out the window while Rod is at his grand piano Stella asks what he is playing. Rod replies, 'It's a serenade. To Stella by Starlight'";

[83] After research on the Web, I discovered the sculptor's official site at http://www.jim-ritchie.com but there was no way to contact him. Thanks to Massimo Del Chiaro, owner of Fonderia d'Arte Massimo Del Chiaro in Pietrasanta (Lucca), where the artist worked years ago, I've obtained an answer from Ritchie: "Yes, I created the record cover for the producer, Dennis Preston and had no contact with the musician". What does his work mean? Ritchie doesn't explain. It's an undeniable fact, anyway, that the drawing seems perfectly summarizes the idea of a compact lump of thoughts and feelings, a concentration of strong emotions, that I feel every time I listen to the record... Interesting to note that in his autobiography titled *A*

Sculptural Life.The life and works of Jim Ritchie (Lulu.com, 2012) at pag. 191 reproduces some drawings, made in 1966-1974, without titles, all made in the same style and with similar abstract subjects to that used for the "Trio" cover;

[84] I. Carr, 1973 Op. cit.;

[85] D. Gelly, *Mike Taylor Remembered*, 2007 Op. cit.. Ron Rubin, who has never appreciated the "glowing reviews"published about the record ("... not one critic said anything about dodgy bass lines and harmonies, and one reviewer commented on "The Way You Look Tonight", which isn't even on the record... Is there no such thing as a mistake?"), he wrote in his journal: "By 2007, the disc had become a 'collector's item'. I sold my spare copy for £ 400 and heard that the LP was on offer on the Net for over a grand. At the time it was made, Mike was working as a dish washer in Lyons... I was paid £ 21.17.6d recording fee.";

[86] R. Bolton, 1975 Op. cit.;

[87] Ibidem;

[88] Ibidem;

[89] When in Autumn of 1967 Hiseman left the flat to get married to Barbara, he is soon in for an unpleasant surprise: "I left the flat to Terry who said he would take over the lease in the Autumn of 1967 after I had married Barbara. Three weeks later I received a phone call from the neighbours downstairs (the flat was on the 1st floor) who said that a bad smell was coming from the flat and they had received no payments from Terry who had disappeared. I returned to the flat, found rotting rubbish in plastic bags in the kitchen and the flat in a terrible state. I spent a several of hours cleaning it all up, because I realised that if Terry had not taken over the lease I was still responsible. I think I did see Terry again a couple of years late - he turned up at a *Colosseum* gig. But only for a moment and I never mentioned the situation...". It was also the last time Mike's friends met Terry and from that moment he disappeared forever...;

[90] T. Leary, R. Metzner and R. Alpert, *The Psychedelic Experience*, University Books, New York 1964;

[91] Anyway the Giant Sun Trolley had a short life, from June 1966 to July 1967. See the Third Ear Band's official archive in the Web at http://ghettoraga.blogspot.com edited by the Author from 2009 with several references to Dave Tomlin;

[92] C. Pariani, *Vita non romanzata di Dino Campana* [The not-fictional Life of Dino Campana], Vallecchi, Firenze 1938 and Guanda, Milano 1978;

[93] A. Roberts, *Albion Dreaming. A popular history of LSD in Britain*, Marshall Cavendish, London 2008;

[94] B. Wells, *Psychedelic Drugs: Psychological, Medical And Social Issues*, Penguin Books, 1973;

[95] P. Corrias (edited by), *Viaggi Acidi. Albert Hofmann intervistato da Pino Corrias* [Acid Trips. Albert Hofmann interviewed by Pino Corrias], Stampa Alternativa, Roma 1992;

[96] Dave Tomlin in Duncan Heining, "The Strange Life and Death of Mike Taylor", 2008 Op. cit.;

[97] R. Bolton, 1975 Op. cit.;

[98] Even if Rubin reports in his journal on the gig of August 31th, lacking an archive that documents the club's activities, and aggravated by the demises of the founders (Stevens passed away in 1994, Rutherford in 2007), it's not easy determine how many times Taylor had actually frequented the Little Theatre that year;

[99] B. Dawbarn, "Roundhouse crowds without the bedrolls", in *Melody Maker*, September 13th, 1969;

[100] D. Gelly, *Mike Taylor Remembered*, 2007 Op. cit.;

[101] Ibidem;

[102] Unfortunately, despite my reiterated requests, for obscure reasons related to copyright questions, Gelly has decided not to supply a copy of the Mike's manuscript, only paraphrasing it. If it could be considered an act of jealousy on the part of one who is conscious of possessing an exclusive document, it's something of which I have a great bitterness for not having had the opportunity to examine the contents of the document (one of the few autographed by the pianist!). Anyway, I'm persuaded as writer Paco Ignacio Taibo II wrote as introduction to his wonderful biography about Ernesto Che Guevara published in 1996, "in history none is owner of documents, but only of interpretations"...;

[103] John Jack: "I seem to have miss-filed the pages for early May... although at this time I was becoming quite ill with work and personal troubles so may not have written any details until what became the final week, with the club having some 250 people coming to the wake... which was also my birthday!". However the Old Place closed just little time later, on May 25th, "after a long struggle for survival", as *Jazz Journal* reported on the June 1968 issue. A group of musicians, among them Graham Collier, Mike Westbrook, John Surman, Chris McGregor and John Jack, established a committee for a fund raising event aimed at founding a new multidisciplinary centre...;

[104] See Eric Clapton with Christopher Simon-Sykes, *The autobiography*, Century 2007; Ginger Baker with Ginette Baker, *Hellraiser. The autobiography of the World's Greatest Drummer*, John Blake 2009; Harry Shapiro, *Jack Bruce, Composing Himself*, Jawbone 2010. In this book there's a small quote about Mike when the author writes on the genesis of Cream's *Wheels of Fire*. Shapiro: "There are certainly no weak links on the studio album. It contains strong contributions from Ginger, who wrote the wonderfully quirky and humorous "Pressed Rat and Warthog" with the much-respected British jazz pianist and composer Mike Taylor" (pag. 111). Not only the main

books but also the official Web site doesn't quote a word related to Mike Taylor as in Baker's (http://www.gingerbaker.com), except for the Pappalardi's short memories, the Bruce's one (http://www.jackbruce.com) or Clapton's (http://www.ericclapton.com)... All attempts by the Author to have interviews with Baker and Bruce (who passed away in October 2014 after a long illness), failed, although Pete Brown's 'intercession', didn't turn out too well either. Brown, even if totally willing to collaborate, admits he doesn't remember anything of significant about that session...;

[105] F. Pappalardi, "How Cream made Wheels of Fire", on Ginger Baker's official Web site http://www.gingerbaker.com;

[106] D. Thompson, *Footnotes from the Archive of Oblivion: rock and pop's forgotten heroes*, CreateSpace Independent Publishing Platform, UK 2009;

[107] 'Missed' for years, Baker would have played the tune on live only in 2005, for the Cream reunion concert at the Royal Albert Hall of London...;

[108] J. S. Wenner, "Wheels of Fire" in *Rolling Stones* #14, July 20th, 1968;

[109] *Beat Instrumental* #65, September 1968, page 40. The controversial opinions of that time reflected the clamorous success of the album, both from public and critics, legitimised in recent years with the inclusion in *500 Greatest Albums of All Time* edited by *Rolling Stones* (Wenner Books, New York 2005). A sort of historic nemesis...In an irony of fate, in 2007 the copyrights for the three tunes composed by Taylor for the Cream amounted to £ 40-50.000. With his wife Ann passed away, paradoxically the only heir became her husband, Gary Drugnik, who had never met Mike!;

[110] Christopher Bird, *Melody Maker*, October 5, 1968;

[111] Burke: "I do have a vivid memory of sitting with Mike, Ann, Dave and Dianne, and listening to the *7th Symphony* by Shostakovich, and *Concerto for the Left Hand* by Ravel. Both outstanding works, which some of us were hearing for the first time. Although we were mostly listening to a lot of Jazz we were all open to new musical experiences...". While Hiseman doesn't remember Mike being passionate for classical music, Tomlin is sure he listened only to Shostakovich;

[112] Unknown journalist, *Gramophone*, July 1969 pag. 94;

[113] M. C. King, *Jazz Journal*, October 1970, p.14;

[114] D. Gelly, *Jazz Journal* n. 65, August 2012;

[115] Jon Hiseman in *Melody Maker*, 1970;

[116] M. Hanson, 2010 Op. cit.;

[117] Among the more influential figures of 20th Century, American John Cage (1912-1992) was musician, composer, avant-garde experimenter (he invented prepared piano), researcher, promoter

of happenings, anarchist, mycologist. His works, along with his books and essays had contributed in a decisive way to extend the borders of music so as to make them vanish. Among his fundamental writings, *Silence* (Wesleyan University Press, Connecticut 1961) and *A Year From Monday* (Wesleyan University Press, Connecticut 1967);

[118] D. Gelly, *Mike Taylor Remembered*, 2007 op. cit. Asking Barry Guy about that evening, he replied me: "I must say that this bit of history eludes me! I am sorry not to offer you further information about this occasion. Perhaps Howard would be the best person to help since he has a good archival memory and may have known Mike personally. Obviously I remember his presence on the music scene, but I became involved in the free music with a different set of guys circling around John Stevens and The Little Theatre club. I do not recall Mike being part of this, but I may be wrong. Check with Howard, that's best". Even if requested to contribute with a memory about it, Riley never replied. Anyway it's significant that Riley had a two-parts interview for the British Library in 1990 about the history of English jazz, where he told to journalist Andy Simons, that Taylor's two albums produced by Denis Preston were among his favourites ever;

[119] *Jazz Journal*, December 1968, page 24. *The Guardian*, reporting the event the day after, wrote: "The Mike Taylor trio, also booked for the concert, never appeared and in their place we had an enjoyable set by Riley, Jon Hiseman (the N.J.O.'s magnificent drummer) and bassist Barry Guy. In this context of free-form trio jazz Guy has no superior and he stole this part of the show...";

[120] Duncan Heining wrote a very good, passionate article on *Jazz Internationale* Web site titled "Jazz and drugs" at http://www.jazzinternationale.com/jazz-and-drugs/;

[121] R. Bolton, 1975 Op. Cit.;

[122] D. Gelly, *Mike Taylor Remembered*, 2007 Op. cit.;

[123] Ibidem;

[124] M. Hanson, 2010 Op. cit.;

[125] From the London British Library's archives, during the sessions of June 22th and 26th 1973 at London Lansdowne Studios an orchestra with fifteen musicians conducted by Ardley recorded "Son of red blues"/"Brown Thurday" (medley); on June 22th and 25th a more restrict band (Ian Carr on trumpet, Barbara Thompson on tenor sax, Peter Lemer on piano, Ron Mathewson on double bass and Jon Hiseman on drums) recorded around 10 minutes of improvisations based on the "Black and White Raga"'s theme;

[126] "Son of the Red Blues", arranged by Ardley, is based on a unrealised original recording made by the Taylor quartet in 1965, where it used Mike's piano solos and excerpts of piano and Tomlin's tenor sax in unison;

[127] J. Fordham, *The Guardian*, October 5, 2007;

[128] D. Heining in *Jazz Wise*, 2008, page. 45, *Op. cit.*; very cleverly Richard Morton Jack

considers also the possibility that Mike Taylor was wearing extra layers of clothing so as to drown more easily;

[129] From the Guildhall School of Music official Web site at

http://www.gsmd.ac.uk/music/news/view/article/
guildhall_jazz_band_to_showcase_rare_repertoire_with_special_guests_for_efg_london_jazz_festi
val/

[130] J. Fordham, *The Guardian*, July 9th 2004.

Acknowledgements

Writing this book about Mike Taylor was a very difficult task because of the scarce sources available and the long time since his death. A two year challenge was to contact people still around and collect all the things existing (magazines, articles, recordings, scores...), conducting interviews, comparing points of view, verifying dates and facts, and recovering official documents and certificates. I hope I have accomplished an acceptable work, above all respectful of Mike Taylor's life and the people involved with him.

Finally, a book like this is always the result of a collective effort. This is based on personal accounts of **Dave Tomlin** (who suggested the title to me, taking it from the famous Jazz standard composed by Johnny Green, and for making a revision of the English text...), **John Mumford** (conclusive revision of the book), **Ron Rubin, Jon Hiseman, Michael Burke, Jak Kilby, Ron A. Ostwald, Pete Brown, Henry Lowther, Evan Parker, John Jack, Dave Gelly, Tony Reeves, Goudie Charles, Digby Fairweather, Lyn Dobson, Norma Winstone, Trevor Watts, Victor Schonfield, Peter Muir.**

Without their inestimable help it wouldn't have been possible to write it.

Many thanks also to **Tony Tomlin** (for his decisive research), **Koro Ito** (archival researches), **Jon Limbert** (rock magazines archivist), **Margaret Richards** (Taylor's original handmade scores photos), **Richard Morton Jack, Bob Stuckey, Barry Guy, John Marshall, Michael Fitzgerald, Alyn Shipton, Paul Wilson, Laura Mills** (Essex Police Headquarters), **Barbara Bridge** (Southend-on-Sea Borough Council's Library Development), **Kathleen Dickson** (British Film Institute), **Cathy Broad** (Librarian Humanist Library and Archives), **Jim Ritchie, Neil Oram, Massimo Del Chiaro, Sara Lemos** (Data Access & Compliance Unit – Department of Justice), **Steven Dryden** (The British Library Sound Archive), **Jonathan Oates** (Ealing Local History Centre), **Hugh Jones** (University of London), **James Marshall** (Local Studies Librarian, Hounslow and Chiswick Libraries), **Denise Hutchings** (H.M. Essex Coroners Office) and to all the few journalists and writers had the rare awareness to write about Mike Taylor throughout the last forty-five years keeping his name alive. Special thanks also to **Natasha Jackson** for her erudite translations of the more difficult parts of the book.

Appendix

MIKE TAYLOR'S BANDS LINE-UPS AS BANDLEADER
A list of line-ups from various sources (photos, reviews, records, Ron Rubin's journal...).

Mike Taylor Quintet (1961)
Mike Taylor (piano) – Dave Tomlin (soprano sax) – Peter *Ginger* Baker (drums) – Charles Goudie (double-bass) – Frank Powell (trumpet)

Source: a recollection by Charles Goudie.

Mike Taylor Quintet (1961-1962)
Mike Taylor (piano) – Dave Tomlin (soprano sax) – Randy Jones (drums) – Charles Goudie (double-bass) – Frank Powell (trumpet)

Source: a track recorded on May 1961 at Herne Bay's Jazz Workshop by Goudie Charles included in *Trad dads, dirty boppers and free fusioneers: British jazz 1960-1975* (CD – Reel Recordings RR026, UK 2012). A memory of Michael Burke about a concert the quintet played on March 15th, 1962 at The Jazz Cellar in Richmond (London).

Mike Taylor Quintet (July 1st 1962)
Mike Taylor (piano) – Dave Tomlin (soprano sax) – Randy Jones (drums) – Ron Rubin (bass) – Chris Bateson (trumpet)

Source: a documented concert at the Modern Jazz Workshop, Herne Bay, on July 1st, 1962 photographed by Terry Taylor. A list of gigs in Rubin's diary.

Mike Taylor Quintet (1962)
Mike Taylor (piano) – Dave Tomlin (soprano sax) – Martin Gail (bass) – Randy Jones (drums) – Frank Powell (trumpet)

Source: a documented concert at The Jazz Cellar, Richmond (London) in November 1962 photographed by Michael Burke.

Mike Taylor Quartet (August 1963)

Mike Taylor (piano) – Dave Tomlin (tenor sax) – Sam Stone (drums) – Ron Rubin (bass)

Source: Rubin's diary about a party at Mannerings (Totteridge, London).

Mike Taylor Quartet (1964)

Mike Taylor (piano) – Dave Tomlin (tenor sax) – Jon Hiseman (drums) – Jack Bruce (bass)

Source: a recollection of Digby Fairweather of a concert at Studio Jazz Club in Westcliff, also quoted by Robert Bolton in his articles of 1974-1975.

Mike Taylor Quartet (January-December 1965)

Mike Taylor (piano) – Dave Tomlin (tenor sax) – Jon Hiseman (drums) – Tony Reeves (bass)

Source: Ron Rubin's diary. On August 29th, 1965 the documented concert at Croydon's Fairfield Hall (London) as backing-band for Ornette Coleman, then in October the recording sessions for *Pendulum* (Columbia 1966).

Mike Taylor Trio (January-July 1966)

Mike Taylor (piano) - Jon Hiseman (drums) – Ron Rubin (bass)

Source: Rubin's diary. This line-up recorded *Trio* on July 1966, published by Columbia in 1967, with the involvement of Jack Bruce on bass.

Mike Taylor Duo (February-November 1967)

Mike Taylor (piano) – Ron Rubin (bass)

Source: Rubin's diary about some concerts at Ronnie Scott's Old Place (London) and at Little Theatre Club (London). In that period also one documented gig in trio with drummer John Stevens (20-09-1967), two in quartet with Henry Lowther (27-10-1967 and 4-11-1967), one in trio with Hiseman (9-10-1967).

Mike Taylor Trio (October 27th, 1967) *rehearsal*

Mike Taylor (piano) – Ron Rubin (bass) – Laurie Allan (drums)

Source: Rubin's diary. A rehearsal at Ronnie Scott's Old Place (London) also documented by photographer Jak Kilby.

Mike Taylor Duo (1968)

Mike Taylor (piano) – Ron Rubin (bass)

Source: Rubin's diary about concerts in April at Ronnie Scott's Old Place. One gig in trio, also with Laurie Allen on drums.

MIKE TAYLOR GIGS/REHEARSALS LIST

All Mike Taylor's verified gigs, included those booked where he didn't play.

1962

15-03-1962 – The Jazz Cellar (Richmond, London)
26-06-1962 – Piedmont Restaurant (Frith Street, Soho, London)
01-07-1962 – Modern Jazz Workshop (Herne Bay)
05-07-1962 – Piedmont Restaurant (Frith Street, Soho, London) *rehearsal*
14-07-1962– Richmond Community Centre (London)
22-07-1962 – Modern Jazz Workshop (Herne Bay)
05-08-1962 – Modern Jazz Workshop (Herne Bay)
12-08-1962 – Modern Jazz Workshop (Herne Bay)
26-08-1962 – Modern Jazz Workshop (Herne Bay)
15-09-1962 – Bernie's Club, George & Dragon (Acton)
16-09-1962 – Club Octave, Hambro Tavern (Southall)
20-09-1962 – Bernie's Club, George & Dragon (Acton)
30-09-1962 – Club Octave, Hambro Tavern (Southall)
07-10-1962 – Modern Jazz Workshop (Herne Bay)
14-10-1962 – Modern Jazz Workshop (Herne Bay)
November   – The Jazz Cellar, Richmond, London

1963

21-04-1963 – Bernie's Club, George & Dragon (Acton)
12-05-1963 – Marquee Club (Oxford Street, London)
26-05-1963 – Bernie's Club, George & Dragon (Acton)
17-08-1963 – *party* at "Mannerings" (Totteridge, London N20)

1964

With Ron Rubin leaving London for Palma de Mallorca from April to October to play bass with Ramòn Farraù Trio, there are no available sources.

A recollection of Digby Fairweather of a concert at Studio Jazz Club in Westcliff, also quoted by Robert Bolton in his articles of 1974-1975, is the only one gig known.

1965

22-01-1965 – London School of Economics (London)
07-03-1965 – Institute of Contemporary Arts (Dover Street, London)
29-08-1965 – Fairfield Hall (Croydon, London)
12-12-1965 – Institute of Contemporary Arts (Dover Street, London)

1966

03-01-1966 – Little Theatre Club (Garrick Yard, London)
30-01-1966 – Marquee Club (Wardour Street, London)
14-02-1966 – Little Theatre Club (London)
18-05-1966 – Regency Club (Stoke Newington)

25-05-1966 – Little Theatre Club (Garrick Yard, London)
29-06-1966 – Little Theatre Club (Garrick Yard, London)

1967

18-02-1967 – UFO Club (Tottenham Court Road, London) *not played*
23-08-1967 – Ronnie Scott's Old Place (Gerrard Street, London)
28-08-1967 – Ronnie Scott's Old Place (Gerrard Street, London)
31-08-1967 – Little Theatre Club (Garrick Yard, London)
05-09-1967 – Les Cousins (Greek Street, London)
20-09-1967 – Ronnie Scott's Old Place (Gerrard Street, London)
09-10-1967 – Ronnie Scott's Old Place (Gerrard Street, London)
27-10-1967 – Ronnie Scott's Old Place (Gerrard Street, London)
                    rehearsal (afternoon) and concert (evening)
04-11-1967 – Ronnie Scott's Old Place (Gerrard Street, London)

1968

19-01-1968 – Ronnie Scott's Old Place (Gerrard Street, London)
04-03-1968 – Ronnie Scott's Old Place (Gerrard Street, London)
11-04-1968 – Ronnie Scott's Old Place (Gerrard Street, London)
08-11-1968 – Conway Hall (Red Lion square, London) *not played*

DISCOGRAPHY

Mike Taylor Quartet - "Pendulum" (LP mono – Columbia SX6042, UK May 1966)

"But not for me"(George Gershwin-Ira Gershwin), "Exactly like you" (Jimmy McHugh-Dorothy Fields), "A night in Tunisia" (Dizzy Gillespie-Frank Paparelli), "Pendulum" (Mike Taylor), "To Segovia" (Mike Taylor), "Leeway" (Mike Taylor)

Mike Taylor – piano, **Tony Reeves** – bass, **Dave Tomlin** – soprano sax, **Jon Hiseman** – drums

Produced by **Denis Preston**

The first Mike Taylor's record on vinyl format is very rare, almost impossible to find. Sometimes it emerges from the Web on commercial site such as eBay but extremely expensive (£ 400/500). The reissue on CD published in April 2007 by Sunbeam Records as SBRCD5034 is quite rare too, valued around £ 70. The artwork on this CD wrongly says that Ron Rubin is the bass player.

Mike Taylor Trio - "Trio" (LP mono – Columbia SCX6137, UK June 1967)

"All the Things you Are" (Jerome Kern-Oscar Hammerstein II), "Just a Blues" (Mike Taylor), "While my Lady Sleeps" (Bronislau Kaper), "The end of a love affair" (Edward C. Redding), "Two autumns" (Mike Taylor), "Guru" (Mike Taylor), "Stella by Starlight" (Victor Young-Ned Washington), "Abena" (Mike Taylor)

Mike Taylor – piano, **Jack Bruce** – bass, **Ron Rubin** – bass, **Jon Hiseman** – drums
Produced by **Denis Preston**.

As with the first one, the second Mike Taylor album is very rare, valued around £ 200/400 on the collector's market. The CD version, edited in June 2004 by Universal (catalogue number: 986 689 4), is rare too, very difficult to find (valued £ 40/50).

Various Artists - "Jazz Explosion" (LP stereo – Lansdowne SLJS1, UK July 1969)

This compilation, "a panorama of contemporary British jazz", features among other artists (Ian Carr, Stan Tracey, Don Rendell, Amancio D'Silva...) also the Mike Taylor Trio with "Abena" from *Trio* (Columbia 1967). On the sleeve notes producer Denis Preston, who personally selected the tracks, writes of Taylor: "... And tribute must be paid to the pioneers... to the inward-looking talent of Mike Taylor, all set for positive-outward appeal when tragic death cut short a fruitful career".

Originally sold for 16 shillings, it is now available on the collector's market for around £ 30-40.

OTHER UNREALISED MIKE TAYLOR'S COMPOSITIONS & RECORDINGS

Here are all the Taylor's compositions known from documents, quotations or original scores survived.

"Straight, No Chaser"
This rendition of the famous Thelonious Monk composition was recorded live on May 1961 at the Herne Bay by **Mike Taylor** (piano) with **Dave Tomlin** (tenor sax), **Frank Powell** (trumpet), **Goudie Charles** (bass) and **Randy Jones** (drums). It's circulating between jazz fans in MP3 and FLAC format.

"The Party" (film soundtrack)
Composed in 1962 for this short film directed by Ron Ostwald (a.k.a. Mark Petersen), the soundtrack was made up with some of the tracks later included in *Pendulum* (Columbia 1965). One of the tracks was titled "Anacleto's Theme". Ostwald remembers: "The theme had a vaguely Mexican feel to it (Anacleto was a Mexican bandit played by Dirk Bogarde in a movie called *The Singer not the Song*). The recording was a primitive affair - we recorded it on Mike Burke's domestic tape recorder through a single microphone - not ideal". This film is archived at British Film Institute of London with the reference number: 253520.

"Conflict" (film soundtrack)
Composed in 1962 for this short film directed by Ron Ostwald (a.k.a. Mark Petersen) by the line-up of *The Party* but never realised.

"Brown Thursday", "Triangle Waltz", "Rama", "Taking a chance on Love"

These compositions were handwritten by Mike Taylor on September 25th, 1964 and given to Trevor Watts to rehearse maybe with the idea to play them live. "Taking a chance on Love" is a Taylor arrangement for the original K. Duke's tune. Only "Brown Thursday" was recorded by the New Jazz Orchestra for the "Mike Taylor Remembered" album (2007), linked with "Son of Red Blues".

"Cardboard Sky"

One of the tracks Tomlin and Taylor composed in 1966 for a planned musical (never realised). Other tracks composed were "Jumping Off The Sun", "Summer Sounds" and "Timewind", (lyrics by Dave Tomlin) later re-arranged by Neil Ardley for the posthumous *Mike Taylor Remembered* (2007).

1. "Lines", 2. "The Sermon of Flowers", 3. "Folk Dances", 4. "Songs"

This is the classification Taylor wrote about his over 200 compositions on a curriculum vitae compiled on November 15th, 1967 to obtain an unemployment benefit as an out-of-work composer.

Among the "ten folk dances" composed by Taylor (Bolton, 1974) just "Folk Dances n. 2" was recorded in 1973 by the New Jazz Orchestra from the original score recovered by Jon Hiseman after Taylor put it in the dustbin outside his flat. "Folk Dance n. 1" became "Summer Sounds, Summer Sights" during the period Taylor was trying to compose a musical with Dave Tomlin (Bolton, 1974), then recorded by the New Jazz Orchestra for "Mike Taylor Remembered" album with the title "Summer Sounds".

Also included in the document the score of a piano piece titled "Paen, Patricia Grace Ellahee, Anna".

"Horn, Gut and Skin Suite"

One of the scores recovered by Jon Hiseman from Mike's flat at Kew.

"A Long Time"

Composed at the time of Kew's flat, (lyrics by Dave Tomlin), is quoted by Robert Bolton in his retrospective of 1974-1975. Probably lost, Tomlin doesn't remember anything about this composition.

Wimbledon Jam Session

Some recordings taken by Jon Hiseman at the end of 1966 at Wimbledon Barbara Thompson's home of a jam session with Mike Taylor (piano), Graham Bond (alto sax), Jon Hiseman (drums), Barbara Thompson (reeds), Tony Reeves (bass) and such Lourie (congas)... Hiseman (August 2014): "I started a project getting all my 2-track tapes into the digital domain last year. I came across a tape with Graham Bond-Mike Taylor and others - and it said "GB & MT" on the box, but with no details I could not tell who it was. However I am sure this is the tape, but Barbara and I have no recollection of the session. The tape recorder did not record for very long because the tapes were on small reels...".

"Pipes"

Quoted by Robert Bolton in his tribute to Taylor's life and work published in 1974-1975, as one of the last tunes composed by the pianist, and played at Barbara Thompson's home. A tape of it seemed to exist.

MIKE TAYLOR'S TUNES RECORDED BY OTHER ARTISTS

Cream - "Wheels of Fire" (LP stereo – Polydor 582/3 031/2, UK 1968)

A classic rock masterpiece double album by the cult trio (**Jack Bruce** on bass, **Ginger Baker** on drums and **Eric Clapton** on guitar) with three tracks composed by Taylor (with lyrics by Ginger Baker): "Pressed Rat and Warthog", "Those were the days" and "Passing the time". The record was remastered on CD in 1997 (as Polydor 531812-2).

At different times the tracks have been included in various compilations: "Heavy Cream" (LP – Polydor UK 1972), "Cream Vol. 2" (LP – RSO 2479 701, UK 1975), "Deserted Cities – The Cream Collection" (CD – Pickwick PWKS 4127P, UK 1992), "The very best of Cream" (CD – Polydor 523 752-2, Europe 1995), "Those Were The Days" (4CDs Box – Polydor 539 000-2, Europe 1997), "Cream Gold" (2CDs – Polydor 0602498801468, Europe 2005), "I Feel Free – The Ultimate Cream" (CD – Polydor 987 136-2, UK 2005).

New Jazz Orchestra - "Le Dejeuner sur l'Herbe" (LP stereo – Verve SVLP 9236, UK 1969)

"Le Dejeuner sur l'Herbe" (Neil Ardley), "Naima" (John Coltrane), "Angle" (Howard Riley), "Ballad" (Mike Taylor), "Dusk Fire" (M. Garrick), "Nardis" (Miles Davis), "Study" (A. Segovia), "Rebirth" (M. Gibbs).

Directed by **Neil Ardley**, the musicians on this record are: **Jack Bruce** (bass), **Jon Hiseman** (drums), **Dave Gelly** (tenor saxophone, clarinet and bass clarinet), **Jim Philip** (tenor saxophone, flute, clarinet), **Dick Heckstall-Smith** (tenor saxophone, soprano saxophone), **Barbara Thompson** (tenor saxophone, soprano saxophone, flute) , **Derek Wadsworth** (trombone), **John Mumford** (trombone), **Michael Gibbs** (trumpet), **Tony Russell** (trumpet), **Derek Watkins** (trumpet), **Harry Beckett** (trumpet), **Henry Lowther** (trumpet), **Ian Carr** (flugelhorn), **George Smith** (tuba), **Frank Ricotti** (vibraphone and marimba).

Produced by **Tony Reeves**

Among the tracks, an original composition by Taylor titled "Ballad" and an arrangement by him of a piece composed by Poland composer Alexandre Tansman titled "Study", but credited to A. Segovia.

The second New Jazz Orchestra's album is very rare, almost impossible to find, and valued on the collector's market around £ 250/300. However a remastered CD edition (1000 copies only), with a booklet edited by Dave Gelly, has been published by Dusk Fire Records in January 2015 (Dusk Fire DuskCD110, UK 2014).

The Rubber Band - "Cream Songbook" (LP - Major Minor -SMCP 5045, UK 1969)
Interpreting Cream's repertoire with arrangements by Michael Lloyd, the band recorded also Taylor's "Those Were the Days".

Colosseum - "The Grass is Greener" (LP - ABC/Dunhill DS 50079, US 1970)
Jon Hiseman's band recorded "Jumping Off the Sun" (with lyrics by Dave Tomlin) for their second album. The same version is included on a 2CD Various Artists compilation titled *2001 – A Space Rock Odyssey* (Castle Music CMDDD094) published in 2001.

Norma Winstone - "Edge of Time" (LP – Argo ZDA 148, UK 1972)
Arranged by Neil Ardley, the record shows a Winstone's interpretation of Taylor's "Song of Love". The original LP, now very rare to find, is available on a CD edition (Dusk Fire Records DUSKCD108, UK 2013). It is available also in Andorra (2000) and Spain (2012).

Various Artists - "Impressed with Gilles Peterson 2. Rare, classic & unique modern jazz from Britain 1963-1974" (CD – Universal 982014, UK 2004)
Following a first issue published in 2003, this compilation edited by BBC Radio 1's Gilles Peterson shows tracks from British jazz musicians as Mike Westbrook, Michael Garrick, Stan Tracey, Tubby Hayes, Neil Ardley. Among them also a tune taken from *Le Dejeuner sur l'herbe* by the New Jazz Orchestra and "Timewind", composed by Mike Taylor, then included in the tribute album titled *Mike Taylor Remembered* (2007).

Cream - "Royal Albert Hall London May 2-3-5-6 2005" (CD - Reprise 9362-49416-2, Europe 2005)
Cream reunion concert of 2005 where they played live also "Pressed Rat & Warthog" by Taylor/Baker. The concert is available also on DVD (Reprise, 2005) and Blu-ray format (Reprise, 2011).

Various Artists - "Mike Taylor Remembered" (LP – Trunk Records JBH 026LP, UK 2007)
"Half Blue", "Pendulum", "See You", "Son of Red Blues", "Brown Thursday", "Song of Love", "Folk Dance n. 2", "Summer Sounds", "Land of Rhyme in Time", "Timewind", "Jumping off the the Sun", "Black and White Raga"

Music direction by Neil Ardley

Recorded by Denis Preston

Tony Fisher, **Greg Bowen**, **Henry Lowther**, **Ian Carr** (trumpet, flugelhorn); **Chris Pyne**, **David Horler** (trombones); **Ray Premru** (bass trombone); **Barbara Thompson** (flute, alto flute, soprano sax); **Ray Warleigh** (flute, alto sax); **Stam Sulzmann** (flute, alto sax,, soprano sax); **Bob Efford** (oboe, tenor sax, bassoon); **Dave Gelly** (bass clarinet, clarinet, tenor sax); **Bunny Gould** (bass clarinet, bassoon); **Peter Lemer** (piano, electric piano, synthesizer); **Alan Branscombe** (vibraphone); **Chris Laurence**, **Ron Mathewson** (bass, bass guitar); **Jon Hiseman** (drums, percussion); **Norma Winstone** (vocal).

Limited LP edition (just 500 copies) become soon very rare. The CD format, made by Dusk Fire

Records (as DUSKCD103) in 2000 copies, was published in England the same year. Booklet notes by Dave Gelly with a personal interesting reconstruction of Taylor's life.

Neil Ardley's New Jazz Orchestra - "Camden '70" (CD – Dusk Fire Records DUSKCD105, UK 2008)

"Stratusfunk" (George Russell), "Tanglewood" (Michael Gibbs), "Shades of Blue" (Neil Ardley), "Rope Ladder to the Moon" (Jack Bruce), "Dusk Fire" (Michael Garrick), "Naima" (John Coltrane), "Nardis" (Miles Davis), "Study" (Mike Taylor), "Rebirth" (Michael Gibbs), "Ballad" (Mike Taylor), "Le Dejeuner sur l'Herbe" (Neil Ardley), "National Anthem & Tango" (Neil Ardley)

Directed by **Neil Ardley**, the musicians on this record are: **Tony Reeves** (bass guitar), **Jon Hiseman** (drums), **Dave Gelly** (tenor saxophone, clarinet and bass clarinet), **Jimmy Philip** (tenor sax, flute, clarinet), **Dick Heckstall-Smith** (tenor/soprano sax), **Barbara Thompson** (soprano/alto sax, flute), **Derek Wadsworth, Mike Gibbs, Robin Gardner** (trombones), **Frank Jellet** (vibes, percussion), **Dave Greenslade** (Hammond organ, Fender Rodhes piano), **Clem Clempson** (guitar), **Harry Beckett, Henry Lowther** (trumpet, flugelhorn), **Nigel Carter, Mike Davis** (trumpets)

Neil Ardley's New Jazz Orchestra CD documents a live recoding of the band at the Jeanetta Cochrane Theatre of London on May 26th, 1970 discovered in the last few years. It contains "Study", a piece arranged by Mike Taylor from the original composition by Poland composer Alexandre Tansman, and "Ballad", composed by Taylor, here arranged by Neil Ardley. Both tracks originally included on the second New Jazz Orchestra album recorded in 1969, *Le Dejeuner sur l'Herbe*. Also a quotation about the Taylor's death - "in mysterious circumstances" - in the included booklet edited by Dave Gelly.

Various Artists - "Trad dads, dirty boppers and free fusioneers: British jazz 1960-1975" (CD – Reel Recordings RR026, UK 2012)

"Phrygie" (Mike Taylor), "Scarpo" (Henry Lowther), "Number Three" (John Stevens), "An Idea" (John Surman), "Shadow" (Joe Harriott), "Quintet" (Ian Carr), "Standfast" (Gary Windo), "Beer Garden" (Elton Dean), "For Those Who Prefer It Mid-Tempo" (Lol Coxhill), "The Small Change" (Norma Winstone)

Compiled by Michael King as a compendium of Duncan Heining's book with the same title (published in 2012), it contains a very rare track composed by Taylor titled "Phrygie". It was recorded live in 1961 at Herne Bay by **Mike Taylor** (piano), **Dave Tomlin** (soprano sax), **Frank Powell** (trumpet), **Goudie Charles** (bass) and **Randy Jones** (drums).

REFERENCES

A., "The New Jazz Orchestra - 'Le Dejeuner Sur L'herbe' ", in *Gramophone*, July 1969, page 94

Atkins, Ronald, "New Jazz Orchestra", in *The Guardian*, November 9, 1968;

Bates, Alan, *Ornette Coleman. The Great London Concert* (sleeve notes of the album Arista Records AL 1900, USA 1975)

Bird, Christopher, "Rebirth of a big band", in *Melody Maker*, October, 5, 1968;

Bolton, Robert, "In the land of warthogs and rhyming piano. Mike Taylor – Part 1: The Innovator", in *Jazz Journal* Vol. 27, December 1974

Bolton, Robert, "In the land of warthogs and rhyming piano. Mike Taylor – Part 2: Composer at Work", in *Jazz Journal* Vol. 28 , January 1975

Brown, Pete, *Wade in the Water*, 4CDs box booklet, Repertoire Records REP 5250, UK 2012

Carr, Ian, *Music Outside. Contemporary jazz in Britain,* Latimer New Dimension, London 1973 (2nd ed. , Northways Publications, London 2008 *with a postscript by R. Cattarell*)

Colaiacono, Paola – Caratozzolo, Vittoria C., *La Londra dei Beatles*, Editori Riuniti, Roma, 1996

Cooke, Jack, "Ornette Coleman at Croydon" in *Jazz Monthly*, October 1965

Corrias, Pino (edited by), *Viaggi Acidi. Albert Hofmann intervistato da Pino Corrias*, Stampa Alternativa, Roma 1992

Cortazar, Julio, "The Pursuer" in *Blow-Up and Other Stories*, Pantheon Editions 2004

Dawbarn, Bob, "Taylor – mystery man of British jazz", in *Melody Maker*, February 15th, 1969

Dawbarn, Bob, "Roundhouse crowds without the bedrolls", in *Melody Maker*, September 13th, 1969

Dawbarn, Bob, "In memory of Mike Taylor", in *Melody Maker*, December 12th 1970

Farbey, Roger, "Le Déjeuner Sur L'herbe with The New Jazz Orchestra", in *Jazz Journal*, February 1972

Fiofori, Tam, "Ornette in London" in *Change* # 1, Fall Winter 1965, pagg. 21-23

Gelly, Dave, "Mike Taylor Remembered *"*, booklet included in *Mike Taylor Remembered* CD (Dusk Fire Record DUSKCD103, UK 2007)

Gelly, Dave, "Le Déjeuner Sur L'herbe with The New Jazz Orchestra", booklet included in *Le Déjeuner Sur L'herbe with The New Jazz Orchestra* CD (Dusk Fire Record DUSKCD110, UK 2014)

Hanson, Martyn, *Playing the band. The musical life of Jon Hiseman*, Temple Music, UK 2010

Heining, Duncan, "The strange life and death of Mike Taylor" in *Jazz Wise* # 115, December 2007-January 2008

Heining, Duncan, *Trad dads, dirty boppers and free fusioneers: British jazz 1960-1975*, Equinox Publishing Ltd, UK 2012

Ingless, Steve, "The Pendulum swings" in *Record Collector* # 4, April 2005

Leary, Timoty – Metzner, Ralph – Alpert, Richard, *The Psychedelic Experience*, University Books, New York 1964

Moore, Barry, "Ornette Coleman – Live" in *Jazz Journal*, October 1965

Morton Jack, Richard - Ingless, Steve, "Pendulum", booklet included in *Pendulum* CD -

Dusk Fire Record SBRCD5034, UK 2007
Morton Jack, Richard "Tony Reeves. Album by album", in *Flashback* vol. 6, Winter 2014
Pieranunzi, Enrico, *Bill Evans. The pianist as an artist*, Stampa Alternativa, Roma 2001
Roberts, Andy, *Albion Dreaming. A popular history of LSD in Britain*, Marshall Cavendish, London 2008
Shapiro, Harry, *Graham Bond. The mighty shadow*, Gullane Children's Books, UK 1992
Thompson, Dave, *Footnotes from the Archive of Oblivion: rock and pop's forgotten heroes*, CreateSpace Independent Publishing Platform, UK 2009
Wells, Brian, *Psychedelic Drugs: Psycological, Medical And Social Issues*, Penguin Books, Harmondsworth 1973)
Wenner, Jann S. , "Wheels of Fire" in *Rolling Stones* # 14, July 20th, 1968
Wickes, John, *Innovations in British Jazz (Vol. One 1960-1980)*, Soundworld, UK 1999

WEBGRAPHY

Gelly, Dave, "Mike Taylor remembered", March 2007 at http://www.trunkrecords.com/turntable/mike_taylor.shtml
Heining, Duncan, "The strange life and death of Mike Taylor", January 23th, 2013 at http://www.jazzinternationale.com/mike-taylor-the-not-so-strange-life-and-death-of-mike-taylor/
Heining, Duncan, "The not so strange and Bizarre Life of Mike Taylor", March 27th, 2013 at http://www.allaboutjazz.com/the-not-so-strange-and-bizarre-life-of-mike-taylor-mike-taylor-by-duncan-heining.php
Morton Jack, Richard, "Mike Taylor: the mystic who looked like a bank clerk" in *Galactic Ramble*, October 22th, 2010 at http://galacticramble.com
Sandy Brown Jazz, "The passing of Mike Taylor, jazz pianist", in *Sandy Brown Jazz* Forum, July 2010-2011, at http://www.sandybrownjazz.co.uk/forummiketaylor.html
Thompson, Dave, "Mike Taylor" (biography) in *All Music* at http://www.allmusic.com/artist/mike-taylor-mn0001541189
Various Authors, "Mike Taylor (Musician)" in *Wikipedia* at http://en.wikipedia.org/wiki/Mike_Taylor_%28musician%29

OTHER WEB LINKS RELATED

Graham Bond Web Site - http://www.grahambond.org/http://www.grahambond.org/
Pete Brown Facebook - https://www.facebook.com/officialpetebrown
Pete Brown Web Site - http://www.petebrown.co.uk
Jon Hiseman official Web site: http://www.temple-music.com/
Jack Bruce official Web site: http://www.jackbruce.com/
Ginger Baker official Web site: http://www.gingerbaker.com/
Norma Winstone official Web site: http://www.normawinstone.com/
Trevor Watts official Web site: http://www.trevorwatts.co.uk/
Evan Parker official Web site: http://evanparker.com/
Dusk Fire Records Web site: http://www.musicsogood.com/duskfire/index.htm
International Times Web site (with Dave Tomlin's writings): http://internationaltimes.it/

ABOUT THE AUTHOR

Luca Ferrari (dopachino@tiscali.it) writes about music from the mid-Eighties. He has collaborated with the main Italian magazines, managed the Third Ear Band, promoted gigs and festivals and written essays and biographies about great rock/folk visionaries such as Syd Barrett, Tim Buckley, Captain Beefheart, Nick Drake, Robyn Hitchcock.

He runs *Ghettoraga*, the official Third Ear Band's esoteric archive, on the Web at http://ghettoraga.blogspot.com

Gonzo Books

There is still such a
thing as alternative
Publishing

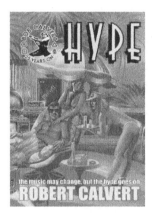

Robert Newton Calvert: Born 9 March 1945, Died 14 August 1988 after suffering a heart attack. Contributed poetry, lyrics and vocals to legendary space rock band Hawkwind intermittently on five of their most critically acclaimed albums, including Space Ritual (1973), Quark, Strangeness & Charm (1977) and Hawklords (1978). He also recorded a number of solo albums in the mid 1970s. CENTIGRADE 232 was Robert Calvert's first collection of poems.

Hype 'And now, for all you speeding street smarties out there, the one you've all been waiting for, the one that'll pierce your laid back ears, decoke your sinuses, cut clean thru the schlock rock, MOR/crossover, techno flash mind mush. It's the new Number One with a bullet ... with a bullet ... It's Tom, Supernova, Mahler with a pan galactic biggie ...' And the Hype goes on. And on. Hype, an amphetamine hit of a story by Hawkwind collaborator Robert Calvert. Who's been there and made it back again. The debriefing session starts here.

Rick Wakeman is the world's most unusual rock star, a genius who has pushed back the barriers of electronic rock. He has had some of the world's top orchestras perform his music, has owned eight Rolls Royces at one time, and has broken all the rules of composing and horrified his tutors at the Royal College of Music. Yet he has delighted his millions of fans. This frank book, authorised by Wakeman himself, tells the moving tale of his larger than life career.

There are nine Henrys, pur
ported to be the world's
first cloned cartoon charac
ter. They live in a strange
lo fi domestic surrealist
world peopled by talking
rock buns and elephants on
wobbly stilts.

They mooch around in their
minimalist universe suffer
ing from an existential
crisis with some genetically
modified humour thrown in.

Marty Wilde on Terry Dene: "Whatever
happened to Terry becomes a great deal
more comprehensible as you read of the
callous way in which he was treated by
people who should have known better
many of whom, frankly, will never know
better of the sad little shadows of
the past who eased themselves into
Terry's life, took everything they
could get and, when it seemed that all
was lost, quietly left him ... Dan Wood
ing's book tells it all."

Rick Wakeman: "There have
always been certain 'careers'
that have fascinated the
public, newspapers, and the
media in general. Such
include musicians, actors,
sportsmen, police, and not
surprisingly, the people who
give the police their employ
ment: The criminal. For the
man in the street, all these
careers have one thing in
common: they are seemingly
beyond both his reach and,
in many cases, understanding
and as such, his only associ
ation can be through the
media of newspapers or tele
vision. The police, however,
will always require the ser
vices of the grass, the
squealer, the snitch, (call
him what you will), in order
to assist in their investiga
tions and arrests; and amaz
ingly, this is the area that
seldom gets written about."

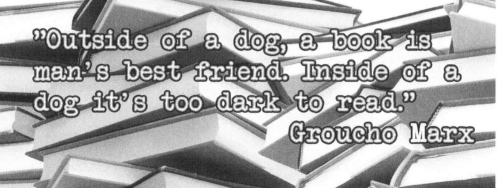

"Outside of a dog, a book is
man's best friend. Inside of a
dog it's too dark to read."
Groucho Marx

Bill Harkleroad joined Captain Beef heart's Magic Band at a time when they were changing from a straight ahead blues band into something completely dif ferent. Through the vision of Don Van Vliet (Captain Beefheart) they created a new form of music which many at the time considered atonal and difficult, but which over the years has continued to exert a powerful influence. Beefheart re christened Harkleroad as Zoot Horn Rollo, and they embarked on recording one of the classic rock albums of all time Trout Mask Replica - a work of unequalled daring and inventiveness.

Politics, paganism and .... Vlad the Impaler. Selected stories from CJ Stone from 2003 to the present. Meet Ivor Coles, a British Tommy killed in action in September 1915, lost, and then found again. Visit Mothers Club in Erdington, the best psyche delic music club in the UK in the '60s. Celebrate Robin Hood's Day and find out what a huckle duckle is. Travel to Stonehenge at the Summer Solstice and carouse with the hippies. Find out what a Ranter is, and why CJ Stone thinks that he's one. Take LSD with Dr Lilly, the psychedelic scientist. Meet a headless soldier or the ghost of Elvis Presley in Gabalfa, Cardiff. Journey to Whitstable, to New York, to Malta and to Transylvania, and to many other places, real and imagined, polit ical and spiritual, transcendent and mundane. As The Independent says, Chris is "The best guide to the underground since Charon ferried dead souls across the Styx."

This is is the first in the highly acclaimed vampire novels of the late Mick Farren. Victor Renquist, a surprisingly urbane and likable leader of a colony of vampires which has existed for centuries in New York is faced with both admin istrative and emotional prob lems. And when you are a vampire, administration is not a thing which one takes lightly.

"The person, be it gentleman or lady, who has not pleasure in a good novel, must be intolerably stupid."

Jane Austen

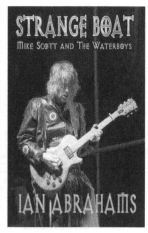

Los Angeles City of Angels, city of dreams. But sometimes the dreams become nightmares. Having fled New York, Victor Renquist and his small group of Nosferatu are striving to re establish their colony. They have become a deeper, darker part of the city's nightlife. And Hollywood's glitterati are hot on the scent of a new thrill, one that outshines all others   immortality. But someone, somewhere, is med dling with even darker powers, powers that even the Nosferatu fear. Someone is attempting to summon the entity of ancient evil known as Cthulhu. And Ren quist must overcome dissent in his own colony, solve the riddle of the Darklost (a being brought part way along the Nosferatu path and then abandoned) and combat powerful enemies to save the world   of humans!

Canadian born Corky Laing is probably best known as the drummer with Mountain. Corky joined the band shortly after Mountain played at the famous Woodstock Festival, although he did receive a gold disc for sales of the soundtrack album after over dubbing drums on Ten Years After's performance. Whilst with Mountain Corky Laing recorded three studio albums with them before the band split. Follow ing the split Corky, along with Mountain gui tarist Leslie West, formed a rock three piece with former Cream bassist Jack Bruce. West, Bruce and Laing recorded two studio albums and a live album before West and Laing re formed Mountain, along with Felix Pappalardi. Since 1974 Corky and Leslie have led Mountain through various line ups and recordings, and continue to record and perform today at numer ous concerts across the world. In addition to his work with Mountain, Corky Laing has recorded one solo album and formed the band Cork with former Spin Doctors guitarist Eric Shenkman, and recorded a further two studio albums with the band, which has also featured former Jimi Hendrix bassist Noel Redding. The stories are told in an incredibly frank, engaging and amusing manner, and will appeal also to those people who may not necessarily be fans of

To me there's no difference between Mike Scott and The Waterboys; they both mean the same thing. They mean myself and whoever are my current travel ling musical companions." Mike Scott Strange Boat charts the twisting and meandering journey of Mike Scott, describing the literary and spiritual references that inform his songwriting and explor ing the multitude of locations and cultures in which The Waterboys have assembled and reflected in their recordings. From his early forays into the music scene in Scotland at the end of the 1970s, to his creation of a 'Big Music' that peaked with the hit single 'The Whole of the Moon' and onto the Irish adventure which spawned the classic Fisher man's Blues, his constantly restless creativity has led him through a myriad of changes. With his revolving cast of troubadours at his side, he's created some of the most era defining records of the 1980s, reeled and jigged across the Celtic heartlands, reinvented himself as an electric rocker in New York, and sought out personal renewal in the spiritual calm of Findhorn's Scot tish highland retreat. Mike Scott's life has been a tale of continual musical exploration entwined with an ever evolving spirituality. "An intriguing portrait of a modern musician" (Record Collector).

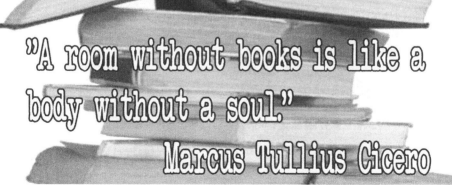

"A room without books is like a body without a soul."
Marcus Tullius Cicero

The OZ trial was the longest obscenity trial in history. It was also one of the worst reported. With minor exceptions, the Press chose to rewrite what had occurred, presumably to fit in with what seemed to them the acceptable prejudices of the times. Perhaps this was inevitable. The proceedings dragged on for nearly six weeks in the hot summer of 1971 when there were, no doubt, a great many other events more worthy of attention. Against the background of murder in Ulster, for example, the OZ affair probably fades into its proper insignificance. Even so, after the trial, when some newspapers realised that maybe something important had happened, it became more and more apparent that what was essential was for anyone who wished to be able to read what had actually been said. Trial and judgment by a badly informed press became the order of the day. This 40th Anniversary edition includes new material by all three of the original defendants, the prosecuting barrister, one of the OZ schoolkids, and even the daughters of the judge. There are also many illustrations including unseen material from Felix Dennis' own collection...

Merrell Fankhauser has led one of the most diverse and interesting careers in music. He was born in Louisville, Kentucky, and moved to California when he was 13 years old. Merrell went on to become one of the innovators of surf music and psychedelic folk rock. His travels from Hollywood to his 15 year jungle experience on the island of Maui have been documented in numerous music books and magazines in the United States and Europe. Merrell has gained legendary international status throughout the field of rock music; his credits include over 250 songs published and released. He is a multi talented singer/songwriter and unique guitar player whose sound has delighted listeners for over 35 years. This extraordinary book tells a unique story of one of the founding fathers of surf rock, who went on to play in a succession of progressive and psychedelic bands and to meet some of the greatest names in the business, including Captain Beefheart, Randy California, The Beach Boys, Jan and Dean... and there is even a run in with the notorious Manson family.

On September 19, 1985, Frank Zappa testified before the United States Senate Commerce, Technology, and Transportation committee, attacking the Parents Music Resource Center or PMRC, a music organization co founded by Tipper Gore, wife of then senator Al Gore. The PMRC consisted of many wives of politicians, including the wives of five members of the committee, and was founded to address the issue of song lyrics with sexual or satanic content. Zappa saw their activities as on a path towards censorship and called their proposal for voluntary labelling of records with explicit content "extortion" of the music industry. This is what happened.

"Good friends, good books, and a sleepy conscience: this is the ideal life."
Mark Twain

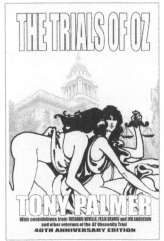

The OZ trial was the longest obscenity trial in history. It was also one of the worst reported. With minor exceptions, the Press chose to rewrite what had occurred, presumably to fit in with what seemed to them the acceptable prejudices of the times. Perhaps this was inevitable. The proceedings dragged on for nearly six weeks in the hot summer of 1971 when there were, no doubt, a great many other events more worthy of attention. Against the background of murder in Ulster, for example, the OZ affair probably fades into its proper insignifi cance. Even so, after the trial, when some newspapers realised that maybe something important had hap pened, it became more and more apparent that what was essential was for anyone who wished to be able to read what had actually been said. Trial and judgment by a badly informed press became the order of the day. This 40th Anniversary edition includes new material by all three of the original defendants, the prosecuting barrister, one of the OZ schoolkids, and even the daughters of the judge. There are also many illustrations including unseen material from Felix Dennis' own collection...

Merrell Fankhauser has led one of the most diverse and interesting careers in music. He was born in Louisville, Kentucky, and moved to California when he was 13 years old. Merrell went on to become one of the innovators of surf music and psychedelic folk rock. His travels from Hollywood to his 15 year jungle experience on the island of Maui have been documented in numerous music books and magazines in the United States and Europe. Merrell has gained legendary international status throughout the field of rock music; his credits include over 250 songs published and released. He is a multi talented singer/songwriter and unique guitar player whose sound has delighted listeners for over 35 years. This extraordi nary book tells a unique story of one of the founding fathers of surf rock, who went on to play in a succession of progressive and psychedelic bands and to meet some of the greatest names in the business, including Captain Beefheart, Randy California, The Beach Boys, Jan and Dean... and there is even a run in with the notorious Manson family.

On September 19, 1985, Frank Zappa testified before the United States Senate Commerce, Technology, and Transportation committee, attacking the Parents Music Resource Center or PMRC, a music organization co founded by Tipper Gore, wife of then senator Al Gore. The PMRC consisted of many wives of politi cians, including the wives of five members of the committee, and was founded to address the issue of song lyrics with sexual or satanic content. Zappa saw their activities as on a path towards censor ship,and called their proposal for voluntary labelling of records with explicit content "extor tion" of the music industry. This is what happened.

> "Good friends, good books, and a sleepy conscience: this is the ideal life."
> Mark Twain